# PROPORTIONAL REPRESENTATION

*Critics of the British Electoral System*
*1820–1945*

# PROPORTIONAL REPRESENTATION

*Critics of the British Electoral System
1820–1945*

JENIFER HART

*Emeritus Fellow of St Anne's College, Oxford*

CLARENDON PRESS · OXFORD

1992

Oxford University Press, Walton Street, Oxford OX2 6DP
Oxford New York Toronto
Delhi Bombay Calcutta Madras Karachi
Petaling Jaya Singapore Hong Kong Tokyo
Nairobi Dar es Salaam Cape Town
Melbourne Auckland
and associated companies in
Berlin Ibadan

Oxford is a trade mark of Oxford University Press

Published in the United States
by Oxford University Press, New York

British Library Cataloguing in Publication Data
Data available

Library of Congress Cataloging in Publication Data
Hart, Jenifer.
Proportional representation : critics of the British electoral
system, 1820–1945 / Jenifer Hart
Includes bibliographical references and index.
1. Proportional representation—Great Britain—History.
I. Title.
JF1075.G7H25     1992     324.6'3'0941—dc20     91–31984
ISBN 0–19–820136–2

Typeset by Cambridge Composing (UK) Ltd
Printed in Great Britain by
Biddles Ltd
Guildford and Kings Lynn

# Preface

I wish to thank those who have read and commented on this work or parts of it, particularly Vernon Bogdanor, Jane Garnett, and A. F. Thompson; also Joanna Ryan, Carol and Francis Graham-Harrison, Margaret Paul, and Jean Floud.

Above all I am grateful to my husband who, bracing himself to take an interest in an unfamiliar subject, has polished and clarified the text.

Many people have kindly answered my queries or supplied useful information. They include Philip Allen, the archivists of the Cornwall Record Office, Dublin University, Reading University, and Trinity College, Cambridge, Robert Blake, Michael Brock, David Butler, Eric Chalker, Harold Colvin, Clifford Davies, Peter Dickson, Jean Dunbabin, Bryan Essenhigh, Michael Freeden, Martin Gilbert, Lawrence Goldman, Shiela Grant-Duff, Brian Harrison, Michael Hart, David Hill, Christopher Hill, Norman Hughes, Bryan Keith-Lucas, Jill Lewis, Ian MacLean, John Maddicott, Colin Matthew, Ron Medlow, Kenneth Morgan, Michael Pinto-Duschinsky, John Prest, David Roberts (Thomas Hare's great-grandson), John M. Robson, Alan Ryan, Robert Skidelsky, Michael Steed, Michael Wheeler-Booth, Anthony Wigram, and Eric Siddique of the Electoral Reform Society from whose extensive knowledge of the subject I have benefited greatly.

The staff of the Bodleian Library have been endlessly helpful and patient.

Elsie Hinkes was a most reliable and efficient typist.

J. H.
November 1990

# Contents

# Introduction

MANY people, if they think about proportional representation at all, assume it to be a difficult, abstruse subject whose understanding requires sophisticated mathematical skills. They also imagine that its advocacy was largely a twentieth-century phenomenon, that its supporters were not numerous, and that they consisted mainly, if not wholly, of rather cranky Liberals.

This book will show that the truth is different. There is nothing complicated about the basic principle that the representation of opinions or parties in legislatures or local government bodies should be in rough proportion to the votes they receive from the electorate, and it is not absurd to be a believer in this principle even if one does not understand the means devised by the experts to ensure its fulfilment.

Early in the nineteenth century a few people in Britain began thinking about the effects of our established electoral procedure, and they became critical of the fact that the system did not always enable minorities to be represented. Therefore in the second half of the century when the franchise was extended dramatically, many of the critics were not Radicals or even Liberals, but anti-democratic Whigs or Conservatives, afraid that the educated and property-owning classes (the minority) would be swamped by the new lower-class electorate. This view prevailed right down to 1918 and led to support for proportional representation from the political Right. Indeed even after 1918 there were advocates of the proportional cause amongst Conservatives. The identification of proportional representation with the Liberal Party is also belied by the fact that for many years the Liberals were by no means solidly behind it; some important ones such as Gladstone, Bright, Chamberlain, and Lloyd George were even hostile. Moreover it also received considerable support in Labour circles.

Between the 1850s and the mid-1880s, and again from 1905 to 1918, a substantial number of people took an interest in electoral procedure and advocated various reforms in order to produce a more accurate representation of the views of the electorate.

These reforms included the limited vote, the cumulative vote, the second ballot, the alternative vote, the election of MPs on a national ticket, and preferential voting with transferable votes in multi-member constituencies. (The meaning of these terms will emerge later in this work, and they are also explained in the glossary.) There resulted numerous pamphlets, articles, books, papers read to learned societies, lectures, public speeches, and debates in parliament. Interest in electoral reform continued after 1918 but at a less intensive level, until its revival in recent years.

It is not the purpose of this book to advocate proportional representation; there are many works which do that. Its aim is to give for the first time a comprehensive account of the numerous and persistent efforts which have been made since the early nineteenth century to change the British system of voting so that the views of the electorate would be more closely represented in parliament and on local authorities. It will therefore focus on the advocates of electoral reform, tracing the genesis of their ideas, analysing their criticisms of the existing system, the various remedies they proposed to meet what they saw as its defects, the arguments they used to support their case, and their organization, activities, and tactics both in and out of parliament. Their opponents' arguments will also be fully examined.

I devote considerable attention to parliamentary debates, for the subject was raised in both Houses far more often than is usually realized, and these discussions convey admirably the flavour of the controversy.

The year 1945 has been chosen as the end date for this study, apart from a brief postscript, as events since then have been adequately chronicled and discussed by others.

The main question to be answered is why the reformers had virtually no success in the United Kingdom except in Ireland. Was this because their opponents did not think there was anything wrong with the existing system? Or because they disagreed with the reformers' accounts of its effects? Or because they did not understand the subject and refused to try to do so? Or because the reformers presented their case badly or over-stated it absurdly, claiming that their proposals were a panacea for all defects in the political system? Or because there was disagreement between the reformers and their opponents as to the purpose of elections and the essence of representative government? Or because it was thought that the change proposed would assist or damage this or that political party? The narrative which follows will show that all these explanations played some part in the reformers' failure, which contrasts poignantly with the world-wide reputation and influence which some of them, particularly Thomas Hare, achieved abroad. Great Britain thus remains one of the few democracies providing no element of proportionality in its representative political institutions.

# I

# The First Critics, 1820–1857

THE origin of the British electoral system can be traced back to the later Middle Ages. At first the members of medieval parliaments were chosen by common consent; the theory was that the unanimous mind of the county or borough was declared. But by the fifteenth century it had become difficult to conduct elections on this basis and a statute of 1430, whose main purpose was to restrict electors to forty-shilling freeholders, introduced the majority principle for shires: those with 'the greatest number' of supporters were to be returned to the parliament. The sheriff, who was the official in charge, no doubt usually 'took the sense' of the meeting in some rough and ready way, such as by listening to the shouts of supporters, but if he felt it was necessary actually to count heads, he declared elected those who had more votes than anyone else. He did not try to ensure that a candidate was elected only if he had more votes than all the other candidates, for electoral assemblies were often tumultuous affairs and a second ballot is a complex procedure in a two-member constituency. The rule of the bare majority was thus established, and MPs continued to be elected, if a poll was held, by simple, i.e. relative not absolute, majorities—a system now known as 'first-past-the-post'. Each voter had as many votes as there were members to be returned for the constituency, which was in almost all cases two.

This practice does not appear to have been questioned in Britain until the beginning of the nineteenth century. Even at the end of the eighteenth century when the representative system came in for a good deal of criticism, this feature of our electoral procedure did not attract attention, no doubt because very few seats were contested, so no poll was held, and critics were focusing on many other aspects of parliamentary reform.

Nor is it strange that the innovative work on the theory of voting being done contemporaneously in France, some of it culminating in constitutional proposals in 1793, had apparently no impact in England. This can be accounted for partly by the fall from favour of Enlightenment writers after the French Revolution, and partly by the mathematical complexities of some of the work on voting theory. Some of the Frenchmen involved made several important distinctions, for example between the sort of electoral method which is appropriate if the electors are choosing one person only, and the best methods if several persons are being elected. The notion of proportionality cannot of course apply if only one person is being chosen, but, it was argued, the aim there should be to secure, if there were more than two candidates, that the person elected was really preferred by the majority of the electors to all the other candidates. An important step forward was taken when J.-C. de Borda pointed out to the French Academy in 1770 that in the choice of the best person among more than two candidates, the one so designated by a simple majority might not be the same as the one arrived at when each was compared with the others.

Many people in France at this time, such as Condorcet, Sièyes, Laplace, and Mirabeau, were discussing wider issues connected with representative systems, particularly the fair or proportional representation of different opinions and elements in the country. They therefore also thought about the methods which should be used if several persons were being elected, and in so doing they made acute analyses of the effects of different voting systems, including the second ballot, list systems, and the limited vote. However these analyses have had to be propounded *de novo* and argued through time and again by later reformers. Indeed the process still continues two hundred years later.

The first Englishman to have thought about the theory of voting and to have devised a scheme enabling minorities to be represented appears to have been Thomas Wright Hill (1763–1851). The son of a baker in Kidderminster, he was apprenticed in Birmingham and became influenced by the dissenting minister and scientist, Dr Joseph Priestley. Hill was unsuccessful in business and in 1803 opened a school at which were educated his remarkable sons who included Matthew Davenport, the criminal law reformer, and Rowland, the inventor of universal penny postage. Thomas Hill was primarily a mathematician, but he had wide intellectual and social interests, and he emphasized in particular the importance of people being able to pursue knowledge which on the face of it had no palpable usefulness. In his concern with voting procedures he may possibly have been influenced by earlier French thinkers on this subject, for he was interested among other things in astronomy and may therefore have known Laplace, who was an associate member of the Astronomical Society of London, founded in 1821, of which Thomas and Rowland were both members. Or he may have been familiar with the work of the French mathematician Gergonne, who published an article in 1820 recommending a system by which voters would group themselves according to their opinions and elect someone to represent them.[1] But it seems more likely that Thomas Hill devised his plan to represent minorities entirely on his own, for it is different from the earlier schemes which had been propounded, and Hill was clearly a most original and ingenious man—as evidenced by his other inventions, including a system of what he terms 'philosophic shorthand'.

None of Hill's writings were published during his lifetime, and his work on electoral matters received no publicity in Britain until much later. It had therefore virtually no influence, or at any rate no direct influence, in this country, but it had some influence on electoral methods in Australia, knowledge of which percolated back to Britain. This happened because a society for literary and scientific improvement, founded by Rowland Hill with others, adopted for its committee a plan of election devised by his father. This involved not only the principle of voters grouping themselves with those whose views most resembled their own and electing someone to represent them, but also a system of transferring surplus votes to second or later choices, and the transfer of votes from weaker to stronger candidates. Rowland Hill later became secretary to the South Australian Commissioners, and was responsible for the recommendation in their third report in 1839 that the government should grant the colony municipal institutions using an

---

[1] For Gergonne, see Poul Andrae, *Andrae and his Invention, the Proportional Method*, English translation by V. Meisling (Philadelphia, 1926).

electoral method which would enable minorities to be represented. This part of the report was said to have been actually drawn up by Thomas Hill. It stated the case for minority representation as follows:

In order to counteract the tendency to exasperated party feeling which is sometimes found to exist in small communities, as well as to make timely provision against the arbitrary power which under popular governments the majority exercise over the minority, we . . . recommend, that the municipal elections may be so conducted that a majority of the rate-payers may not have the power to exclude the minority from returning their due proportion of members to the Common Council.[2]

Curiously, however, the electoral method proposed did not incorporate any transfer of votes, but was in simpler form essentially the same as that recommended by Gergonne. Electors were by voluntary classification to form themselves into as many equal electoral sections or quorums as there were members to be elected; and each quorum would, provided it could agree on a unanimous vote, return one member to the Council, so that the parties in the Council would bear the same proportion to each other as they bore in the elective body. Aldermen were to be elected by the Council in the same manner. This electoral system was put into operation in the town of Adelaide, which therefore had, according to a knowledgeable commentator, W. E. Hickson, the only municipal constitution which had not a tendency to give exclusive domination to one class or party. Hickson also pointed out that this was the first instance on record of a government department having recognized the principle that the minority should be represented.[3]

Thomas Hill's electoral method falls short in not providing for the expression on one voting paper of several choices, and it is not compatible with secret voting in public elections; but he

[2] PP 1839 XVII. Third Annual Report of the Colonial Commissioners for South Australia, 19.

[3] William Edward Hickson, 1803–70. Owned property in City of London. On Handloom Weavers' Commission, 1837. Proprietor and editor of *Westminster Review*, 1840–52. See his article 'The Corporation of London and Municipal Reform' in *Westminster Review*, 39 (May 1843), 570, and his evidence to the Commissioners inquiring into the state of the Corporation of London. PP 1854 XXVI, 319.

can nevertheless rightly be regarded as the first inventor of the core principles of the system of proportional representation with the single transferable vote which was advocated sixty years later by the British Proportional Representation Society.[4]

Before this, in 1831, a different, simpler proposal had been made to assist minority representation. This was what later came to be known as the limited vote. The fact that its advocate was the poet and writer of light verse, Winthrop Mackworth Praed,[5] might at first sight appear strange, but it can be explained. Praed had held radical or at least liberal views in his Cambridge days in the early 1820s, had sharpened his wits in discussions and debates with Macaulay, then a Tory, and Charles Austin, and was a member of John Stuart Mill's London Debating Society. But in the late 1820s he became alarmed at the democratic tendencies of the reformers and, as Leslie Stephen put it in the *Dictionary of National Biography*, 'his fastidious and scholarly temperament made contempt for demagogues more congenial than popular enthusiasm'. Having bought the Cornish seat of St Germans for £1,000, he entered parliament as a Tory late in 1830, and soon got to grips with the details of the Reform Bill, many parts of which he attacked. During some of his numerous speeches he pointed out that the custom of allowing voters to have as many votes as there were members to be returned by each constituency rested merely on usage, long prescriptive usage, originally adopted without reflection and subsequently acquiesced in without dispute. Praed, who was clearly not a disciple of Burke in his attitude to prescription, thought this practice was undesirable because it often allowed a bare majority of the voters to return both members. It may be observed that he did not address his mind to the electoral effects of single-member constituencies. This is understandable because at that time the majority, over five-sixths, of United Kingdom constituencies returned two members each. In England proper there were only five single-

---

[4] For T. W. Hill, see *Remains of Thomas Wright Hill, together with notice of his life by himself*, with a continuation by M. D. Hill (1859); *Selections from the Papers of the late Thomas Wright Hill* (1860) which includes an anonymous Memoir; and George Birkbeck Hill, *Life of Sir Rowland Hill* (1880).

[5] W. M. Praed, 1802–39. MP, Tory, 1830–2 and 1835–9.

member constituencies. Praed admitted that sometimes compromises were struck thus enabling the minority to be represented, but one could not rely on these (they were an 'insecure
gate') and in any case people generally felt horror of compromises between parties entertaining different opinions. If, as the
Reform Bill proposed, some counties were to have three members instead of the traditional two, because they were so
populous, and voters were to have three votes each, the
position would be even more indefensible. So he suggested that
in these seven counties no elector should be able to vote for
more than two candidates. He made it clear that he was chiefly
worried by the thought that a minority of 'property and intelligence' would be swamped by the votes of the populous masses,
and so he can be seen as merely an anxious defender of the
interests of the propertied classes. But he also thought about
some aspects of the machinery of representative government
more closely than his contemporaries, and devised a novel
remedy to what he saw as an error in the original construction
of the representative assembly of this country.

Praed acknowledged the strangeness of his proposal, though
he considered it very important, reasonable, and easy to operate. When he first made it, on 13 August 1831, the only
comment it elicited in the House of Commons, which was thinly
attended, was from Lord Althorp speaking on behalf of the
government. In spite of Praed's full, lucid, and thoroughly
argued speech, Althorp's remarks reveal that he did not understand the results which the existing 'block vote' as it was later
known might easily produce, for he said the minority must be
very small indeed if all the three members returned were men
professing the same politics.[6] Praed complained a few days after
the debate that he could not get Peel or any of their leaders
except Herries to listen to his proposal. (Actually Peel in general
thought very well of Praed and in 1834 gave him a post in his
government.) But, Praed added, since the debate many MPs,
some unknown to him, had asked him to explain particular
points in his statement; encouraged by so much favourable

---

[6] The term 'block vote' has given rise to some confusion. It is used here to
describe the system under which each voter in a multi-member constituency,
that is a constituency returning two or more members, has one vote for each
seat that is to be filled. See also Glossary.

interest he thought of pushing his idea to a division at a later stage. When he renewed his proposal in January 1832, Althorp was a little more forthcoming, saying that he could not deny that there might be something advantageous in it, but that he did not see how it could be adopted at the present moment. The initial interest apparently shown by some MPs seems to have evaporated, for no one took up Praed's suggestion and the proposal never went to a division.[7]

Praed's failure to get any further with his plan is not difficult to explain. Apart from anything else he must have alienated many MPs with his contempt for their lack of rationality and power of argument. They cannot have welcomed being told by a new and young MP that 'however strong may be the prejudice with which they may regard the introduction of a perfectly new principle into our representative system, it is still a naked prejudice'.[8] Macaulay described Praed's conduct on one occasion as 'silly, conceited, and factious' and said it had disgraced him even more than his bad speaking. On another occasion he said that with all his talent Praed lacked tact. Admittedly little weight can be attached to these strictures, for their original friendshii had broken under the strain of party animosity: Macaulay considered that Praed had used him basely, and he did not even appreciate Praed's poetry, describing it as 'a display of showy superficial Etonian scholarship'. Nevertheless these comments may be an indication of the effect Praed produced on some other contemporaries.[9]

Praed died when still young in 1839 and thus did not live to see the adoption of his proposal in 1867 or to take part in the mid-century discussions about electoral systems. Even when still an MP in the 1830s, he does not seem to have concerned himself further with this question. Thus he did not propose any form of minority representation for the election of town councillors when the important Municipal Corporations Bill of 1835 was

[7] *HC Deb.*, 3rd ser. 5 (13 Aug. 1831), 1359–73; and 9 (27 Jan. 1832), 991–2, 1006, 1013. *The Political and Occasional Poems of William Mackworth Praed*, ed. Sir George Young (1888), pp. xvi–xvii.

[8] *HC Deb.* 5 (13 Aug. 1831), 1360.

[9] Thomas Babington Macaulay, *Letters*, ed. Thomas Pinney (1974–81), 15 July 1831, 30 Apr. 1831, and 22 Dec. 1843.

passing through parliament. Nor did anyone else. However this statute does contain a very small experiment in vote limiting, inserted it seems by the government. For it provided that in the election of auditors and assessors, who were to determine disputes about the registration of voters, burgesses were to elect two of each, but that no elector should vote for more than one person for each job. This provision was in practice not very significant, but in 1836 it was cited as a model to be followed for the election of local commissioners for charitable trusts. It had been agreed that the management of such trusts should be separated from the control of town councils; so the government introduced a bill to effect this. In order to counteract as far as possible the influence of political feelings in the election of trustees, it was proposed that they should be elected not as were town councillors, but under a system which limited the elector to voting for only half the number required, thus enabling, it was argued, the minority to be represented fully and fairly. The bill passed through the Commons but was blocked in the Lords where in August 1836 Lord Lyndhurst attacked this voting system as absurd. He said an equal number of each party might be elected, resulting in bitter conflicts. Peel had objected to the scheme on the opposite ground, namely that trusts would be placed in the hands of one political party, thus illustrating the difficulties contemporaries faced in predicting the effect of changes in the electoral system.[10]

Whilst this discussion about charitable trusts was taking place, the limited vote was proposed in yet another connection, namely for town councils in Ireland. The reform of Irish municipal corporations had been before parliament for some time. The two Houses were at loggerheads on the issue in 1836, as a majority in the Lords wished not to reform Irish municipal institutions but to extirpate them altogether. One of their fears was that as the bulk of the electors would be poor Roman Catholics, Protestants, being the main property owners, would be unfairly taxed through the rating system. Earl Grey, who was very anxious that the Lords should pass the bill, suggested as a palliative that voters should be able to vote for only five-

---

[10] *HC Deb.* 34 (7 June 1836), 201–3; 35 (19 July 1836), 314–18; and *HL Deb.* 35 (4 Aug. 1836), 897–9.

eighths of town councillors, thus enabling minorities to retain their due share of influence. He had not thought up the device himself, but was persuaded to put it forward by Edward Stanley who had been Chief Secretary for Ireland in his government from 1831 to 1833. One or two peers evinced some interest in Grey's proposal, but, as Lord Wharncliffe said, it was not sufficient to reconcile the differences between the two Houses at that moment. The Duke of Wellington was typically more forthright: he had heard of the idea before; it was altogether impracticable and anyway he entertained objections to such a scheme under any circumstances.[11] The proposal was not incorporated in the bill then or when it was finally passed in 1840.

In the 1840s, at least until the end of the decade, there does not appear to have been much discussion in Britain about electoral methods, partly because, though there was considerable pressure for an extension of the suffrage, it was clear that this had no chance of success. Then, as earlier, foreign ideas and work on voting methods do not seem to have influenced the British. For instance no one at the time or indeed for many years seems to have noticed a scheme proposed in 1844 by an American, Thomas Gilpin. This is understandable given the then generally patronizing and critical attitude of the British to American political institutions, and that Gilpin's plan originated in an obscure quarter, namely in a paper he gave to the American Philosophical Society of Philadelphia. The American Congress had just (in 1842) introduced districting, that is compulsory single-member constituencies for elections to the House of Representatives. This was to replace the existing practice under which many Congressmen were elected on a general ticket from their states at large, which resulted in the non-representation of the party in a minority in the state. It was thought by many people that districting would enable minorities to obtain fairer representation, but Gilpin saw clearly that this would not necessarily be so. He pointed out that locally based elections might not give minorities a chance to be heard, and he proposed instead what was later called the 'free list' system. Under this each party would put up a number of candidates equal to the

---

[11] *HL Deb.* 34 (27 June 1836), 927–8, 953-4, and 959. Grey was the second earl.

number of seats to be filled in each constituency, say twenty. Each voter would have twenty votes, but only one vote could be given to any candidate. Each party would be allotted a number of representatives bearing the same ratio to twenty as its vote bore to the total vote, the names first on the party list being elected first.[12]

Similarly ideas and schemes which were being thrown up in France in the 1830s and 1840s do not appear to have made any impact in Britain. This too is understandable because they tended to emanate from radical or Utopian socialist thinkers, but it meant that some of their valid points were not appreciated even when politically neutral. For instance when answering in 1846 opponents of electoral reform in Geneva who had based their case on 'the principle of majorities'—namely the principle that the minority should be bound by the majority—Victor Considérant[13] argued that it was an error to confound two votes perfectly distinct by nature, the representative and the deliberative: one should not confuse bestowing an authority of trust and making a decision. However a scheme emanating from a very different quarter, namely from a man who had been a minister in the reactionary Restoration period, the Comte de Villèle, also does not seem to have aroused any interest in Britain when it was put forward in 1839. Villèle, who was known as a manipulator of electoral colleges, proposed that electors should gather in the *chef-lieu* of each *département*, and group themselves in colleges of equal size according to their political persuasions. The number of colleges would be determined by the number of deputies per *département*. But this scheme of proportional representation would only work if the number of electors was small, as it was in France at the time. It was also incompatible with the secret ballot.

In the late 1840s, after the Whigs had returned to power, it seemed possible that the government, galvanized into action by

[12] Thomas Gilpin, 1776–1853. Successful paper manufacturer. Gilpin's father had been banished from Philadelphia at the time of the American revolution because of his supposed sympathy with the British. As a result Thomas was very aware of the disadvantages facing unrepresented minorities. His work was not noticed in America for twenty years.

[13] Victor Considérant, 1805–93. Socialist and disciple of Charles Fourier, who had advocated a plan of proportional representation in 1834.

Lord John Russell, would in due course propose legislation to extend and rationalize the franchise; by the early 1850s this became fairly certain. The likelihood of a wider, perhaps much wider, franchise alarmed some people, and they began to think of how to protect the interests of the more educated members of the community who it was thought would be in a minority among voters. Other aspects of the representative system such as inequalities in the size of constituency electorates were also being commented on or criticized. This interest in electoral matters generally and the probability of legislation stimulated thought about the specific effects of the mechanism of voting.

It was necessary first to analyse what happened or could happen under the existing system—that is, electing MPs in local constituencies by simple majorities, each voter having as many votes as there were members to be returned for the constituency. In 1850 Nassau Senior, who was an economist with wide political and intellectual interests, discussed in an article what tended to happen with one-, two-, and three-member constituencies. He considered (rightly) that single-member constituencies were apt to disfranchise all but the members of a single party, but that two-member constituencies often over-represented minorities because the parties made compromises. In three-member constituencies he thought the minority party would probably get one representative, even supposing three votes per voter. In fact he was over-optimistic about minority representation in three-member constituencies, for in the seven counties returning three members each at general elections between 1832 and 1865, all three members were of the same party one-third of the time. But Senior at least saw that the number of representatives a constituency returned was, as he put it, 'one of the most important questions connected with representation' which had to be resolved if, as he wished, the will of the majority was to preponderate whilst the minority secured a fair hearing.[14]

The next year, 1851, angered by the overwhelming vote in the House of Commons against papal aggression, the *Spectator*

[14] Nassau William Senior, 1790–1864. Professor of Political Economy at Oxford, 1825–30 and 1847–52. Member of many Royal Commissions. The article was in the *Edinburgh Review*, 9 (Apr. 1850), 508–58, reviewing George Cornewall Lewis's *Essay on the Influence of Authority in Matters of Opinion*.

considered that the existing mode of election gave no security for representation of opinions opposed to the majority. The pope had reinstated the Roman Catholic hierarchy in England, thus provoking a violent John Bullish storm in the country against popery. The government's bill to counter the papacy's plans was passed in the Commons by 438 votes to 91. But this was in fact not a strong case on which to hang arguments for the representation of minority views, because they were eloquently voiced by, amongst others, Gladstone in his famous speech in favour of religious toleration. The *Spectator* admitted that the distinction between town and country constituencies did at the moment normally produce the representation of various opinions in parliament, but it forecast that this would not last because urban and rural areas would come to agree more, so that the majority in each constituency would tally more and more with the majority in the whole country. There were thousands of persons about the country, the *Spectator* averred, who studied subjects like foreign and colonial policy and social progress at home, but in each constituency they formed only a small minority. The result was that parliament registered only the net balance of local majorities, and did not try to create an enlightened public opinion.[15] This article was clearly inspired, if not written, by the editor, R. S. Rintoul, a brilliant radical Scottish journalist who had been an ardent advocate of the Reform Bill of 1832, and incidentally the author of the famous slogan 'the Bill, the whole Bill, and nothing but the Bill'.

The analysis was taken a step further in 1852 by W. R. Greg, who was beginning to become well known as a contributor to the periodical literature of the day on political and other subjects.[16] He was reviewing a pamphlet which argued at great length that electoral districts should be equalized according to their population, returning one or two MPs each. (At that time some MPs represented constituencies with a population vastly greater than that of others.) Greg pointed out with some justification that under such a system all MPs could be of the

---

[15] 'Representation of Minorities', *Spectator*, 18 Oct. 1851, 997.
[16] William Rathbone Greg, 1809–81. He stood for parliament as a Liberal at Lancaster in 1837, but was defeated and never tried again. There is an interesting account of him by John Morley in his *Miscellanies*, iii (1886).

same party; at present it was only by a happy accident that minorities were represented at all; injustice was neutralized by the variety of our constituencies. In another article the same year Greg introduced the concept of the 'wasted vote', arguing that many people were at present virtually disfranchised because their votes were wasted, i.e. had no effect on the outcome of the election. This had the added result, he considered, of preventing some good individuals from getting into parliament, though there were in every constituency electors who appreciated their value. Although later generations looking back on the 1850s have seen them as the heyday of the independent member, Greg obviously felt that party pressures were inhibiting MPs from thinking for themselves, those that did being condemned as crotchety, subtle, and inconsistent. So, anticipating many later supporters of proportional representation, he made a plea for a system which would enable non-party men to be elected. He himself was such a man, his views cutting across those of the two main parties. A year later, when reviewing several works on electoral matters, Greg argued that one should distinguish between the principle which should determine a decision after the discussion of a bill in parliament and the principle which should determine the decision of electors when choosing representatives. He was, probably without knowing it, making the same point as Considérant had made seven years before.[17]

The same year, 1853, saw the publication of a pamphlet entitled *Minorities and Majorities: Their Relative Rights. A Letter to Lord John Russell on Parliamentary Reform*. The author was James Garth Marshall.[18] This was an important publication which broke new ground, for Marshall introduced the concept of proportionality, and talked about the rights of majorities as well as of minorities. He considered that a defect in the mechanism of our representative system had been noticed by some people, but that it had not been adequately investigated or discussed. The mode of voting which had sprung up as it were by chance

[17] *Edinburgh Review*, 95 (Jan. 1852), 213–80; 96 (Oct. 1852), 452–508; 98 (Oct. 1853), 566–624.

[18] James Garth Marshall, 1802–73. MP, Liberal, 1847–52. He was well connected, having married the daughter of his brother-in-law, Lord Monteagle, who had been in Melbourne's governments.

did not give fair and proportionate representation to the various political parties and opinions either in each constituency or in the whole country, whether they were opinions held by majorities or minorities. A considerable minority could be entirely excluded from the House of Commons, and even partial or local exclusions were evil. Marshall urged that 'we should divest ourselves of the traditional prepossession that the majority have somehow or other a right to more than their share, and are ill-used if they do not get it'. He too tackled the 'majority rule' objection to the representation of minorities, namely the objection that it was a principle of all established governments that the minority should be bound by the majority. He considered that a minority excluded from the House of Commons was in a much worse position than if they had merely been outvoted in an assembly at which they had the right to be present, for the right of being heard and explaining their views is taken away from them not on one question only, but on all questions, not just on a single administrative act but on questions of permanent legislation.

The effect of the electoral system on local government also came under scrutiny in 1853. Thus W. E. Hickson, who had considerable experience of the working of the Corporation of the City of London, was critical of the fact that the system did not guarantee the minority, as well as the majority, representation in municipal assemblies. He applied the same principle to national assemblies; representation in these should be a reflex, as far as possible, of the nation itself. Hickson stressed that the principle of minority representation, which was indispensable to any system of real representation, was as yet little understood, and that the public mind was not sufficiently awakened to a number of important questions connected with the subject.[19]

Another good example of the kind of questioning which was taking place at this time is afforded by George Cornewall Lewis who, when reviewing Marshall's pamphlet in 1854, pointed out (as had Praed in 1831) that our electoral system was the result of accident rather than design, and that the origin of the custom

---

[19] PP 1854 XXVI, 319. Q. 2974. Commission of Enquiry into the Corporation of London.

according to which each elector voted for as many candidates as there were MPs to be returned by the constituency was unknown. Some people, Lewis said, regarded this custom which had become a rule as an unchangeable law of nature, but he considered it no less arbitrary than the rules regarding customs duties on sugar; we must be allowed to question its necessity and universality without being charged as politically heterodox.[20]

After analysing how the electoral system worked and what was actually or potentially defective in it, these various commentators turned to remedies. The most novel proposals, made by the *Spectator* in 1851, were that there should be enlarged constituencies in which a minimum number of votes would secure the return of an MP—the germ of what later became known as the quota or quorum—and that electors could withdraw themselves from their local constituency and register themselves as national voters, the quota provision applying there too. This idea was supported for a time by Greg, who suggested that twenty-six seats in parliament should be allocated to these national representatives, but neither he nor the *Spectator* worked out any further details of the scheme.

Other radical ideas were discussed and discarded. These included a proposal that the whole country should constitute one constituency. For this scheme two alternative and equally novel methods of voting were put forward. One was that the electors should have as many votes as there were MPs in parliament, viz. 658. This was known as 'collective voting' or sometimes as the 'ticket system'. It could have the adverse effect, it was pointed out, of disfranchising all but the members of a single party. The second proposed method of voting went to the other extreme and allowed every voter to vote for only one candidate from a list which included all the candidates for the whole national constituency. This would have enabled very small parties and the most skilfully organized to get represented.

---

[20] George Cornewall Lewis, 1806–63. Statesman and author. He held a number of different posts in Whig governments from 1847 onwards. His article was in the *Edinburgh Review*, 100 (July 1854), 226–35.

One remedy which found some favour was the cumulative vote, a system under which constituencies would elect more than one MP (for example, three) and electors could accumulate their three votes on one candidate or scatter them around between candidates as they wished. The cumulative vote should not be confused (as it sometimes is) with plural voting, a system which entitles some electors to more votes than other electors, because for instance they own more property, pay more rates, or are more educated. It is easy to confuse cumulative and plural voting because the two can be combined: that is, an elector entitled to more than one vote may be allowed to accumulate his votes on one candidate. This brand of plural voting was used in the nineteenth century for the election of various local authorities, the most notorious being Poor Law Guardians and members of local Boards of Health. When plural voting is not combined with cumulative voting, the plural elector votes in more than one constituency, for example where he lives, and where he has a business, or as a graduate of a university. Plural voting based on property or educational qualifications was sometimes advocated for parliamentary elections in the mid-nineteenth century; but no form of plural voting of course is consistent with the assumption made by most advocates of minority representation that minorities should be fairly, but not over, represented.

The cumulative vote seems to have made its first appearance in the report of a committee of the Privy Council in 1850 when it was considering the establishment of a representative legislature in the Cape of Good Hope, the whole country being one constituency. Earl Grey, the third earl, who was the Colonial Secretary at the time, liked the idea because he thought it would enable a minority of electors to be represented on the Legislative Council. He secured its adoption in the Cape, where it was used with the desired result until 1909.

The cumulative vote was first recommended for the British parliament by both Greg and Marshall in 1853 with a minimum of three representatives per constituency. Marshall indeed seems to have invented the expression. He revealed in his pamphlet considerable understanding of the effects of different electoral mechanisms. Thus he saw that rearranging electoral districts would not necessarily result in the representation of a wide diversity of opinions in parliament, as some people thought, unless political parties were concentrated in different constituencies. But in fact, he pointed out, most constituencies contained supporters of several political parties; there was a much greater intermixture than was usually realized. Marshall worked out in considerable detail what could happen with the cumulative vote on various assumptions. He also foresaw and answered some of the objections which could be made to it, but neither he nor Greg anticipated all the drawbacks to it which became manifest after it was adopted for the election of school boards in 1870. The cumulative vote also found favour with John Stuart Mill for a time. Early in 1853 he read the pamphlet of his old friend Marshall, thought carefully about the proposal, and by 1857, if not earlier, was supporting the cumulative vote as a simple way of ensuring that every considerable minority could be represented in a fair proportion to its numbers. Moreover it had for Mill the additional advantage of enabling intensity of preference to carry weight as well as the mere fact of preference.

Another remedy which got some support was the limited vote. First put forward by Praed in 1831, and kept just alive in the 1830s, it was revived in the 1850s by W. E. Hickson and more importantly by Lord John Russell. Hickson recommended it in a rather extreme form in 1853 for elections to the corporation of the City of London. He proposed that there should be ten representatives for each ward of the city, but that every elector could vote for only one of them.[21] This would have enabled a minority as small as one-eleventh of the electorate to be sure of representation if it did not nominate more than one candidate. His suggestion was not adopted by the commissioners of inquiry, but was referred to favourably by Cornewall Lewis in 1854.

Lord John Russell's 1852 Reform Bill did not provide for the limited vote or for any device to protect minorities, but his 1854 bill which was longer and more elaborate gave three members to constituencies with populations of more than 100,000, limiting voters in these constituencies, of which there were then fifty-three, to two votes each. When introducing the bill, which applied only to England and Wales, Russell referred to the

[21] PP 1854 XXVI, 319.

advocacy of minority representation in many writings and pamphlets, though it seems likely that he got the idea of the limited vote from Praed whom he considered very talented and whose loss he had deplored. He claimed that sometimes 2,000 to 4,000 people had voted for the unsuccessful candidate and only 100 to 150 more for the successful one. The excluded felt sore and irritated by being perpetually shut out from a share in the representation of the place. In a county it might be the Liberal party who were excluded, in a great town the Conservative party. Moreover the larger constituencies became, the more their MPs should represent the community at large. Under his proposal, he said, when the minority exceeded two-fifths of all the electors, they would have one representative of the three to be returned. He thought his scheme would help to prevent angry contests at elections.

The only comments made in parliament on Russell's proposal were critical. J. G. Phillimore (Liberal) regarded the idea as whimsical to say the least, asking mockingly whether Russell would apply the principle to proceedings in the House, so that out of every three measures, the majority should carry two and the minority one. Joseph Hume, though a radical, said he was against the idea of minority representation because all our institutions were grounded on the principle of a majority and he was against any innovation on that principle. John Bright also made a derisory comment: it was like making the last in the race the winner, thus illustrating how little he understood the rationale of the scheme, and foreshadowing his later profound antipathy to all forms of minority and proportional representation. Russell had no further opportunity to explain and advocate his scheme for the limited vote, as the bill never reached its second reading, being withdrawn to his great distress in the spring of 1854 because of the outbreak of the Crimean war.[22]

Several years later Russell said that his proposal was not popular in the country and not very palatable to the House. He still thought it was a fair and just proposition, but he did not include it in his 1860 Reform Bill.[23] One well-informed commen-

---

[22] *HC Deb.* 130 (13 Feb. 1854), 498–500 and 519–21; (16 Feb. 1854), 735; 132 (11 Apr. 1854), 836–44.
[23] *HC Deb.* 156 (1 Mar. 1860), 2062.

tator (Cornewall Lewis) described the attitude of the opposition more bluntly: he said that critics of the 1854 bill wrongly regarded the representation of minorities as strange, unnatural, irrational, unconstitutional, oligarchic, and anti-popular.[24] Certainly the whole episode showed how little understood was the principle of minority representation and the machinery for its implementation. Thomas Hare (the subject of the next chapter) writing in 1857 seems to have been justified in saying that the coldness approaching contempt with which Russell's suggestion was received showed the tyranny of thought due to inveterate habit. It is however interesting to observe that contemporaries were able to see that the limited vote could sometimes serve a useful purpose, for it was adopted for the election of the governing body of Oxford University, Hebdomadal Council, when it was reformed in 1854.[25]

The pioneering work on electoral systems which has been described above did not attract wide contemporary attention, partly because many other issues concerning the representative system were also being discussed, but it did play a part in stimulating thought about the theory of representation. The standard answer to those who advocated the better representation of minorities was that the object of elections was not to express the opinions of the voters or to represent individual or local interests, but to choose people who would, in Burke's words, 'consult for the general good of the whole community'.[26] To this the reformers replied that the existing system failed abysmally on this count too: representative government was not a success in so far as the choice of MPs was concerned, for they were the fittest in respect neither of their interests, their culture, nor of their wisdom.[27] This was the main issue which triggered off the work of the progenitor of proportional representation—Thomas Hare.

[24] Op. cit. at n. 20 above.
[25] Oxford University Act, 1854, sec. 21.
[26] See, e.g., John E. Eardley-Wilmot, *Parliamentary Reform: A Letter to Richard Freedom . . .* (1854).
[27] See, e.g., Herbert Spencer, *Westminster Review*, 12 NS (Oct. 1857), 454–86. Spencer had no faith in the devices suggested by the reformers, but he was very critical of the composition of the House of Commons, at least two-thirds of whose members were in his view unsuited to their tasks.

# II

# Thomas Hare and
# John Stuart Mill

IN the spring of 1857 there appeared a pamphlet of fifty-three pages entitled *The Machinery of Representation*. The author, Thomas Hare, was little known outside legal circles, but the pamphlet, which went into a second edition the same year, attracted, according to Hare, so much attention that he was soon emboldened to write a whole book 370 pages long on the subject. The result was the publication in January 1859 of *A Treatise on the Election of Representatives, Parliamentary and Municipal*. Three further editions of the *Treatise* were published in 1861, 1865, and 1873. By the summer of 1875, 1,500 copies of the book had been sold, although it was not all easy reading, and for ten years thereafter annual sales averaged twenty-five. A copious literature grew up for the promotion or discussion of Hare's electoral system which attracted attention in many parts of the world.

The story of Hare's life is remarkable. Born in 1806, he was the illegitimate and only son of Mary Ann Hare of Leigh, Dorset, his father being Thomas King, a yeoman farmer. Little else is known about his family background except that his mother at some stage married a Mr Barrett and that Thomas Hare appears to have remained on friendly terms with relatives on his father's side and probably with his father. There is no evidence that he was related to the more famous Hares, Archdeacon Julius and his brother Augustus, even though he quotes freely from their book, *Guesses at Truth* (1827), and from Julius's edition of Niebuhr's *History of Rome* (1828–32). After slight schooling in Dorset where he lived on a farm, Hare came to London and obtained work as a clerk in a solicitor's office at a few shillings a week. He later described his youth with some justification as a continuous series of struggles; for after long hours at the office, he set himself in the evening unaided to study the law, and such was his energy and tenacity that he was admitted a student of the Inner Temple at the age of 22 in 1828. Meanwhile he had written a pamphlet in support of relaxation of the Navigation laws. This was seen in manuscript by Huskisson, the President of the Board of Trade, and was published in 1826 at his wish. Huskisson was a Canningite Tory with advanced opinions on free trade. Hare became Huskisson's private secretary in, it seems, 1828, but a possible future in the political world was cut short by Huskisson's death before Hare's eyes in 1830 at the opening of the Liverpool to Manchester railway.

It is not clear how Hare supported himself from 1830 to 1833 when he was called to the Bar, but he is said never to have lacked work after 1830. He practised in the Chancery court, and by 1837 was well enough off to marry. His wife came from Dorset which suggests that he had kept in touch with his home. He was also soon engaged in compiling various legal works. In 1853 he left the Bar, and became an Inspector of Charities at the start of the Charity Commission at a salary of £800 p.a. His main motive for the move was to secure a better and guaranteed income, as he had by then eight children. Indeed less than two years after his appointment as Inspector, when one of the Commissioners died, Hare put himself forward (unsuccessfully) to the Prime Minister and Lord Chancellor as a suitable successor, the job being worth £1,200 p.a. It seems that his work in the Charity Commission, which involved a good deal of travelling round the country, broadened his interests from narrow legal problems towards various social issues, particularly the dwellings of the poorer classes and the depopulation of villages. He thought great results could be effected for the good of the community and especially for the working classes in both town and country by a proper use of charity property, combined with improved local government. He was worried about class antagonisms and saw the need to get into parliament those people who wanted to promote the social advancement, comfort, and happiness of the people. His work at the Commission must also have given him opportunities to become acquainted with the parliamentary scene, because new schemes for charities made by the Commissioners had to be laid before parliament and passed as bills. The Commissioners, who were not represented in parliament, found great difficulty in getting the assent of the two Houses for their proposals in the face of opposition by interested parties. So Hare's mind turned towards the questions of how candidates were selected for the House of Commons, what sort of people became MPs, and how the existing electoral machinery worked. In his view it separated those who could act in harmony, and this deprived them of influence. In particular, people wanting social reforms should, he considered, be able to elect members who would devote themselves mainly or exclusively to such objects, and even those seeking wide organic changes in our national institutions should be able to send exponents of their views to parliament.

This was the background to his 1857 pamphlet. It was written in April 1857 just after the general election which saw the defeat of several prominent Liberal and Radical politicians who had been critical of the Crimean War, Palmerston's jingoism, and the government's treatment of China.[1] The defeated candidates included Cobden, Bright, Miall, Layard, W. J. Fox, Milner-Gibson, and several Peelites. It seemed to Hare that no amount of political knowledge, official experience, public service, high character, or integrity of purpose could ensure a man a seat in parliament, and that the past few years showed how the absence of all such qualities did not exclude men without them. Moreover the situation would get worse, he thought, if the franchise was extended. So he proposed a remedy. Hare did not, it seems, share all the political views of the more radical of the defeated politicians, but he felt it was wrong that people who had the support of thousands of electors throughout the country should not be returned to parliament.

It is worth looking at the main features of Hare's 1857 scheme, as only thus can one grasp his striking originality and ingenuity, but also his complete inability to see what would be practicable. Electors would be able to vote for any qualified candidate throughout the kingdom. The names of all candidates, running into thousands, would be placed on a list. Returning officers

---

[1] Henry Fawcett wrote in 1860 in his pamphlet on Hare's proposals that 'vengeance upon China was the popular cry which in 1857 defeated many of the most eminent men in the house', 27.

were to send the local register of electors annually to a general registrar of electors. He would place the names of all electors in the kingdom (of whom there were then about 1,200,000) on a general register 'alphabetically and numerically', and would send back every year to returning officers their local registers with distinct letters and numbers for each elector. The number of votes required to get into parliament was then to be worked out by dividing the total number of registered electors by the number of seats in parliament, 654 at that time. The result was known as the quotient or quota. The friends of every candidate would normally form a committee, and the candidate or committee would receive the names of the electors who intimated their intention of voting for him. He would accept twice the number of names he needed to be elected—presumably to be on the safe side in case some electors did not fulfil their promises. If more than this number notified their support, they would be told to transfer it to some other candidate.

On the first of the three polling days the name of the candidate for whom a voter had voted would be recorded by the poll clerk in three columns. One of these would be sent to the general registrar, one would be left in the poll book, and one would be kept by the elector. The moment a candidate obtained the quota, he was declared elected either by the returning officer if all the votes came from his area, or by the general registrar if the votes came from more than one locality. If too many candidates for one constituency obtained the quota as a result of the votes of the electors in one place—and this could happen if constituencies varied greatly in size as they did then—machinery was provided to allocate candidates to another seat. A candidate who received more than the necessary quota of votes could decide which of the electors who voted for him he would like as his constituents, and send the names, letters, and numbers of the surplus voters to the general registrar. The registrar would then give 'excess polling papers' to the candidate, who would send them to the surplus voters who could vote again on the second polling day. Similarly a candidate who did badly on the first polling day could withdraw from the contest, obtain 'withdrawal polling papers' from the registrar, and send them to his supporters who could vote again. These electors would know the state of the polls and could vote for candidates who had some votes, but not the quota, or for entirely new ones even if not on the registrar's list.

The good results confidently anticipated by Hare were manifold. Having an unrestricted choice from among a thousand or so candidates instead of perhaps only two, the elector would be roused and animated. He would make enquiries in a wide field, and examine the works and actions of candidates through their lifelong careers. This would greatly improve political education. The elector would know his vote would be effective, so he would prize it and would take the trouble to get on to the register and actually to vote, which he often did not do under the existing system. A better quality of candidate would emerge, and the contemptible tactics of borough politicians would end. Bribery would be reduced because a candidate would only need to bribe if he had nothing but money to recommend him. MPs would become less subservient to their constituents because, appealing to the entire nation, they would not depend on the caprice of a local constituency and be at the mercy of petty jealousies and intrigues. Hare also hoped that leading men would come to realize that there were other and better things to be desired than the triumph of any party. He wanted to see the two great parties thinking of the national good rather than rivalling each other. Altogether it was an idealistic vision of a political system where harmony and concert would reign.

In the second edition of the pamphlet Hare admitted that the subordinate details of the proposal in the first edition were liable to grave objections, in imposing great labour on candidates and protracting the poll. So he suggested some amendments to his original scheme. These provided for only one poll instead of three and transferred the bulk of the work from candidates to the general registrar. The main lines of the original scheme were unchanged, but in the second edition more attention is given to dissemination of the list of candidates. Any person could offer himself as a candidate by sending his name to the clerk of parliament who was to publish daily, after the dissolution of parliament until polling day, a list of all candidates with their addresses and specify the constituency or constituencies for which they were candidates. No limit seems to have been placed on these. The clerk was to send to every returning officer as many copies of this list as there were electors in his constituency. Electors were entitled to one copy each. They could insert on their voting papers the names of all or any number of candidates on the list, putting them in order of preference. The poll clerk was to keep a record of the order in which voting papers were delivered to him. Any candidate getting as many first preferences as the quota number was immediately declared elected and could not be voted for by any other electors. His name was to be cancelled on all other voting papers—of which there might be thousands or indeed tens of thousands, though this is not mentioned by Hare—by a stamp provided for the purpose, a detail which he typically prescribed. (Sometimes one thinks that in such attention to detail he must have been influenced by Bentham, though there is no evidence that he was.) This was an ingenious device to prevent a candidate getting surplus votes. The voting papers, other than those on which the successful candidate or candidates were named first, were to be sent to the general registrar. He was then by a fairly elaborate process gradually to exclude the candidates with least support, and to appropriate the votes for them to the next or subsequent preferences of the electors. According to Hare, who had some justification for the view, the mechanism would give full and complete weight to every electoral preference which the voting papers indicated. He was also justified in claiming that this scheme reduced the labour imposed on candidates by his first scheme, but the work it required of returning officers and of the general registrar was correspondingly greater and more complex.

The main comment elicited by the 1857 pamphlet was that it did not solve the problem of how to prevent lower-class votes swamping those of the higher classes if the suffrage were extended. This problem was in Hare's mind as in that of so many other people at the time, but it was not by any means his main concern. However his scheme would have enabled the educated minority to get due representation and a proper hearing in parliament, and Hare, unlike some people, did not advocate their disproportionate representation.

Although Hare's job at the Charity Commission was no doubt fairly exacting, he did not have to work as hard as when he was at the Bar. One of his daughters recollected that before 1854 evening readings with his family had long been given up for legal work. Now he had more leisure not only to educate his four daughters—an activity to which he attached great import-ance—but also to read widely himself, to think about political subjects, and to write and publish in 1859 a substantial book. It was probably at this period that he read many of the numerous works referred to in the *Treatise*. The list of these is impressive for they include the following: Burke's *Speeches*; Guizot, *Histoire des origines du gouvernement représentatif*; Calhoun, *Disquisition on Government*, and *Discourse on the Constitution and Government of the United States*; Buckle, *History of Civilisation*; Grote, *History of Greece*; Niebuhr, *History of Rome*; Hallam, *The Middle Ages*; Macaulay, *History of England*; Blackstone, *Commentaries*; Montes-quieu, *De l'esprit des lois*; J. S. Mill, *Civilisation*, and *Principles of Political Economy*; Gibbon, *Decline and Fall of the Roman Empire*; Sismondi, *Fragments de son journal et correspondance*; Lord John Russell, *Essay on the English Constitution*; Lord Grey, *Essay on the Reform of Parliament*; Cornewall Lewis, *Essay on the Influence of Authority on Matters of Opinion*; *Guesses at Truth*.

Hare also referred in the *Treatise* to some of the contemporary periodical literature discussing electoral problems. This included the article in the *Edinburgh Review* of January 1852 in which the author (Greg) mentioned the idea put forward in the *Spectator* in 1851 of having a number of national MPs, so that any electors who so pleased could withdraw themselves from the local register and inscribe themselves among the voters for these national representatives. It is therefore just possible that it was from here that Hare derived one of the main features of his scheme, namely that of allowing electors to vote for any candidate in the whole country, though his references to Greg's article do not mention this part of it. But even if this is so, Hare still remains a remarkably original thinker, for it is clear that it was he who thought out the extraordinary machinery which he considered was required to implement the idea. There seems little doubt that he had not seen Gilpin's paper of 1844 though they both use the expression 'quota'. Nor was he acquainted with Rowland Hill's proposals of 1839 for town councils in South Australia, or with Hickson's recommendations of 1853 for London local government. Neither had he heard of the electoral method devised by a Dane, C. C. G. Andrae, and actually put into operation in Denmark in 1855, though Hare's scheme was substantially the same as Andrae's.

Hare's book is a strange and uneasy amalgam of broad general reflections on such subjects as government, society, public opinion, and divine law, and meticulous details in the form of thirty-three extremely technical clauses of an electoral law with explanations of how it would work. The general reflections rely heavily on Burke, Guizot, and Calhoun, from whose works lengthy passages are quoted with reverence and no analysis. Guizot was for many people a major figure in political life in the mid-nineteenth century. He was well known in Britain as well as in France and his numerous works were much read; so it is not strange that he figures so prominently in Hare's *Treatise*. He is incidentally throughout quoted by Hare in French although his book on representative government had already been translated into English in 1852.[2]

However the important place occupied by the works of the American statesman John C. Calhoun may at first surprise the modern reader. He was known in Britain from the 1830s onwards as a prominent Southern politician, an ardent advocate of States' Rights, and a defender of slavery, but his writings, published after his death in 1850, did not have wide currency in this country. It is perhaps not fanciful to suggest that Hare may have been interested in Calhoun because of a certain similarity between their early lives. For Calhoun was the son of a farmer in South Carolina, self-educated to a large extent, with a law training, a voracious solitary reader and a great admirer of Burke. Later their careers diverged, as Calhoun soon went into politics, married a rich wife, and rose to be Vice-President of the USA and a Senator. But Calhoun's main attraction for Hare lay in the doctrine which he developed to support his views, namely the principle of 'nullification'. The essence of this was that if the federal government passed legislation (allegedly) injuring one of the states, it was exceeding its powers; the offended state then

[2] Hare may have taught himself French as he had so many other things, or learnt it from two of his daughters who were sent to school in Paris where they acquired a perfect knowledge of the language which they imparted to the rest of the family. Moreover Hare, who had a passion for foreign travel, spent his summer vacations abroad, often walking through France, accompanied by some of his children.

had the right to ignore the law and declare it null and void. The legislation which sparked off this controversy was a protective tariff imposed to assist northern manufactured goods which would have damaged the South's export trade. (Hare was a keen free-trader.) Subsequently the Southern states objected to federal laws which protected slaves who had escaped to non-slavery states from being returned to their masters. When in the 1840s Calhoun began to systematize his theories, he developed the doctrine of nullification further through the device of the 'concurrent majority'. The essence of this was to give every interest in the state an effective part in making and executing laws, or in vetoing them. Decisions to be effective would have to be agreed by a majority of the members of every interest, so that every substantial minority would have the power of self-protection. The completeness of the check of the minority over the majority should vary with the degree of difference between the conflicting interests and the extent of possible exploitation.

Calhoun's system if embodied in political machinery would clearly have provided the different interests, orders, classes, and portions of the community with entrenched powers to veto any action of the government. The state would have been at the mercy of Rousseau's 'particular wills'. Hare, one can presume, did not wish to pursue Calhoun's principle to its logical conclusion, and he was saved from having to do so by arguing that Britain did not need the devices recommended by Calhoun as it had a different constitution: the British parliament was composed of King, Lords, and Commons and, as stated by Blackstone, the consent of all three is required to make any new law binding the subject. However, on reflection Hare had to admit that in fact the three co-ordinate branches of parliament were not of equal power and that the House of Commons was becoming in practice the dominant body. It was therefore very important to ensure that it was properly composed: it should not be the creature of numerical majorities, but should represent all the varieties of disposition and interest which make up society. In such an assembly the majority would necessarily be 'concurrent'. This would happen because, according to Calhoun quoted by Hare, every group of constituents would select representatives who they thought would command the confidence of the others, for in order to advance its own peculiar interests it would have to conciliate the others. This would somehow lead to the representatives desiring to promote the common interests of the whole, though these do not (conveniently we may note) conflict with the separate interests of each. Hare was attracted by Calhoun's idealistic picture of a system in which, under the impulse of an exalted patriotism, all were impelled to acquiesce in whatever the common good requires. If, as Hare recommended, every distinct variety and combination of thought, sentiment, feeling, opinion, and interest were represented, they would form pillars to support and give unity to the constitutional edifice.

Hare's criticisms of contemporary political life in his book are similar to those made in the 1857 pamphlet, but the moral denunciations are fiercer and more numerous. At times it reads like the jeremiad of an evangelical preacher thundering away about the sins of the world. The electorate do not ask themselves what they ought to do, only what will be successful. Many of them, including the most intelligent classes, are apathetic and do not register, or if registered do not vote. The electoral body forms itself into adverse parties which cramp and distort people and excite hostility where none really exists. They form foul cabals. They succumb to the temptations of selfishness, hypocrisy, and untruth. The forces of thought and conscience are lowered so that true and individual opinions are not expressed. There is universal idolatry of money, and every effort is devoted to the acquisition of material riches. The character of the elected too is generally poor. Candidates are selected in secret by a process which excludes many good people. They suppress and conceal their opinions in order not to lose votes by their candour, and the links between MPs and their constituents are selfish and sordid. With very few exceptions the representative assembly is filled with an inferior class of men who are not adequate to their tasks. The main cause of this lamentable state of affairs is in Hare's view that constituencies are arbitrarily formed electoral bodies. He sees electoral boundaries as mystical, artificial lines, which restrict the elector to candidates of his locality. So the remedy is to allow him to vote for any of the thousands of persons who put themselves forward as candidates.

The 1859 scheme is in general structure similar to the second edition of the 1857 one, though more elaborate and radical, particularly because it involved in effect the possibility, indeed probability, of a completely new electoral map. For the right to return an MP could be conferred, after petition to Her Majesty in Council, on *inter alia* any borough or ward of a borough, any parish or part of a parish, any division of a county, and on any corporate body, college, or society. A petition had to be agreed to by a majority of the electors in each of these communities. The initiative to obtain separate representation would therefore rest with the local or corporate body. Any person could oppose such a request when it was being considered by Council, and Council's orders had to be laid before parliament. Hare suggests guide-lines on which Council should act and states (optimistically) that the question would always be one of a purely administrative character, in which party feelings could hardly enter. No limit would be placed on the number of constituencies which could be thus created, and Hare anticipates an increase over the existing number. A limit was not necessary because the number of constituencies did not affect the number of MPs who would be returned; for to be returned a candidate had to get the quota of votes, which was the quotient secured after dividing the total number of electors in the whole country by the number of members of the House of Commons as then prescribed by law, and only 654 candidates could achieve this. Hare did not incorporate in his scheme any alteration in the size of the House of Commons.

The scheme put no limit on the number of candidates who would be on the national list, as it was open to anyone to offer himself 'for the political service of his country'. It is not clear how candidates or at any rate some candidates would decide which and how many constituencies they would stand for. It seems that a candidate could put himself forward for a constituency even if not asked for by its electors, though Hare envisages that a candidate will usually communicate with the constituency or constituencies to which he presents himself. If a candidate was standing for several constituencies, the order in which the constituencies were listed would be important, as it would affect how votes were transferred if he did not get returned by the constituency first on his list.

The elector can as before vote for any of the thousands of

names on the list to which he has been given access, and he can put as few or as many names as he likes on his voting paper in order of preference. He can even put down all the names on the gazetted list, though this might, according to Hare, amount to two or three thousand. However he supposes an average of only 40 names on each voting paper. Hare most considerately provided that if a voter was unable to write he could cut out the names of candidates from the gazetted list and stick them on his voting paper. The voter's preferences would show how he wished his vote to be transferred from one candidate to another until it reached a candidate whom he had named who would require the vote to make up his quota. The system thus ensured that as far as possible votes were not wasted on candidates who had more support than was necessary for their election. The voters whose votes were assigned to a candidate made up his constituency, which might or might not have a territorial basis.

The duties imposed by the 1859 scheme on returning officers and on the three national registrars (for England, Scotland, and Ireland) for counting, appropriating, and transferring preferences are roughly the same as in 1857, but they are expanded and refined on by Hare in numerous ways. Their meticulous details need not be described here, but we must digress to explain briefly the method by which the quota is determined under a system of proportional representation, the quota being the number of votes which necessarily secures the election of a candidate.

Some people are puzzled by the notion of the quota,[3] but it is in fact simple and easy to understand with the following example. If there is only one seat to be filled, it is clear that the quota is one more than half of the votes cast, for no other candidate can obtain this number. Thus the candidate who obtains 51 out of 100 votes in a single-member constituency is sure of election. Similarly in a two-member constituency, if each voter has only one vote, any candidate who obtains more than a third of the votes must be elected. The quota in this case would be one more than one-third, namely 34, for if there are

---

[3] This is true even of a modern professional historian writing in 1972 about electoral reform in 1884: thus Andrew Jones in *The Politics of Reform 1884* talks of the quota as 'that magic number' (97, n. 4).

100 votes, only two candidates can poll as many as 34 each. Similarly in a three-member constituency the candidate who obtains one more than one-quarter of the votes (26 out of 100) is sure of election; and in a four-member constituency one more than one-fifth, and so on. In general terms the quota is found by dividing the total number of votes cast by one more than the number of seats to be filled and by adding one to the result so obtained. It will be observed that this method of calculating the quota is not exactly the same as Hare's. He proposed simply dividing the number of voters by the number of seats in parliament. (At first he had proposed taking the number of registered electors as the dividend; in the second edition of the *Treatise* this is changed to voters.) The quota thus obtained would have resulted in many MPs being elected by less than the quota because it would have been larger than necessary. This would have been undesirable because they would have had the same weight in the representative body as members elected by a full quota. Hare saw certain problems about how to calculate the quota, but he did not perceive this defect in his system. It was however pointed out in 1868 by the mathematician and lawyer H. R. Droop, and the method he advocated, which is the formula described above, has generally been accepted by advocates of proportional representation with the single transferable vote as the correct one. It is strange that Hare did not incorporate it into the 1873 edition of his book.

The suffrage was not an especially crucial issue for Hare, as he points out in his book that his system of representation could work with any suffrage, provided it did not differ (as it then did) according to one's place of residence. He was in any case in favour of a uniform franchise for counties and boroughs. Otherwise he argues for a test of capacity, and considers the then £10 qualification about right, though he recommends that it should be adjusted to allow for inequalities in rent in different places. He was not in favour of an educational test, partly because it would be very difficult to apply, but also, and more interestingly, because it would exclude men of much practical knowledge and good sense and would operate severely on the elderly. The book ends indicating how a much simpler version of the scheme could be introduced for the election of local councils, and with a very reasonable plea for a better structure of government in the metropolis, a subject to which Hare gave continuing attention for many years.

Hare's book was published in January 1859 and quickly attracted attention. John Stuart Mill, to whom Hare had sent it, read it at once and by 7 February was recommending Edwin Chadwick to read it without delay. It seemed to Mill 'most masterly in theory and of the greatest possible practical value'.[4] Mill had clearly not seen Hare's 1857 pamphlet. At that time and indeed until he saw Hare's book he was in favour of the cumulative vote. This is evident not only from various letters he wrote in 1857 and 1858, but also from his pamphlet *Thoughts on Parliamentary Reform* which was published at the end of January or in early February 1859 just before he saw Hare's book. It had in fact mostly been written five or six years before, but Mill decided to complete and publish it then as a Reform bill was about to be introduced by the government. In this pamphlet of fifty pages, four are devoted to the need for, and means of, securing the representation of minorities. Mill discusses briefly the devices of the limited and cumulative vote, preferring the latter, as he thought Marshall's pamphlet was able and conclusive on this issue. It was bad luck for Mill that so soon after the publication of his long-matured pamphlet, that part of it relating to the representation of minorities was rendered obsolete by his discovery of personal representation as advocated by Hare.[5] So when a second edition of the *Thoughts* came out later the same year, Mill appended to it the relevant parts of the article he had contributed to *Fraser's Magazine* for April 1859, explaining that his opinions had been greatly enlarged by Hare's speculations.

Meanwhile during March Mill was recommending the *Treatise* to other people, including the economist J. E. Cairnes, Herbert Spencer, Alexander Bain, and Cornewall Lewis. He had 'not been so delighted with any political treatise for many years'. It

---

[4] *The Later Letters of John Stuart Mill, 1849–73*, vols. xiv–xvii of the *Collected Works of John Stuart Mill*, ed. Francis E. Minneka and Dwight N. Lindley, University of Toronto Press (1972–81). Letter No. 359, 7 Feb. 1859. Mill's letters will subsequently be referred to as 'L' with number and date.

[5] Hare at first described his plan as 'personal representation', but it soon came to be known as 'proportional representation', as he was advocating the fair and adequate representation of all interests, classes, and opinions.

was 'a combination of theoretic wisdom and practical sagacity very rarely found in any writings on such subjects'. Hare's 'plan supersedes all that I or anyone else has said about grouping of boroughs, representation of minorities etc. . . . by realizing all these ends through a self acting machinery in a degree of perfection almost ideal'. Mill thought Hare's book was 'both a monument of intellect, and of inestimable practical importance at the present moment'. Hare's suggestions appeared to him to be 'the real basis of a reconciliation between Radicalism and Conservatism'. Had he seen it before writing his pamphlet he would have made it 'very different'.[6]

Mill also wrote to Hare on 3 March 1859 praising the book. He told Hare that he appeared 'to have exactly, and for the first time, solved the difficulty of popular representation; and by doing so, to have raised up the cloud and gloom of uncertainty which hung over the futurity of representative government and therefore of civilisation. That you are right in theory I never could have doubted, and as to practice, having begun with a great natural distrust of what seemed a very complicated set of arrangements, I ended by being convinced that the plan is workable, and effectually guarded or guardable against fraud.' Mill continued that he was as sanguine as Hare about the moral and political effects of the scheme. He entirely concurred both in the principles of the book and in its practical proposals, and agreed with most even of Hare's incidental remarks on things in general.[7]

Soon Mill was showing the most amazing optimism about the adoption of the scheme. Thus he was talking about 'when the time actually comes for legislating on your [Hare's] principles'. When once the plan is understood, it had 'a fair chance, if sufficiently promulgated, of being widely and enthusiastically taken up by the élite of the nation'. If kept before the public, the plan 'will be adopted as soon as any really large concession of the suffrage has to be made to the working classes'. He saw no obstacle to its adoption except the novelty of the idea. He even thought (wrongly as it turned out) that of all prominent

[6] L 362, 2 Mar. 1859; L 370, 4 Mar. 1859; L 374, 17 Mar. 1859; L 376, 20 Mar. 1859.
[7] L 365, 3 Mar. 1859.

public men Gladstone was the likeliest to appreciate it. Hare had in fact already sent his book to Gladstone in March 1859 suggesting, unsuccessfully, that his scheme should be examined by a committee of the House of Commons.[8]

Mill made his conversion public in his (April 1859) article in *Fraser's Magazine* entitled 'Recent Writers on Reform'. About half of it is devoted to outlining and praising Hare's plan. Mill considered Hare's book 'to be the most important work ever written on the practical part of the subject (parliamentary reform)'. Hare had raised the principle of the representation of minorities 'to an importance and dignity which no previous thinker had ascribed to it. As conceived by him, it should be called the real, instead of nominal, representation of every individual elector.' For the first time, a way was really shown to that reconciliation and simultaneous recognition of the best principles and ends of rival theories, which the generality of political writers have despaired of. Hare had not only illuminated it with the light of an advanced political philosophy, but embodied it in a draft Act of parliament, prepared with the hand of a master in the difficult art of practical legislation. This 'masterly contrivance' would be 'unspeakably beneficial'. When Hare was showing how his scheme would raise the tone of the whole political morality of the country, he 'rises into a noble enthusiasm, which is irresistibly attractive when combined, as it is with him, with a sober and sagacious perception of the relation between means and ends, and a far-sighted circumspection in guarding his arrangements against all possibilities of miscarriage and abuse'. Hare's scheme would allay the fears of people about the extension of the suffrage, because the educated and propertied classes would at least be represented in parliament and though in a minority could influence the working classes. Ultimately if his scheme were adopted, it would not be necessary to have plural voting.[9]

Although Mill remained an ardent Hare enthusiast, he did

---

[8] L 373, 12 Mar. 1859; L 380, 29 Mar. 1859; L 386, 7 Apr. 1859; Gladstone to Hare, 12 Mar. 1859, in St John's College, Oxford.

[9] *Fraser's Magazine*, 59 os (Apr. 1859), 489–508. The other works discussed in the article are John Austin, *A Plea for the Constitution* (1859), and James Lorimer, *Political Progress Not Necessarily Democratic; Or Relative Equality the True Foundation of Liberty* (1857).

occasionally venture a tentative note of criticism or advice about the presentation of the scheme. Thus in June 1859 he hoped Hare would give 'brief and pungent answers' to the popular objections against the plan at the meeting of the National Association for the Promotion of Social Science to which Hare was to present a paper; and in August 1859 Mill recommended Hare to produce a brief popular explanation of the plan and its purposes.[10] Hare would clearly have been incapable of this, but it was done in due course by Henry Fawcett who had met Hare in October 1859 at the meeting where Hare had read a paper.[11] Fawcett had seen, as Mill put it, that Hare like many discoverers had much to learn in the art of presenting his discoveries with a view to popular effect. Mill therefore helped Fawcett prepare his pamphlet *Mr. Hare's Reform Bill, Simplified and Explained* which was published in March 1860. Fawcett was at this time a young Fellow of Trinity Hall, Cambridge, interested in political and economic questions and a great admirer of Mill's works. He boldly invited Mill and Hare to the 1859 Christmas feast at his college. Hare came, but Mill did not. However Hare effected a meeting between Fawcett and Mill (and himself) on 8 February 1860. This was Mill's first meeting with Hare. Leslie Stephen in his life of Fawcett says that no practical results followed from Mill's contact with Fawcett and that Fawcett's pamphlet attracted very little notice. Indeed he says it was even suppressed (though he does not make it clear by whom) because the scheme was not ripe for practical application.[12] It is true that Fawcett, when he started on a political career, as he soon did, saw the difficulties involved in embodying the complete scheme in any political programme, but his plan was to bring its discussion forward as much as possible. This was also Mill's aim and between the two of them they succeeded in doing this.

Fawcett's pamphlet managed to compress the essentials of Hare's book of 370 pages into thirty-one, the scheme itself being reduced from Hare's thirty-three clauses to seventeen. Under the simplified plan, constituencies remained as they were then, and candidates offered themselves for only one constituency,

---

[10] L 399, 17 June 1859; L 409, 24 Aug. 1859.
[11] Henry Fawcett, 1833–84. Professor of Political Economy at Cambridge, 1863. MP, Liberal, 1865–84. Postmaster-General, 1880–4.
[12] Leslie Stephen, *Life of Henry Fawcett* (1885), 185.

though voters could vote for any candidates in the country. Fawcett accepted Hare's main criticisms of the existing electoral machinery, and without indulging in apocalyptic denunciations of the tone of political life, he was confident that the adoption of Hare's plan would effectually check bribery and corruption. At this time Fawcett put more emphasis than Hare on the dangers of extending the franchise without some such protection for minorities; but a few years later he thought that as the working classes were greatly divided in their opinions, it would be safe to extend the suffrage without waiting until the representation of minorities had been safeguarded. Mill on the other hand thought that the working classes were united on points which involved class interests or prejudices, and was disagreeably surprised by Fawcett's view which told against the need for such a plan as Hare's.[13] Although he was a mathematician by training, Fawcett did not get diverted into the intricate discussions which took place for many years about the machinery for transferring voters' preferences, and in later years he ceased to care for some of the details of Hare's plan. But he remained throughout his life a staunch supporter of the principle of proportional representation, and would, it seems, have resigned from the government in December 1884 with Leonard Courtney when the government adopted a measure incompatible with the principle, had he not died the previous month. Hare agreed to Fawcett's amendments to his scheme but did not embody them in subsequent editions of his book.

Besides seeing the need for a brief explanation of Hare's plan, Mill also saw the danger of Hare's supporters becoming identified with Toryism. They should not be unguarded enough to give any handle for representing the scheme as anti-democratic. Their only chance was to come forward as Liberals, carrying out the democratic idea, not as Conservatives, resisting it. Hare had apparently been thinking of trying to get support from the House of Lords.[14]

Mill also became gradually aware (as Hare clearly was not) of the danger of making people feel bored by the subject before they understood it. More interestingly Mill criticized Hare for

---

[13] L 721, 3 Oct. 1864; L 732, 2 Dec. 1864.
[14] L 438, 4 Feb. 1860; L 440, 5 Feb. 1860.

introducing so many of other writers' 'generalities' which were associated in most minds with unrealizable objectives; Hare should have shaped the generalities in his own mind and clothed them in his own language. Mill was moved to make these comments having seen Hare's article in *Fraser's Magazine* of February 1860 on 'Representation in Practice and Theory'. This article contains a great many quotations, including over a dozen from Carlyle, and some from F. D. Maurice, Ruskin, and others. Mill felt strongly on this point, on which he also expressed himself to his stepdaughter: Hare's paper rather disappointed him; it was 'overlaid with quotations of rhapsody from Carlyle and generalities from Maurice and Ruskin, as applicable to any other subject as to this'.[15] It is strange that it was only then that Mill seems to have been critical of Hare's habit of quoting the often rather vacuous statements of other writers in order to support his position. This is particularly odd in the case of Guizot and Calhoun. For although Mill had earlier admired Guizot as a historian, by 1849 he described one of Guizot's works (*De la démocratie en France*) as 'so vague and general as to be almost intangible', and he considered that the tract's 'denunciation of democracy is made up of vague and declamatory generalities'.[16] Mill read Calhoun's *Disquisition* and *Discourse* in 1854 when they were sent to him by the Legislature of South Carolina. When thanking them for the beautifully bound volume he wrote that whilst he was far from agreeing with it on all points, he considered it to be a really valuable contribution to the science of government. But when writing to his wife he expressed different views: he considered the style rather diffuse and that there was 'not a word to take the writer out of the category of hewers of wood and drawers of water. He is in some points a very inferior likeness of my father. One did not expect that in an American, but if in any, in this particular man.'[17]

In spite of Mill's criticisms, Hare did not alter his style of writing and continued to include many quotations from other people's works in the hope of thereby strengthening his case.

---

[15] L 436, 2 Feb. 1860; L 437, 2 Feb. 1860.

[16] L 4, 6 Feb. 1849 (to Hickson), and 'Vindication of the French Revolution of February 1848' (1849). *Collected Works of John Stuart Mill*, xx. 328–9.

[17] L 133, 18 Feb. 1854.

Thus an article by him in *Fraser's Magazine* of April 1860 continuing the February one was redolent with passages from Ruskin, Carlyle, Bain, Guizot, and others.

But in all essentials Mill's admiration for Hare and his scheme remained unadulterated, reaching a climax in his famous chapter VII of *Considerations on Representative Government* published in 1861. His diagnosis here of what is wrong with British political life is broadly similar to Hare's. Most MPs were of poor quality and low intelligence, largely due to the faulty selection process; there existed hundreds of able men of independent thought who had no chance of being returned to parliament. Mill also agreed that minorities were not adequately represented, but he puts more emphasis than Hare did on the dangers of class legislation in a democracy and rather less on the apathy and moral turpitude of the electorate. When he turns to the remedy for these infirmities, he accepts Hare's scheme as the complete answer. It could produce almost ideal perfection in representation and also attain several other important ends. The machinery was very simple. The scheme was perfectly feasible and had transcendent advantages. These advantages are so numerous that 'they place Mr. Hare's plan among the very greatest improvements yet made in the theory and practice of government'.[18] It would produce the proportionate representation not just of two great parties, but of every minority large enough to be entitled to a representative. The tie between elector and representative would be strengthened because the MP would represent persons, not mere bricks and mortar, though localities if large enough could still be represented by a local candidate. Parliament would contain men of superior intellect and character, the very élite of the country. The majority of MPs would admittedly still represent the uninstructed classes of the community, but they would have to meet the arguments of the instructed few, and might occasionally be convinced that they were in the wrong. Conflict and antagonism were essential to prevent stagnation and decay in any community. The system of personal representation would supply a rallying point for opinions and interests which the ascendant

---

[18] J. S. Mill, *Considerations on Representative Government*, Everyman's Library (1962), 263.

public opinion viewed with disfavour. This was essential to guard against the deteriorating influences which assail the weak side of democracy.

Mill referred briefly in his book to the 'ostensible objectors' to Hare's scheme. He dismissed those who 'profess to think the plan unworkable' by saying that they are generally people who have barely heard of it, or have given it very slight and cursory examination. He also answered those who criticized the abandonment of geographical areas as the only unit to be represented. The only serious obstacle to the scheme envisaged by Mill was unfamiliarity with it; this could be removed with time—years rather than centuries.

In later editions of *Representative Government* (especially the third edition of 1865), Mill conceded that several critics of Hare's plan had examined it carefully; nevertheless their objections were unreal or easily surmountable. He was no doubt correct in saying that it would be perfectly easy to guard against fraud at the central office. He also gave thoroughly reasoned answers to the two conflicting objections that the scheme would give undue power to small sections of the community, or to the great organized parties. Mill admitted that under any plan organization would exist and be an advantage, but he argued with justification that under Hare's scheme neither the two great parties nor the smaller sectarian groups—'knots of men bound together by a common crotchet'—would be able to elect more MPs than the number of their adherents warranted. Moreover he contemplated that another interest, the independent voters, who wanted to be represented by 'unpatronised persons of merit', would also get organized and be able to return men who were an honour to the nation. If necessary, in order to assist the representation of this group, the number of preferences a voter could express on his voting paper might be limited, for example to twenty or fifty; this would prevent independent voters filling up their lists with mere party candidates. Finally Mill tackled the objection of complexity. He considered this was exaggerated, and proposed that the scheme should be tried as an experiment in a limited field, such as a municipal election; this would enable people to convince themselves that it was not impracticable. It is true that one can illustrate preferential voting and the transfer of votes by small-scale experiments—this was frequently done later on by the Proportional Representation Society—but these experiments are very different affairs from the totality of Hare's scheme with its national list and elaborate machinery. Although Mill admitted that 'such experiments would be a very imperfect test of the worth of the plan', he was underplaying the differences between using the scheme for one local authority and for a general election over the whole country.

After the publication of *Representative Government* in 1861, Mill remained optimistic about the prospects of Hare's scheme. He was encouraged by the fact it was attracting attention and support in Australia, America, and on the continent of Europe, especially in Germany, Switzerland, and France.[19] Australian interest in Hare's ideas was sparked off by Mill's article in *Fraser's Magazine*. This was read in 1859 by Catherine Spence who had emigrated to South Australia from Scotland with her parents in 1839.[20] Hare's system brought back to her mind the provision in the Adelaide Municipal Act, put in at the instance of Rowland Hill, enabling a certain minimum of ratepayers (one-twentieth of the whole) to get together in groups and elect a member of the town council to represent them. Spence's father, who was for a time clerk to the Adelaide council, had explained the system to her and shown its implications for minority representation. She also read Hare's book and was delighted because she felt it showed how democratic government could be made 'real, and safe, and progressive'.[21] But on reflection she recommended a modification of his scheme by abandoning the idea that candidates could appeal to the whole country, and introducing instead manageable electoral districts. She published this in 1861 in a pamphlet, *A Plea for Pure Democracy*. Though Mill and Hare apparently thought well of the pamphlet, they did not abandon the national constituency idea. If they had, the cause of proportional representation would probably have made greater progress.

The parliament of New South Wales discussed the Hare

[19] L 495, 5 July 1861; L 526, 12 Jan. 1862; L 536, 6 Mar. 1862; L 557, 9 Oct. 1862.
[20] Catherine Helen Spence, 1825–1910. Novelist and journalist.
[21] C. H. Spence, *Autobiography* (Adelaide, 1910), 23.

scheme extensively in 1862 in connection with a proposal to make the Upper House elected instead of nominated. Mill was quoted at length and many speakers showed considerable understanding of the scheme. Although a majority supported it on second reading, the measure lapsed when the ministry resigned. Hare's ideas were also referred to in a debate in the parliament of Victoria in 1863, when it was discussing the cumulative vote.

In 1865 Spence published a three-volume novel, *Mr Hogarth's Will*, in which the hero reveals an unusual knowledge of the Adelaide Municipal Act and of limited and cumulative voting systems, and of course advocates Hare's scheme. The same year Spence came to Europe and met Hare and Mill. They had much in common besides electoral reform, for Spence had long believed that women were fit to share in the work of the world and that making it pleasant for men was not their only mission, as she put it later in her *Autobiography*. She was also very interested in land reform and land values taxation. In the 1890s she travelled again extensively, to Great Britain where she stayed with Hare's daughters, and to Belgium and the United States, speaking at many meetings about proportional representation. On her return to Australia she became president of the newly formed Effective Voting League, whose work met with some success, as proportional representation was introduced during her lifetime in the Australian state of Tasmania and later in New South Wales. In both cases the method used was the one favoured by Spence—the single transferable vote.

Foreign interest in Hare's scheme seemed to Mill to augur well for its reception and success in England, once people gave their minds to it as a question of the day. He acknowledged that few in practical politics had begun to concern themselves about it, but these few were an increasing body. Right ideas now that they were promulgated were making rapid way among thinking persons and future teachers of all parts of the world. Mill also noted with approval that the scheme had been discussed in 1864 for two days at the Amsterdam congress for the Progress of the Social Sciences, and that Louis Blanc had been writing from London letters to the French newspaper *Le Temps* showing that he fully understood Hare's plan and appreciated its advantages, indirect as well as direct. Even more encouraging for Mill was the fact that something nearly identical with Hare's scheme had actually been in operation and found workable in Denmark for several years.[22] It is strange that no one in England seems to have been aware of this until the summer of 1864 when a report from the British legation in Copenhagen was published.[23] In May 1865 Mill felt that the question had for the first time passed into the domain of popular discussion in England: it was being noticed in country newspapers and was making 'unexpected proselytes', such as Thomas Hughes and John Lubbock.[24] Hughes was well known as a Christian Socialist and author of *Tom Brown's Schooldays*; Lubbock was a banker and man of science. Both of them were standing for parliament in 1865. In fact Lubbock was still thinking about the scheme, but not yet supporting it. Mill was also pleased to have the support of the scholar and man of letters Francis Newman,[25] but in retrospect it seems that this must have been of doubtful value, as Newman typified the sort of eccentric 'crotcheteer' with whom opponents of proportional representation have so often associated its supporters. He was anti-vaccination, anti-vivisection, a keen vegetarian, pro-female suffrage, a maverick Christian, a friend of Mazzini and Kossuth, and he dressed in a peculiar way. No wonder that his brother, John Henry, said of him, 'Much as we love each other, neither would like to be mistaken for the other.'[26]

The cheaper editions of Mill's *Representative Government* were selling very well in 1865, and the fact that he was getting support for his candidature for parliament from people who had liked his books and not from any of the organized political parties clearly showed, he considered, the correctness of his contention that a substantial number of isolated individuals had independent views which they wished to get represented in parliament.

---

[22] L 580, 26 Jan. 1863; L 592, 24 Feb. 1863; L 537, before 11 June 1862; L 721, 3 Oct. 1864. Louis Blanc, 1811–82. Prominent French socialist living in exile in England after the revolution of 1848.

[23] PP 1864 LXI, 576–99. Election of Representatives for the Rigsraad. The Report, by Robert Lytton, gives a masterly account of Hare's ideas and scheme, relating them to theories of representation.

[24] L 826, 29 May 1865.

[25] Francis William Newman, 1805–97.

[26] Oldcastle, *Cardinal Newman* (1890), 5.

In January 1866 Mill thought that he or Hare might live to see the plan in actual operation in England, or at all events in America, but he sensibly poured scorn on Hare's suggestion that the House of Commons might be induced to appoint a committee to inquire into the best means of 'liberating and stimulating individual thought and action'. 'Are there six persons in the house of commons', Mill wrote, 'who think it any business of theirs to liberate and stimulate individual thought and action, or who would desire to do so even if they knew what it meant?' Even outside the House of Commons, he added, only a small number of people were converts to Hare's plan.[27] There seem in effect to have been two conflicting strands in Mill's thinking about support for the scheme, an optimistic one and a more realistic one. But the explanation is that he was coming more and more to distrust the attitude of most politicians—middle- and upper-class—and to place his faith in working men. Thus he wrote in 1862 that practical politicians were only too glad to turn from the whole subject. In 1864 he compared English politicians unfavourably with foreign ones, and he was not surprised that they did not 'catch at' the plan, 'for when were they in advance of the public in adopting any new idea?' Radical MPs showed extreme narrowness of mind and were afraid to concede anything, or admit any fault or danger on the democratic side; there was more chance of being listened to on such subjects as the representation of minorities by the working classes than by their well-dressed friends. He criticized (understandably) the new (1865) edition of Lord John Russell's book on English government, castigating the Introduction for 'pompous emptiness' and 'mental feebleness'.[28] Russell had there written that when the question could be fairly entertained, he hoped the suffrage would be extended 'on good old English principles, and in conformity with good old English notions of representation'. He would 'be sorry to see the dangers of universal suffrage and of unlimited democracy averted, or sought to be averted, by . . . contrivances altogether unknown to our habits, such as the plan of Mr Hare, though

[27] L 902, 4 Jan. 1866; L 907, 11 Jan. 1866.
[28] L 537, before 11 June 1862; L 721, 3 Oct. 1864; L 747, 4 Feb. 1865; L 782, 23 Mar. 1865.

sanctioned by the high authority of so profound a thinker as Mr Mill . . . It is difficult to believe in this age of the world that there are models of government, still untried, promising a cup of felicity and of freedom which England has not yet tasted . . . The subject is full of unknown pitfalls, and it is far better for the great Liberal party in the country to . . . trust to . . . no subtle inventions of ingenious theorists, than to be parties to a plausible scheme.'[29]

Support for Mill's view that politicians here did not study the subject carefully was supplied by the revelation that as late as May 1866 Earl Grey thought Mill was still in favour of the cumulative vote. Grey had blundered before too by referring to Hare as 'Julius' instead of 'Thomas' and by getting wrong the title of Hare's book which he called a pamphlet. Similarly Lord Robert Montagu had shown in his intervention at a meeting of the Social Science Association in 1866 that he confounded the results of Hare's plan with those of the opposite one. (He thought that under Hare's plan 658 MPs all of one party would be elected.) This was for Mill an illustration of the manner in which English politicians, specially of Montagu's class, make themselves acquainted with new ideas. By contrast Mill was encouraged by a debate at the Working Men's College in the summer of 1867, where the representation of minorities had been supported; 'for the working men do not share the indifference of the middle class to superior cultivation, and are much more willing than the middle class to give full and thoroughgoing effect to a principle'.[30]

Mill's view of politicians must have been greatly reinforced by the cold reception they gave to his proposal to incorporate the Hare scheme, albeit in a modified form, into the Reform Bill which was going through parliament in 1867. Ten days after he had proposed extending the suffrage to women, late at night, Mill moved an amendment to the redistribution clauses, embodying the main features of the Hare scheme, namely that electors should be able to vote for any candidate in the United Kingdom, putting as many names as they liked in order of

[29] Lord John Russell. *An Essay on the History of the English Government and Constitution* (1865), 239–42. The book first appeared in 1821.

[30] L 949, 21 May 1866; L 695, 13 May 1864; L 1007, 18 Nov. 1866; L 1130, after 7 Aug. 1867.

preference on their voting papers. Candidates who obtained the quota were elected. The rules governing the counting of votes and the transfer and appropriation of preferences were to be framed by the Speaker of the House of Commons and laid before parliament.

In a speech which occupies thirteen columns of Hansard, Mill argued that at least a third and perhaps a half of electors were at present unrepresented in parliament, either because they had voted for candidates who were defeated, or because, where there was no contest, they would not have supported the MP who was returned if there had been a contest, or because they could take no part in the selection of candidates. So the remedy was to allow anyone to put himself up as a candidate, and for the electors to be able to vote for any candidate. This would not, Mill averred, destroy the local character of representation because most voters would in fact vote for a local man or someone connected with the place by a special tie, but it would raise the level of local candidates as they would be facing national competition. Mill met the argument that under the existing system those who are defeated in one constituency can console themselves with the knowledge that their party is victorious in other places by saying that one wanted a House of Commons that represented all the feelings of the people, not just their party feelings, and that electors should be able to show their confidence in particular men. He then showed that his proposal was a legitimate corollary from the distinctive doctrines of Conservatives and Liberals. It complied with conservative principles because it would prevent manual labourers monopolizing the whole of the legislature and would ensure the variegated character of representation. It also complied with the principle of democracy, the radical creed that everybody, every class, should be represented in proportion to numbers. He argued ingeniously that those who are anxious for safeguards against the evils they expect from democracy should not neglect the safeguard which is to be found in the principles of democracy itself.

In the course of his speech Mill paid a glowing tribute to his 'eminent friend Mr Hare—a man distinguished by that union of large and enlightened general principles with an organising intellect and a rare fertility of practical contrivance, which together constitute a genius for legislation'. But considering his passionate commitment to the cause, Mill in general put his case for the amendment in a fairly restrained way, except when he was eulogizing Hare or forecasting that his plan would result in a prodigious gain to policy, morality, and even civilization. Moreover he was realistic in not expecting to obtain the immediate assent of the House to his proposal, but he was pathetically over-optimistic in expecting that many MPs would consider the subject seriously. On the contrary they treated him with scant respect or even courtesy, being inattentive or laughing at him. This was recorded by Lady Amberley who listened to the debate with two of Hare's daughters; they were naturally disgusted at the behaviour of MPs, which was also commented on adversely by Viscount Cranborne (later Lord Salisbury) although he did not share any of Mill's opinions. The debate on Mill's amendment was brief. Cranborne agreed that there was an evil at present, namely the danger of nomination caucuses and local party machines, but he considered Mill's remedy impracticable. Nevertheless he urged that it should be properly discussed and he even thought that it might be a good plan if some MPs, say fifty to 100, could appeal to the whole country as their constituency and be returned independently of local and party considerations. Cranborne's reproof to the House for its reception of Mill's speech had no effect on one of the five members who contributed to the debate, for Sergeant Gaselee ridiculed Hare's plan as 'an emanation from Gooseberry Hall'— a reference to Gosbury Hill where Hare lived—and asked the Commons to turn from the amusement they had had to more serious business. Sensing the temper of the House, Mill wisely did not press his amendment to a division and withdrew it.[31]

Apart from all the obvious reasons for the failure of the proposal at that time, there was the added fact that Mill was not by nature or experience a politician versed in the parliamentary arts. It was said of him later that he seemed when addressing the House of Commons like a man performing a difficult and disagreeable duty; that he was hardly fluent, deliberating on every sentence; that he often paused for some

---

[31] *HC Deb.* 187 (30 May 1867), 1343–62. Mill's speech, entitled 'Personal Representation', is reprinted in his *Collected Works*, xxviii. 176–87.

minutes for an appropriate phrase and that his oratory, in Gladstone's words, 'came as from a statue'.[32] Afterwards Mill said that he never expected any better reception in parliament or the press for the scheme of personal representation, and he had enough sense to realize that it was too soon to form an organized combination to work for the plan, especially among MPs.[33] Nevertheless he must have been disappointed at the parliamentary proceedings, for he had been planning the amendment with Hare for months.

Mill intervened occasionally in subsequent debates on the Reform Bill, particularly when the House was discussing the cumulative vote for three-member constituencies, which he regarded as an 'almost insignificant makeshift' but nevertheless one of considerable efficacy, resting in part upon the same principles as Hare's system of personal representation. This was surely a dubious statement, but Mill could not shake off his long-standing though strange loyalty to the cumulative vote. He answered the objection raised by some people that the proposal would weaken the executive by saying boldly that it was not desirable that a government should be strong by having a large majority in the House if it only had a small majority in the country.[34] Mill was a teller when the House voted on the proposal, which was lost. He did not speak in the debate on the limited vote on 8 August 1867, but he voted for it and it became law.[35]

Mill's virtual intoxication with Hare's scheme raises various questions. How did a man who was usually deliberate and cautious in his judgements come to form an opinion so precipitately and to stick to it with such obduracy? Were MPs really as low-grade as he and Hare made out? What experience had Mill had of elections and political life generally? Did he think out carefully and closely how Hare's scheme would actually work and see the problems it would have posed?

[32] W. L. Courtney, *Life of John Stuart Mill* (1889), 159. See also Leslie Stephen's impressions of Mill speaking in the Commons. He described him as 'trembling with nervous irritability'. *National Review*, 248 (Oct. 1903), 215.

[33] L 1104, 30 June 1867; L 1129, 6 Aug. 1867.

[34] *HC Deb.* 188 (5 July 1867), 1102–7.

[35] Discussed more fully in Ch. III.

When Mill first read Hare's *Treatise* in January 1859, his wife had only recently died (in November 1858) and he was suffering acutely from this crushing calamity. He was also depressed at the loss of liberty in many countries. It is therefore not unreasonable to suggest that this may at any rate partly account for the rather unbalanced avidity with which he took up a scheme which looked like solving the problems attendant upon the spread of democracy, problems which had worried him for thirty years. He had always been interested in particular in the quality of representatives: Hare's plan would, he thought, ensure that power would be exercised by the fittest persons available. Having taken instantly to the scheme, it seems as if he was thereafter reluctant to look carefully into how it would actually work. He was not really interested in the machinery and details of the proposed electoral system, but he was committed to the notion that it was simple and practicable. The difficulties seen by others were merely 'supposed' and would largely disappear after a little experience. Alexander Bain, who knew him quite well, considered that his natural temperament was confiding rather than sceptical, and that when he had not knowledge enough to check what other people said, he was ready to take them at their word.[36] Mill had not been involved in electoral or party politics since the 1830s, the attempt to establish the Philosophical Radicals as a third party having clearly failed by 1841. So he was willing to accept uncritically Hare's denunciations of the political mores of the times, and the cure he proffered. Further, not being himself a trained lawyer or practised in the art of drafting Acts of parliament, he was over-impressed by what he saw as Hare's mastery of a difficult art. Other people, battling their way through the thirty-three clauses of Hare's bill, reacted rather differently to its highly technical and legalistic language.

Apart from the fact that Hare's plan provided Mill with a solution to problems attendant upon an extension of the suffrage, there was much in Hare's system of values with which Mill agreed, in particular the importance of independent thought and action. For Mill the choices a man makes are what go to make up his self; and it was important to have the widest

[36] Alexander Bain, *John Stuart Mill, a Criticism* (1852), 158.

possible range of choices available, as our choices create as well as reflect our characters.[37] Hare's scheme offered electors a gigantic, some might say a bewildering, choice of candidates, as there would probably be a thousand or more on the list from which they could select which and how many to vote for. Similarly Hare's understandable belief that his proposals would result in improved political education fitted in well with Mill's passionate desire for progress—improvement in the quality of human beings. Moreover Mill agreed with Hare's views on various other issues such as the limitation of MPs' expenses, opposition to the secret ballot, non-payment of MPs, and, most important of all, votes for women.

It is also significant that Mill, who had been a recluse for many years, acquired in Hare 'a real friend' as he himself put it in 1865. A year later he classed Hare amongst 'the friends one values most'. Mill had many acquaintances and admirers, but, it would seem, few close friends. Two weeks after he first actually met Hare, he told his daughter, 'I like Hare more and more. I like very much the expression on his face.'[38] One of Hare's daughters recorded later that Mill and his stepdaughter became intimate friends of Hare and his family, that they often visited the Hares' home at Kingston upon Thames, staying there for the weekend, and that Hare and some of his family often dined and spent the night with Mill at Blackheath. They also stayed with him once in France for two weeks.[39] Mill must have found the atmosphere of the Hare household congenial as the daughters were keen feminists, and visitors included many interesting people. Indeed so agreeable was this family circle that he was not disconcerted by the religious atmosphere which pervaded it. Hare had been much influenced by the Tractarian movement and remained all his life a keen High Churchman. Family prayers were said twice daily in the chapel at Gosbury Hill, but Mill expressed no disapproval of this practice, seeming, according to Hare's daughter, even to admire and approve of the family's adhesion to their point of view. Indeed so solid was Mill's admiration for Hare that their friendship was not shaken

[37] See *A System of Logic* (1843), Bk. VI, ch. ii, §3.

[38] L 826, 29 May 1865; L 1007, 18 Nov. 1866; L 447, 21 Feb. 1860.

[39] From undated memorandum by Mrs K. Clayton in the possession of David Roberts, Hare's great-grandson.

by a difference of opinion over the American Civil War. Mill explained away Hare's support for the South by saying that he had probably 'not much studied the subject' and was not 'well in possession of the antecedent facts'.[40]

Mill's sponsorship of Hare's plan gave him 'a letter of introduction to the public' as the *Economist* put it in June 1859, thus securing Hare more attention than he might otherwise have received. But in the long run the cause of proportional representation would probably have been better served if Mill had looked more critically at the practicality of the scheme, for then his enthusiastic backing of it could not have been so easily discounted by those for whom 'philosopher' was a term of denigration.

[40] L 536, 6 Mar. 1862.

# III

# The First Campaign:
# Part I, 1859–1883

THOMAS HARE was a man of great energy, determination, and self-confidence, and as a staunch believer in individual initiative he did not leave the publicity for his book—the *Treatise*—to others. Soon after publication in January 1859, he sent copies of it to many people, including, among politicians, Gladstone, Edward Cardwell, John Bright, Sir Edward Lytton, and Lord Grey. They all wisely thanked him before reading it.[1] During the rest of his life (he died at the age of 85 in 1891) he wrote at least twenty-five papers or articles on representative machinery and numerous letters to the press. He also gave evidence to two parliamentary select committees and was involved in many other activities to promote his ideas at home and abroad.

After giving in October 1859 the first of many papers at a meeting of the recently formed National Association for the Promotion of Social Science, Hare wrote in 1860 two articles in which he criticized the work and composition of parliament, which had in his view deteriorated substantially since 1832: he thought the Reform Act of that year had opened the doors to rich, reckless, unscrupulous, and shameless men; and he showed how under his scheme one could combine the representation of localities with the election of the best and wisest persons.[2] He also wrote a letter to *The Times* proposing two modest amendments to the current Reform bill.[3] One of these was that no elector was to have more than one vote, however many representatives the constituency returned. At that time in

---

[1] Correspondence in St John's College, Oxford.
[2] *Fraser's Magazine*, 61 os (Feb. 1860), 188–204; and (Apr. 1860), 527–43.
[3] *The Times*, 15 Mar. 1860, 10–11.

many constituencies electors had two votes; in seven constituencies they had three votes; and in one four votes. In the United Kingdom as a whole electors had more than one vote in 62 per cent of constituencies. Hare argued that there was absolutely no reason for this diversity except the historical one that it existed; and he pointed out with some justification that if that consideration were to prevail, it would be an argument fatal to any Reform bill which had ever been passed or projected. The other amendment he proposed was a limitation of £50 on candidates' election expenses.

In June 1860 Hare gave evidence to a House of Lords select committee on the Elective Franchise in Counties and Boroughs.[4] He was questioned about the proportion of electors who voted in different constituencies. He had written to many people of eminence in different departments of life, including science, law, medicine, and literature, asking them what they did themselves and observed others doing as regards voting. He got quite a good response, but the committee, adopting a legalistic attitude, refused to hear from him what were the opinions of others or even to look at the letters he had received. However they allowed him to give his conclusions. His calculations showed that the proportion of registered voters entitled to vote who actually voted fell as constituencies became larger; so he concluded that educated and property-owning electors tended not to vote in large constituencies because their votes would probably not be effective. This gave him a chance to expound his scheme to the committee, but nothing came of this as the committee issued no report. Later in June 1860 he gave a long paper to the Statistical Society of London entitled 'On the Application of a New Statistical Method to the Ascertainment of the Votes of Majorities in a More Exhaustive Manner'. He explained his system of contingent voting and outlined the good effects he considered it would produce on the morality of electors and the quality of their representatives.[5] He made similar points in an article in 1862 whilst commenting on the

---

[4] PP 1860 XII, 4 June 1860, 451–7.

[5] *Journal of the Statistical Society*, 23 (Sept. 1860), 337–56. Hare used the expression 'contingent voting' because the voter was indicating on his voting paper that if it so happened that his first choice did not need his vote, he would like it transferred to his next choice, and so on.

recent University Elections Act, which allowed university electors to vote by proxy for university MPs, and he answered
sneers that his scheme of voting by what he called 'exhaustive
majorities' was Utopian or 'worthy of Laputa'.[6] In the same year
at the Social Science Association June meeting, Hare referred to
the considerable interest his scheme had aroused abroad, in
America, Australia, and Europe.

Meanwhile in the spring of 1861 there had appeared a second
edition of the *Treatise*. In this Hare claimed that he had made 'a
great simplification of the proposed method of election', and
predicted with his inveterate optimism that the system, thus
'freed from apparent complication', would be likely to make
more rapid progress towards a general acceptance.[7] But in fact
the simplification was minimal: the book was of the same length
as the first edition, and the draft electoral law had been reduced
by only one clause to thirty-two clauses.

In 1863, Hare showed in an article[8] how his plan could be
adapted to produce improved and real local government in
London, linking this in particular with the need for better
housing, a subject which concerned him deeply and on which
he had published in 1862 a separate long pamphlet, *Usque ad
Coelum*.[9] In this he had pointed out that through no fault of
their own it was impossible for working men, even when
earning an average wage, to find decent accommodation in
London at a price they could afford. He was not in favour of
their migrating to the suburbs where they would be cut off
socially and far from their work. His solution was that the mass
of existing small houses should be extended upwards by three
or four floors. Landlords should be cajoled or forced to do this
by a reformed local authority with powers of compulsory
purchase; it was no use expecting that a solution to the problem
would emerge if left to private enterprise. The scheme could be

[6] *Macmillan's Magazine*, 5 (Feb. 1862), 295–301. The reference to 'Laputa' is to
the fabled island in Swift's *Gulliver's Travels* which epitomizes the rationalist's
daydream.
[7] Advertisement to the New and Revised Edition of Hare's *Treatise* (1861),
p. iii.
[8] *Macmillan's Magazine*, 7 (Apr. 1863), 441–7.
[9] This title was derived from the legal maxim 'Cujus est solum, ejus est usque
ad coelum' which Hare wanted abandoned, so that the unoccupied space above
a building no longer belonged to the owner of the ground beneath.

made financially sound by mixing in retailers' businesses and higher-class people who would occupy the lower floors; the working classes would be on the top floors and would benefit from proximity to educated people of good taste. Communal facilities would also be provided; and he urged that resources should be better organized by reformed local government for common benefits such as physical activities like gymnastics, swimming, and riding, and education for all classes. Altogether it was a typical Hare scheme, bold, original, ingenious, benevolently inspired, and well argued with support from Mill's works—*A System of Logic*, his article on Coleridge, and *Principles of Political Economy*.

In March 1865 there appeared the third edition of the *Treatise*. It was thirty pages longer than the previous editions, containing a new preface, many appendices, and other additions, but the price had been reduced from ten to six shillings. The preface contains a reply to the three main 'supposed objections' which had been made to his method: its too great complexity, its incompatibility with local constituencies, and its liability to party organization and abuse. The proposed electoral law still contains thirty-two clauses. The appendices exhibit the progress of the idea in other countries—Switzerland, Germany, France, Denmark, America, Holland, and Belgium.

In April 1865 at a meeting of the Social Science Association, Hare read a paper entitled 'Such an organisation of the Metropolitan elections as would call into exercise the greatest amount of the knowledge and judgment of the constituencies and as far as possible discourage all corrupt and pernicious influences'. Mill was present and reported that the meeting was full and went off well.

Later in 1865 in an article, Hare made the perceptive observation that the poor are more interested in good government than the rich because they have far smaller resources to compensate for or indemnify themselves against the mischiefs of evil government. So it was necessary to arouse the upper classes from their indifference to political action; one way of doing this was to allow them separate representation through the mechanism of a general electoral college.[10] Hare outlined the same proposal

---

[10] *Fortnightly Review*, 2 os (Oct. 1865), 439–42.

at the Social Science Association meeting of October 1865, throwing in the acute observation that the objections to his scheme which he had heard in former discussions were not those of electors, but of candidates, and these in his view were of no importance.

The next year, 1866, saw two articles by Hare.[11] In the first one he discarded altogether the argument for what had been called the 'representation of minorities', whether by cumulative or restrictive (i.e. limited) voting. These devices would in his view not add appreciably to the power of individual expression; on the contrary they would aggravate the slavery of individuals to the leaders of parties. Minorities in Hare's view already obtained too many seats by using illegitimate means, and because of an artificial distribution of the franchise. He was presumably thinking here of small borough constituencies, of which there were a great many. The second article covered the same general ground and also answered various objections made in an article by J. Boyd Kinnear.[12] The debate between them shows how unsatisfactory it often was to talk about majorities and minorities without specifying what minority one had in mind. But Hare was justified in claiming for his electoral method a more important purpose than that of a plan for representing minorities. He also tackled the objection that his scheme would encourage people to hold strong opinions on small points—which were commonly dubbed 'crotchets'—and not to think enough of the general good. Hare saw no reason to think that advocates of particular causes (such as the opening of museums on Sundays) would be more ignorant of the general welfare than others who had no view on such questions; to support his position he said that some of the ablest minds in the past first found their way into parliament as the advocates of special interests.

[11] *Fortnightly Review*, 3 os (Jan. 1866), 559–65; and 4 os (Mar. 1866), 350–8.

[12] John Boyd Kinnear, 1828–1920. A Scottish barrister turned journalist. He was in many ways rather similar to Hare, being an individualistic philanthropic Radical; but he was critical of Hare's electoral scheme and did not even mention the representation of minorities in his book *Principles of Reform* (1865), an omission adversely commented on by Mill in a letter to him (L 861, 19 Aug. 1865). Kinnear's article is in the *Fortnightly Review*, 4 os (Feb. 1866), 49–64. There is an interesting account of him by Christopher Harvie in the *Journal of the Scottish Labour History Society*, Nov. 1970.

Hare's activities during 1866 also included giving evidence to a House of Commons select committee on Metropolitan Local Government.[13] He pointed out that his electoral scheme if applied to a municipal council for the whole of London, which he regarded as highly desirable, would undermine one of the current objections made against such a council, namely that it would be a too powerful body near the seat of the central government. If it was elected under his plan, it would not represent only the overwhelming weight of numbers, which the government saw as a source of danger, but a balance of all social forces and interests. Hare was questioned vigorously and at some length about his proposals. Assisted by Mill who was a member of the committee, he answered with skill and verve, but patiently even when, as so often, members showed they did not understand essential ingredients of the scheme, like the transfer of votes so that none should be wasted. He also tried to reassure them that people who would look after local interests would still be elected as well as more eminent and philanthropic individuals. An interesting difference of opinion emerged between him and the chairman (Acton Smee Ayrton) who, although a Radical, suggested that an inert state of society was very convenient. Why should one try to make people into active and contentious electors when nobody wants this? he asked. Hare replied that 'there are a vast number of social improvements that want to be carried out' in London.[14] The committee never reported its views on Hare's proposals as it was not reappointed in the next parliamentary session, but it seems unlikely that any converts were made. The same year (1866) Hare gave two papers to the Social Science Association, one in February on local government and the other in October with the comprehensive title 'A Grouping of Parliamentary Electors that combines a Just and Equal Distribution of Seats, and the Free Expression both of Individual and Public Opinion, with the smallest degree of Disturbance from Corrupt Influence'. His proposed electoral law summarized in a footnote had by then thirty-seven clauses.

\*

[13] PP 1866 XIII, 378–91.     [14] Ibid. Q. 2771.

After the failure of Mill's initiative in parliament in 1867, Hare turned his attention towards getting support for his scheme from the working classes. In October of that year he suggested to the President of the Reform League, Edmond Beales, that they should hold conferences during the parliamentary recess on the distribution of seats and the organization of constituencies. In a letter of nineteen pages, Hare reviewed the history of the British constitution, criticized the fiction of virtual representation—a fiction believed in by Gladstone—and suggested the way in which the conferences should be conducted: they would collect facts, there would be thorough discussion, errors would be corrected, and just deductions would be made. Parliament would not be able to disregard the reports which ensued; on the contrary they would influence opinion just as the *Federalist* papers had had a wide and good influence on the American Constitution. The Reform League, founded in 1865, was the most important of a long line of often ephemeral societies striving for electoral reform since the collapse of the Chartist movement. Though its large membership was predominantly working class, it had links with middle-class Radicals and Liberals, including Mill. It was therefore the most obvious organization for Hare and his associates to approach. The council of the League studied and discussed Hare's ideas and, it appeared, thoroughly understood his theory.[15]

Hare addressed the first meeting of the conference with the Reform League in March 1868, saying that he would do little more than refer to the paper about his scheme which had been circulated. He then typically spoke at great length, ending up with a flourish of rhetoric: his proposals would regenerate the political system, substituting earnest effort for timid conventionalism and insincerity, and calling for leaders who could really teach and guide. A long discussion ensued, objections being answered by Mill and Fawcett. The conference met again twice in March. The task of the Hare party was a delicate one, as they had to reconcile the stress laid by some supporters of proportional representation on its value as a tool to represent the minority of propertied and educated voters if the suffrage was

---

[15] W. Morrison to G. Howell, 29 Feb. 1868. Howell Collection, Bishopsgate Institute, London.

extended, with its capacity to ensure the return of many working-class MPs, which they undoubtedly wanted, the better to represent working men's interests and feelings. Fawcett tried to meet this dilemma with the mysterious paradox that the scheme aimed at the representation of minorities in order the better to represent majorities. A representative from the USA supported him by saying that it had been disastrous to introduce universal suffrage without electoral reform in America: Republicans were grossly over-represented and there was not one free-trader in Congress though many electors held free-trade views. Hare spoke what he called 'a few words', explaining the scheme and saying that he wanted to make 'the exercise of the franchise the proudest act of citizenship—one which directly associated the voter with the great and noble aspirations of his time'.[16]

The conference appointed a committee of nine people, of whom five were working-class, to confer with Hare and draw up a simple explanatory statement of the details of his system. The result was a report, issued in May 1868, based on a very elaborate draft prepared by Hare. The report got round the suspicions of Hare's scheme which some Reform League members must have felt by saying that the true interests of mankind are the same: there is nothing in the enlightened pursuit of the real welfare of one class antagonistic to that of another. With the assurance that the scheme would enable the best and noblest of contemporaries to get power, the report was unanimously adopted by the conference on 13 June 1868 and it was resolved to form an association to improve representative government.

The society which the Reform League conference decided to form was called the Representative Reform Assocation. A provisional committee was appointed by the conference. The president was Hare, the secretary George Howell, who had been secretary of the Reform League, and the treasurer Walter Morrison MP. Morrison was no doubt selected as treasurer because he was extremely rich, having inherited a large fortune from his father, James Morrison, who was probably the richest

---

[16] *The Times*, 23 Mar. 1868, 7c.

commoner of the nineteenth century in the United Kingdom.[17] Apart from these officers, the main people involved in establishing the society were Mill, Fawcett, Leonard Courtney, and George Holyoake, in conjunction with Beales, Charles Bradlaugh, George Odger, W. R. Cremer, and others of the Reform League. The aims of the society were to promote the real and complete representation of constituents, to give the largest choice to electors, to study how to accomplish these objects, and to be a centre of communication with foreign societies having similar designs. Many foreigners were elected corresponding members. The minimum subscription was one shilling. Premises were acquired in the summer of 1868 together with a library of relevant publications.

The Representative Reform Association was quite active at first. Thus in 1869 it persuaded the government to add Fawcett to the House of Commons select committee which was inquiring into the conduct of parliamentary and municipal elections, but it was unsuccessful in getting the committee to hear evidence from Hare and Howell, although the advocates of Hare's scheme or something like it were confident that it would greatly reduce or even eliminate bribery at elections. In 1870 the Association organized a conference with members of the Labour Representation League, a body created in 1869 to secure the return of working men to parliament. Hare showed the conference the bearings of a system of proportional voting on the direct representation of labour in parliament, and a committee was appointed to prepare a practical plan for getting proportional representation in London and other large towns. The next year (1871) the Association considered what amendments to propose to the secret ballot bill which was then before parliament, and pressed for the publication of a memorandum which had been prepared by Hare at the request of the government to send to foreign enquirers. But the main outcome of the Association's activities was the introduction by Morrison in 1872 of a bill into parliament providing for proportional representation in England and Wales, with the aim of starting discussion on the subject whilst there was a lull in party politics.[18]

---

[17] See W. D. Rubinstein, *Economic History Review*, 2nd ser. xxx (Nov. 1977), 602–23, 'The Victorian Middle Classes: Wealth, Occupation, and Geography'.

[18] The bill is discussed fully beneath.

The Representative Reform Association continued to watch events in parliament and to plan how to take any opportunity that offered to advocate its views, but by the end of 1874 it had petered out as an organization. Howell was busy with other work, and Morrison, who had been the Association's mainstay financially and in other ways, refused to go on subsidizing it and paying Howell's salary. At its start he had borne at least two-thirds of the expenditure, and had continued to contribute to it generously, though more and more reluctantly. The membership was always small and subscriptions inadequate. Another factor which contributed to the dissolution of the Association was that Morrison lost his seat in parliament at the general election of 1874. He was understandably discouraged: he told Howell that he was tired of being 'in my sole person the association', adding that 'The country can stand and understand and appreciate the advantages of the cumulative vote and such small palliatives of our wretched electoral system, but the idea of personal representation is too much for them for a century to come'.[19] The Association may have been more successful in encouraging movements for proportional representation abroad than in its work at home, for it established links with foreign societies and sent them literature.

The question whether the interests of working men would have been better represented in parliament during the years 1868–1900 if the Hare scheme had operated is discussed in Appendix A.

In spite of these activities and his work at the Charity Commission,[20] Hare found time to continue writing and lecturing, and did not abandon the platform provided for him by the Social Science Association which was, it would seem, amazingly generous in the number of opportunities it gave him to expound his ideas. Thus he read a paper in 1868 on 'The Means of Manifesting Public Opinion in the Election of Representatives to Parliament', pointing out that people like members of the

---

[19] Morrison to Howell, 5 Nov. 1874.

[20] In 1872 Hare was promoted to be an Assistant Commissioner with a seat on the Board. He had been pressing his case for promotion for many years. (See correspondence in St John's College, Oxford.) He did not retire from the Charity Commission until 1887, aged 81.

Social Science Association were largely ineffective at elections. This was followed in 1870 by a paper on the constitution of local governing bodies. He was no doubt right in saying that the calibre of local representatives needed some improvement, but the method of election he proposed would not have been compatible with secret voting which was being widely advocated at that time: a candidate's name would be placed at the top of a piece of paper; electors who supported him would write their names underneath his, and when he had obtained the quota, he would be elected. In 1871 Hare read a paper on the working of the cumulative vote in school board elections, arguing that although it had some advantages over the usual electoral system, it wasted votes and was inferior to his scheme in a number of ways. The year 1874 saw yet another paper by Hare to the Social Science Association on how municipal councillors should be elected. In this he pointed out one ingenious facet of his scheme, namely that in local elections a district would get more representatives the more registered electors actually voted, since more candidates would probably achieve the quota; this would therefore stimulate individual exertion. Hare's last paper to the Association was delivered in 1879 on the distribution of seats in parliament. In this he described once again the advantageous effects of his scheme, particularly a reduction in the estrangement of classes.

The Social Science Association provided Hare with an excellent forum for the dissemination of his views, as there came to its annual meetings in provincial centres, particularly in its early years, not only politicians, officials, experts, and intellectuals with wide-ranging interests, but also the general public in large numbers. Regular but smaller meetings were held in London. Many members of the Association were attracted to Hare's ideas, as his scheme offered the prospect of electing to parliament men of experience and expertise in social and other questions; but electoral reform, either along Hare's or any other lines, was not endorsed by the Association's Council or campaigned for by them, as were various other reforms, for example in the fields of education and sanitation. Mill had been on the Council but resigned from it in 1860.

In 1873 the fourth and last edition of the *Treatise* was published. It was thirty pages longer than the third edition, but the

electoral law had been reduced to twenty-eight clauses. The
new edition adapted Hare's proposed law to the secret ballot
which had been introduced in 1872. It also described the
working of the cumulative vote in the state of Illinois in the
USA, and of preferential voting for the board of Overseers of
Harvard University. In 1874 when reviewing Mill's *Autobiography*, Hare took the opportunity to advocate his scheme;[21] and
he wrote two further articles on electoral matters, one in 1875
and one in 1878.[22] In the first article he answered objections
made by Leslie Stephen, and repeated a point he had made on
a number of occasions, namely that it was the tyranny of the
minority not of the majority which had to be overcome, thus
illustrating the confused state of the arguments for proportional
representation, as Mill had always focused on the tyranny of
the majority. His second article emphasized the uplifting effects
of the right kind of electoral reform: the election of an MP could
be converted into an intellectual and moral exercise, from being
as it too often was a demoralizing game; a generous rivalry in
the manifestation of public spirit would be provided.

How successful were these activities? Hare's ideas undoubtedly
attracted considerable attention, partly because he had acquired
Mill as a disciple. The *Treatise* was widely reviewed and even
those who were critical of the scheme paid Hare high compli-
ments. Thus the *Saturday Review* spoke of his extreme ingenuity
and technical skill. The *Economist* wrote of his grasp of principle
and command of detail, and of the exact, thorough, and
consistent thinking displayed in a remarkable book which
deserved thoughtful study; its lucidity was unusual in political
writing. The *Economist* had previously reviewed Hare's 1857
pamphlet, describing it as the production of an able man which
suggested points of great interest. And even Walter Bagehot,
who became Hare's most famous and influential critic, considered that his scheme had 'high intellectual interest'.[23]
   Amongst those sympathetic to Hare, there were some,
besides Mill and Fawcett, who advocated his scheme virtually

[21] *Westminster Review*, 45 NS (Jan. 1874), 122–59.
[22] *Fortnightly Review*, 18 NS (July 1875), 102–7, and 23 NS (Jan. 1878), 75–84.
[23] *Saturday Review*, 26 Feb. 1859, 244–6. *Economist*, 11 June 1859, 649. *Economist*, 25 July 1857, 819. *Fortnightly Review*, 4 (Mar. 1866), 272.

in its entirety. These included F. D. Maurice, the Christian Socialist, and Lord Hobart, who both published articles about Hare in *Macmillan's Magazine*.[24] Though the editor of this recently founded journal, David Masson, was a man of letters, he was interested in Hare and thought well of him. He considered Hare's views to be 'of the very greatest importance, constituting when taken collectively, a real stroke of inventive genius in a department of practical politics in which it was supposed, a little while ago, by almost everyone, that the "last word" had been spoken through the mouths of our ordinary politicians' with no hope of further progress.[25] Maurice was mainly attracted by Hare's confident assertion that one could effect moral progress in the community by a change in electoral machinery, but it may be doubted whether he fully understood how the machinery would work. Lord Hobart probably did thoroughly understand the scheme, for he was capable of close thinking having been a clerk in the (very efficient) Board of Trade for over twenty years and an astute writer on current political topics. Mill considered he had 'about the best theoretical head in the whole nobility'.[26] Hobart regarded Hare as a man of high ability and considered that his plan would get rid of the chaos of the present electoral system, and allow every elector to be represented, as he should be, thus substituting reality for fiction. He believed that it offered a complete and satisfactory solution to several problems, namely the irrationality and inequality of the existing arrangements, the need to ensure that the wealthier and more instructed part of the nation would be properly represented if the suffrage was extended, as Hobart thought it should be, and the prevention of bribery at elections. Unfortunately for the cause, Hobart, like Hare, seemed to contemporaries to be Utopian, especially when he forecast that the scheme was too deeply founded in truth to fail of ultimate adoption.[27]

The *Westminster Review* carried an enthusiastic notice of Hare's *Treatise* in July 1860, and the *Law Magazine and Review* a favour-

---

[24] Frederick Denison Maurice, 1805–72. Vere Henry Hobart, 1818–75. *Macmillan's Magazine*, 2 (June 1860), 89–97, and 13 (Jan. 1866) 259–72.

[25] *Macmillan's Magazine*, 5 (Apr. 1862), 480.

[26] L 902, 4 Jan. 1866.

[27] Letter to *The Times*, 7 Sept. 1869, 4f.

able notice of it in 1861, prophesying that his suggestions would eventually be adopted. It urged lawyers to study the book; several of them clearly did and some became keen Hare supporters. The most famous of these is John Westlake, later professor of International Law at Cambridge, who was a Hare supporter even before he married one of his daughters in 1864. Fawcett's wife, who was a whole-hearted Hare enthusiast, explained the scheme clearly and recommended it warmly in two articles in *Macmillan's*.[28]

Indeed for many years Hare's scheme had some supporters in this country, as well as many abroad, and in spite of the problems which it posed, they worked to get it adopted. Others were in favour of it and would have liked to see it adopted, but thought this was impossible at any rate for the time being, given the public's ignorance about electoral methods and their antipathy to understanding the subject. Others, who saw great merit in Hare's two key devices—the quota and preferential voting with the transfer of surplus and useless votes—thought out how these ideas could be applied in a simpler system. They saw that to treat a country the size of the United Kingdom as a national constituency posed many problems. For instance how could one inform two-and-a-half million electors about perhaps as many as 2,000 candidates at a general election? Even those who thought Hare's system admirable feared that electors would suffer from an *embarras de richesses* and be at a loss what names and how many to insert.[29] They also saw that to combine, as Hare proposed, local and national constituencies would lead to many complications. They therefore abandoned the idea of voluntary constituencies and suggested compulsory ones, but not of course the existing ones, at least not as many as there were then, for a proportional system must involve multi-member constituencies with a minimum of three members and preferably more.

This emendation of the Hare scheme was first advocated by Catherine Spence in her pamphlet of 1861, but as this was published in Australia it received little attention in England.

---

[28] *Macmillan's Magazine*, 22 (Sept. 1870), 376–82, and 23 (Apr. 1871), 481–7. Millicent Fawcett, née Garrett, 1847–1929. She also worked for many women's causes, and for Liberal Unionism.

[29] H. F. Amedroz, in 2nd ed. of *The Franchise* (1865).

However a few English people in due course had the same idea—for instance H. F. Amedroz in 1865, and more importantly H. R. Droop who read a paper entitled 'On Methods of Electing Representatives' to the Juridical Society in 1868. Droop was a barrister who had been a mathematician and a Fellow of Trinity College, Cambridge.[30] He considered the existing system of election by simple majority rude and primitive; he saw drawbacks in cumulative and limited voting; he granted that to the highly educated political thinker the liberty of choice offered by Hare was very tempting, but he thought that for the majority of people a choice of six to eight candidates should suffice. So he showed how Hare's 'bold and highly elaborated scheme of personal representation' could be applied to a limited number of representatives, three or more, in local constituencies. Droop also proposed a simpler method than that recommended by Hare for the transfer of votes when this was necessary and a better method for calculating the quota. In 1871 Droop argued for the application of proportional representation to the election of local government bodies, and in 1881 he gave a long paper to the Statistical Society of London surveying again the various methods of electing representatives.[31] Altogether he showed himself to be one of the best-informed and most level-headed thinkers amongst the reformers.

Droop was a member of the Representative Reform Association and may thus have been the instigator of the bill introduced into parliament in 1872 by the Association's treasurer, Walter Morrison.[32] Morrison was a clever and learned business man who had become Liberal MP for Plymouth in 1861. His interest in proportional representation probably owes its origin to his visit to the USA on the grand tour after coming down from Oxford in 1858. This visit made him aware of the disadvantages of single-member constituencies and simple majority voting. Moreover he was in favour of the better representation of labour in parliament (though not of universal suffrage), and considered this could not take place under the existing electoral

[30]   Henry Richmond Droop. *c*.1831–84.
[31]   *Journal of the Statistical Society*, 44 (June 1881), 141–202.
[32]   Walter Morrison, 1836–1921. MP, Liberal, 1861–74; Liberal Unionist, 1886–92 and 1895–1900. For information about Morrison, see the *DNB*, and Geoffrey Dawson's article in the *National Review* (Feb. 1922), 854–66.

system, but would result if proportional representation were introduced. Though a great admirer of Mill and obviously acquainted with his writings on representative government, he saw difficulties in Hare's scheme as it stood, and thought it necessary to simplify it and to proceed gradually. His bill therefore divided the country (England and Wales) into 69 constituencies (instead of the existing 317), returning between three and sixteen members each. Voters could put the names of candidates for their constituency in order of preference, but could not exceed the number of MPs to be elected for that constituency. Any candidate getting the quota of votes necessary in that constituency was declared elected, the quota being found by dividing the number of voting papers by the number of MPs to be elected for that constituency. Any surplus votes given to a successful candidate were transferred to the voter's next choice, as were votes for the lowest candidates who were excluded as long as there remained more candidates than vacancies.

Morrison made a restrained speech when introducing his bill. He stressed that great masses of opinion, for example that of miners and Catholics, were unrepresented at present, and that a minority of electors could return a majority of the House of Commons. He considered it significant that in four different countries (America, Denmark, England, and Geneva) independent enquirers, acting without concert, and ignorant of one another's existence, had hit upon what was virtually the same remedy for the evils attendant upon representative institutions. In a thinly attended House, the debate was brief with only two MPs, Thomas Hughes and Thomas Collins, offering any support to Morrison, and one of these, Collins, actually voted against the bill.[33] The government representative, H. S. P. Winterbotham, made the curious point that the bill was of too abstract a character to call for an immediate decision by the Home Office. It was defeated by 154 votes to 26. The twenty-six who voted for the bill were all Liberals except for one Radical; those who voted against were divided evenly between Conservatives and Liberals.[34]

---

[33] Thomas Hughes, 1822–96. MP, Liberal, 1865–74. Principal of Working Men's College, 1872–83. Thomas Collins, *c*.1826–84. MP, Conservative, 1851, 1857–65, 1868–74, and 1881–4.
[34] *HC Deb*. 212 (10 July 1872), 890–926.

Morrison's scheme was in essence the system known later as the single transferable vote, which gradually emerged amongst most advocates of proportional representation in England as their preferred electoral method, being adopted in 1884 by the recently formed Proportional Representation Society as the best system. Hare's scheme of course involves a single transferable vote, but in order not to cause confusion it is referred to here as his scheme, and the term 'single transferable vote' is reserved for schemes which do not treat the whole country as one constituency and suppose multi-membered constituencies of at least three members. Meanwhile others proposed different emendations of Hare's scheme, usually in an effort to simplify the machinery whilst preserving its essential principles. One of these variants made candidates responsible for determining to which other candidates their surplus votes—that is votes in excess of the quota—would be transferred with the aim of reducing the tasks of electors and electoral officials. Every candidate after nomination day would publish a list of the other candidates, in whatever order he pleased, showing to whom he would transfer any surplus votes he received, so that electors would ostensibly know how their votes were liable to be transferred. But this scheme was in fact far from simple; and it seems unlikely that it would have done much to ease the work of returning officers.[35]

One idea put forward in the 1870s was to introduce a proportional system of representation by stages, starting with the large towns and the more populous counties. Leonard Courtney, who was to become for some years the most prominent person in the movement for proportional representation, was an advocate of this plan for a time, but it did not then get much support.[36]

Some suggestions made at this time were not emendations of

---

[35] Walter Baily, *A Scheme for Proportional Representation* (1869), and *Proportional Representation in Large Constituencies (1872).* Also Archibald E. Dobbs, *General Representation: On a Complete Readjustment and Modification of Mr Hare's Plan* (1871). Baily and Dobbs were both barristers.

[36] Leonard Henry Courtney, 1832–1918. Leader writer on *The Times*, 1865–80. Professor of Political Economy, University College, London, 1872–5. MP, 1876–1900, Liberal and later Liberal Unionist. Held government offices, 1880–4. Deputy Speaker, 1886–92. Became Baron Courtney, 1906. See *Fortnightly Review*, 20 NS (July 1876), 74–92, and *Nineteenth Century*, 6 (July 1879), 141–56.

the Hare scheme, as they did not incorporate his basic principles, but they owed their origin to the stimulus provided by his
pioneering work and to the general opening up of the subject
of proportional representation. One proposal was to merge
boroughs in their counties for electoral purposes and to make
counties or divisions of counties into multi-membered constituencies with about twelve seats each. The voter would be
limited to voting for only two-thirds of the number of MPs to
be returned by that constituency, but could accumulate his
votes on candidates as he wished.[37] Another proposal was what
came to be known as 'the second ballot', namely the holding of
a second poll one or two weeks later when at the first poll no
candidate got an absolute majority, i.e. more than 50 per cent
of the votes. One of its advocates was Sir Charles Dilke,[38] but it
never acquired as much support in the United Kingdom as it
did for a time in other European countries.

One interesting development during the 1870s and 1880s was
the beginning of the study of electoral statistics. Hare and Mill
had not bolstered up their case for proportional representation,
in the way which later has become so common, with statistics
revealing the disproportionate representation of political parties. This was partly because one of their central aims was to
minimize the role and influence of parties in the political
process. But others began looking at regional and national
statistics. For instance it was pointed out that Kent was represented between 1868 and 1874 by six Conservative MPs and no
Liberals, although 21,000 people had voted Liberal in 1868 and
only 2,000 more had voted Conservative. This observation was
made at a meeting of the Statistical Society of London in May
1874 at which a pioneering paper in the field of electoral studies
was read. The author, John Biddulph Martin, a banker, was not
primarily interested in the relation of votes to seats; he was
mainly trying to find out why the result of the general election
of 1874 was so different from that of 1868, for, he said, in 1868

[37] E. H. Knatchbull-Hugessen, *Macmillan's Magazine*, 27 (Nov. 1872), 67–76.
Hugessen at that time held a minor office in the Liberal government.
[38] In his pamphlet *Parliamentary Reform* (1879). Charles Wentworth Dilke,
1843–1911. MP, Radical, 1868–86, and 1892–1911. In Liberal government,
1880–5.

the Liberals had a majority in parliament of at least 100 seats and in 1874 the Conservatives had a majority of 50. Did some previously Liberal electors defect and vote Conservative, Martin asked, or did they abstain? Or was the result due to an influx of new voters? In order to answer these questions he produced far more compendious and reliable figures than anyone had up till then, and he also drew attention to the many difficulties which beset such enquiries.[39] These difficulties were due mainly to the large number of uncontested seats at this time—212 in 1868 and 187 in 1874; but the existence of many constituencies returning more than one member also created problems for the electoral statistician. Moreover it was not always easy to be sure about the politics of some candidates, or to know how to classify Irish MPs.

In 1879 Courtney showed how the wrong party could actually get the majority of seats in one county by citing what had happened in Lancashire in 1868: the Conservatives got 2,000 fewer votes than the Liberals, but more seats—twenty-two as against the Liberals' eleven. This, as he pointed out, was not because the electoral districts in Lancashire were of unequal size, but because the Liberal votes were concentrated in a few urban districts whilst the Conservative votes were only just in a majority in county districts.[40] Others went further and averred that looking at the whole country the wrong party could get the majority of seats in parliament. They considered that this had happened at the general election of 1874. One commentator calculated that the Liberals should have been returned with a majority of 17 instead of the Conservatives with a majority of 75 in Great Britain,[41] and another, a mathematician, put the correct Liberal majority for the UK as high as 52.[42] These two writers confined their analyses to places where there had been a contest. Others made calculations based also on uncontested seats, and they too concluded that Liberal voters would have

[39] *Journal of the Statistical Society*, 37 (June 1874), 193–225.

[40] *Nineteenth Century*, 6 (July 1879), 141–56.

[41] Alfred Frisby, 'Voters *not* Votes. The Relative Strength of Political Parties as Shown by the Last Two General Elections', *Contemporary Review*, 38 (Oct. 1880), 635–46.

[42] Robert B. Hayward, 'Proportional Representation', *Nineteenth Century*, 15 (Feb. 1884), 293–304.

been in the majority in 1874 if there had been a contest everywhere.[43] These figures were naturally controversial. On the other hand the parliamentary majority secured by the Liberals at the general election of 1880, which amounted to 128 for Great Britain, was generally considered to be at least twice too big in relation to the votes cast.

Even Lord Salisbury delved into electoral statistics, though he apologized to the readers of the *National Review* for the offence of obtruding statistics upon them, thus illustrating the novelty of their use.[44] He was worried about the likely effects on the Conservatives of an extension of the franchise in the absence of a redistribution of seats. In some respects he showed a more acute understanding of the possible working of the existing electoral system than many of his contemporaries, pointing out for instance that it would be possible for one party to get all the seats even though it had only a small majority of votes. But he was wrong in thinking that the system always favoured the Liberals—a conclusion he came to because he only looked at the election of 1880—instead of seeing that it would often favour, i.e. over-represent, whichever party got the most votes. This was pointed out by H. M. Bompas, who was a lawyer with an interest in politics and elections.[45] He condemned Salisbury's figures as entirely fallacious and worked out that if the Conservatives had got 8 per cent more votes than the Liberals in 1880, instead of vice versa, the Liberal majority of 128 would have been changed into a Conservative majority of at least 218. It is difficult to evaluate his estimates, but he was correct in pointing out the increasing tendency of the majority in parliament greatly to exceed that in the country at large.[46]

It is sometimes thought that Hare and his disciples were responsible for the provision in the Reform Act, 1867, of the limited vote in constituencies returning three members each.

[43] 'Representation and Misrepresentation', *Westminster Review*, 65 NS (Apr. 1884), 392–420.

[44] *National Review*, 4 (Oct. 1884), 145–62.

[45] Henry Mason Bompas, 1836–1909. He had published a pamphlet on Hare's scheme in 1870. He stood for parliament as a Liberal unsuccessfully in 1878, 1880, and 1885. He became a judge in 1896.

[46] 'Lord Salisbury and Redistribution', *Contemporary Review*, 46 (Nov. 1884), 714–17.

These constituencies were the seven counties which had been given three members in 1832,[47] and the four (large) boroughs— Birmingham, Leeds, Liverpool, and Manchester—whose representation was raised from two to three members by the 1867 Act. Glasgow was added in 1868. The voter in all these places was limited to two votes. Similarly the voter in the City of London, which returned four members, was limited to three votes. It is true that Mill and other advocates of a general scheme of proportional representation voted for the limited vote in August 1867, just as they had previously supported the (unsuccessful) proposal for cumulative voting in three-member constituencies as being a start towards a better electoral system;[48] but the initiative and drive for both of these proposals came from a different quarter—namely the group of MPs, known as the Cave of Adullam, who were passionately hostile to the extension of the suffrage embodied in the bill. Thus Robert Lowe and others, desperately alarmed by the proposal to give votes to what they saw as the lowest class of society, had since February 1867 been arguing for the safeguards of plural, cumulative, or limited voting.[49] As Mill pointed out, they had not previously shown much interest in the broad case for proportional representation and only took up the question when they saw it would help them. So the arguments made by the anti-democratic supporters of cumulative and limited voting were based not on a thorough understanding and criticism of the existing electoral system, but merely on the need to provide for the representation of wealth, property, and intelligence to counteract in the phrase of the time 'the influence of numbers'. Other supporters of the cumulative and limited vote, usually though not always Liberals, argued more widely for the general principle of the representation of minorities which some of them saw as the logical consequence of democracy.

The amendment to the Reform Bill providing for the limited vote was actually initiated in the House of Lords by Lord Cairns

---

[47] Berkshire, Buckinghamshire, Cambridgeshire, Dorset, Herefordshire, Hertfordshire, and Oxfordshire.

[48] *HC Deb.* 188 (4 July 1867), 1042–4; (5 July 1867), 1074–8, 1085–8, 1102–7.

[49] They did not always distinguish clearly between these three devices. Nor have some recent historians, e.g. Maurice Cowling and F. B. Smith in their books on the 1867 Reform Bill.

who had been a Law Officer in previous Conservative governments and who was generally unsympathetic to the bill.[50] In
1859 he had delivered an astringent attack on Lord John Russell
for having proposed a greater extension of the suffrage than
that then contemplated in the Conservative government's bill.
He did not question the working classes' loyalty and patriotism,
but that was no reason for giving votes to all of them any more
than it was an argument for giving votes to women; our
representative system should preserve an equal balance
between the classes and not, by giving weight to numbers,
allow one class to outvote every other class.[51] So too in 1867 he
feared the transfer of political power from a select and privileged
class to a new electorate. The amendment he proposed would,
he argued, enable men of intelligence and independence to be
elected in the large towns, thus safeguarding the interests of
property.[52] The Lords passed the limited vote by 142 votes to
51. When it returned to the Commons Disraeli announced that
although the government had strongly opposed the new clause
in the Lords, it would now support it in deference to the spirit
of compromise and conciliation in which the bill had been
carried through the other House.[53] It passed in the Lower
House after fierce opposition by 253 votes to 204. When an
attempt was made in 1870 to get the limited vote repealed, the
case for keeping it was based to a considerable extent on the
fact that it was too soon to repeal a provision so recently passed,
rather than on the desirability of fairer representation.[54]

Nor were Hare and his supporters responsible for the provision in the Education Act, 1870, enabling votes to be accumu-
lated at elections to the school boards which were to be set up
to supply and manage schools in any area where they were
deficient. The bill as introduced by the government provided
that the boards should be elected by town councils in boroughs
and by vestries in other areas. Objection was taken to this on
the ground that the boards would consist entirely of the party
which was in a majority on the electing body; so it was proposed

---

[50] Hugh McCalmont Cairns, 1819–85. Created a peer in 1867.
[51] *HC Deb.* 153 (22 Mar. 1859), 612–13.
[52] *HL Deb.* 189 (30 July 1867), 433–41.
[53] *HC Deb.* 189 (8 Aug. 1867), 1110–11.
[54] *HC Deb.* 202 (15 June 1870), 129–83.

that they should be elected by ratepayers, in the hope that minority views would have some chance of representation. An amendment to this effect was introduced by Sir Charles Dilke.[55] 'Minority' and 'majority' in this context normally referred to views on religious issues which generated strong passions in connection with education. However some people realized that Dilke's amendment would not guarantee minority representation; so they proposed cumulative voting: each voter would have as many votes as there were board members to be elected (which was between five and fifteen) and could give all his or her votes to one candidate, or distribute them among candidates as he or she thought fit. The initiative for cumulative voting came from Lord Frederick Cavendish, who was a Liberal MP interested in educational questions. Gladstone, though in his own words 'a rather stiff opponent of the minority principle' for parliamentary elections, and whilst (typically) considering the question one of great difficulty, accepted the amendment on behalf of the government because he thought the proposal would reduce acrimony and animosity in elections. He also reassured himself by thinking (wrongly) that the plan was not altogether novel, confusing it with plural voting. It was agreed to after a short debate with no vote.[56] When the next year (1871) an effort was made to get cumulative voting rescinded, supporters of a full system of proportional representation with preferential voting (i.e. Walter Morrison and Auberon Herbert)[57] resisted the proposal on the ground that the cumulative vote, though inadequate, was at least helping some minorities, like Roman Catholics and women, to get on to school boards.[58]

The main forums used at this time by protagonists of proportional or minority representation were the periodical journals and learned societies; but they did not abandon the arena of parliament even after the defeat of Morrison's bill in 1872. The first of many efforts to keep the subject alive was made by Thomas Collins in 1873. Dilke had moved a resolution 'to

[55] *HC Deb*. 202 (4 July 1870), 1398.

[56] *HC Deb*. 202 (4 July 1870), 1420–5.

[57] Auberon Herbert, 1858–1906. MP, 1870–4. An advanced Radical on all issues.

[58] *HC Deb*. 207 (12 July 1871), 1525–39.

redress the inequalities of the distribution of electoral power'. Collins proposed adding to it 'by the application of the cumulative vote or otherwise, so as to secure a better proportional representation of the people in the respective constituencies'. Dilke wanted to reduce the huge differences between the number of electors and population which MPs represented. He did not indicate how this should be effected, but Collins assumed probably rightly that he was not proposing any change in the existing electoral system other than the equalizing of electoral districts. Collins pointed out that this would not secure a better proportional representation of the people; indeed, he said, it would merely aggravate the present evil. His remedy was to have constituencies of three to five MPs and the 'modern and scientific principle of cumulative voting'. He had no sympathy whatever with Hare's plan of personal representation but wanted to ensure that minorities were represented. Dilke opposed Collins's amendment on the ground that it was like counting ones chickens before they were hatched. The amendment was withdrawn and Dilke's motion was heavily defeated,[59] but the debate stimulated Lord Grey to write to *The Times* advocating a royal commission to look at all the remedies which had been suggested, including Hare's scheme.[60]

The next move made by supporters of proportional or minority representation was to advocate the cumulative vote for the election of aldermen by town councils. They introduced bills to effect this annually from 1873 to 1878. The first of these was sponsored by Morrison and Collins, and after they were defeated at the general election of 1874, by Fawcett and others, five of whom were Conservative and one Liberal. They secured three debates on the subject, which enabled them to point out that as things stood a majority of only one on a council could result in the total exclusion of the minority party from the aldermanic bench, thus keeping exclusive power on the council

[59] *HC Deb.* 215 (6 May 1873), 1561–90.
[60] *The Times*, 10 May 1873, 8c. This was Henry George, the third Earl Grey (1802–94). He had been Colonial Secretary in various Whig governments. He was familiar with current schemes for the reform of the electoral system and was sympathetic to Hare's objective, but thought his scheme too complicated. He preferred the cumulative vote. See the 1864 edition of his book *Parliamentary Government considered with Reference to the Reform of Parliament*.

in the hands of the majority party regardless of the opinion of the ratepayers. But the issue of minority representation on town councils tended to become submerged in other questions such as who should elect aldermen, i.e. other aldermen, town councillors, or ratepayers, and how to keep party politics out of local elections. One of the bills secured a second reading, but none of them came near reaching the statute book.[61]

In 1875 Dilke resumed his efforts, moving a resolution in parliament for an inquiry into 'the various methods of bringing about a juster system of political power, with a view of securing a more complete representation of the people'. He discoursed on the anomalies which existed then in the vastly different size of the electorate which returned MPs; this varied from 76 in one constituency to over 20,000 in another. These discrepancies were clearly Dilke's main concern rather than the faulty basis of the whole electoral system which worried supporters of proportional representation, but he had moved a little from his position in 1873 for he had learnt from Lord Grey's letter to *The Times* that there were competing schemes for the removal of the anomalies. This was a good moment, he said, to hold an impartial and scientific inquiry into these various plans in order to avoid hurried legislation. Fawcett seconded the resolution. He said he was not advocating any particular system of representation, but he in fact hinted that equal electoral districts would not prevent a waste of voting power or give every section of opinion its due share of representation. The demand for an inquiry was also supported by G. J. Goschen, who mentioned in particular the need to collect information on the working of the limited vote introduced in 1867 for certain constituencies. This, if it had been done, would have produced a better-informed debate than that which took place when the device was ended in 1885. But Disraeli poured scorn on Dilke's arguments, eulogizing anomalies and making sarcastic remarks about the clever, thoughtful, doctrinaire philosophers who had produced a variety of schemes. Dilke's resolution was defeated by 190 votes to 120.[62]

---

[61] *HC Deb.* 217 (16 July 1873), 482–91; 225 (14 July 1875), 1425–49; and 240 (6 June 1878), 1323–5.

[62] *HC Deb.* 225 (15 July 1875), 1533–54. George Joachim Goschen, 1831–1907. MP, 1865–85, and 1887–1900. First Liberal, then Liberal Unionist, then Conservative. Held office in Liberal and Conservative governments.

The next year (1876) Fawcett had an opportunity to say a few words about the need to have some plan which would not give the representation entirely to the majority, during the debate on G. O. Trevelyan's resolutions advocating a uniform franchise for boroughs and counties and a redistribution of political powers.[63] Fawcett seems to have been contemplating a very moderate reform involving only the larger constituencies.[64] He did not speak during the long debate on the same resolutions in 1877, and the only mention of minority representation was made by Lord Edmond Fitzmaurice who wished to see an extension of minority voting, i.e. the limited and cumulative vote, both of which he considered were working well.[65]

In 1878 a resolution on the subject was moved by R. P. Blennerhassett, the young Liberal MP for Kerry who had spoken on this issue in parliament only once before—in 1872 when he urged that Morrison's bill should apply to Ireland.[66] He now moved that 'in the opinion of this House it is desirable that the whole electoral body should be enabled to enjoy that direct representation which is at present confined to majorities; that no effectual security exists for the due representation of minorities; and that, as far as possible, all opinions should have an opportunity of being represented in direct proportion to the number of electors by whom they are held'. In a long speech he recommended Hare's scheme, but proposed that a committee should be appointed to work out the best plan. He based his case partly on the need to remedy defects in the present system, but he also laid great emphasis on the importance of mitigating the evil effects of the further extension of the franchise which would take place sooner or later. Power was being transferred from capital to labour, he said; previously excluded classes would get absolute and exclusive control of government; it was therefore very important to ensure that the more educated and better off would be adequately represented. Blennerhassett

[63] George Otto Trevelyan, 1838–1928. MP, Liberal, 1865–86 and 1887–97. Held various offices in Liberal governments 1868–95.

[64] *HC Deb.* 229 (30 May 1876), 1456.

[65] *HC Deb.* 235 (29 June 1877), 533.

[66] Richard Ponsonby Blennerhassett, 1850–1913. MP, Liberal, 1872–85. Barrister.

regarded his proposals as consistent with liberalism as well as conservatism, because they would undermine the 'iron weight of party' which crushed out independence. He received some support from A. J. Balfour[67] who thought a modification of the Hare plan would improve the calibre of representatives and prevent waves of political opinion having too much effect; but he considered it was unnecessary to raise the issue at the moment as the House had only recently rejected a reform bill. It was on this occasion that Courtney, who had become an MP in 1876, made the first of his many speeches in parliament on the subject. He put forward a number of arguments and figures to support the resolution, but then said the present generation would not accept the scheme; it could only be realized in the far distant future. After outlining the recent history of minority representation, he advocated the extension of the limited vote, mentioning one vote per voter in constituencies of five or six members as a possible arrangement. Two other MPs, one Conservative and one Liberal, spoke in favour of a widespread adoption of the present 'three-cornered' or 'triangular' constituencies, as those with the limited vote were then often known. The resolution was not voted on as the House, lacking a quorum, adjourned.[68]

A fairly similar debate took place the next year (1879) when Blennerhassett moved an amendment to Trevelyan's motion to extend the franchise to counties, by adding to it 'and to provide, as far as possible, for the fair representation of minorities'. He seems to have been in an even greater panic than the year before about the results he anticipated from an extension of the suffrage: he thought it would 'practically disfranchise every class which is now enfranchised' since the better sorts of electors might not get a single representative if the existing electoral system were not altered. 'Those that want' would get, in effect, exclusive control over the government of the Empire, whilst 'those that have' would be condemned to political annihilation, social downfall, and economic disaster. He did not discuss the merits of different schemes enabling minorities to be repre-

---

[67] Arthur James Balfour, 1848–1930. MP, Conservative, 1874–1922, when he became an earl. Held office in many governments from 1885 to 1929, being Prime Minister from 1902 to 1905. A philosopher as well as a statesman.

[68] *HC Deb.* 238 (8 Mar. 1878), 979–1020.

sented, though he made it clear that he did not regard the restricted (i.e. limited) vote or the cumulative vote as adequate safeguards, and that in his view the Hare scheme provided fair representation. The only support Blennerhassett received came from Courtney who emphasized that Trevelyan's proposal to enfranchise the agricultural labourer would not ensure him representation, and that Dilke was mistaken in thinking that equal electoral districts would prevent a minority of electors from returning a majority of members. In the course of a long speech Courtney made a number of other criticisms of the working of the existing electoral system, but he must have left the House wondering what remedy he recommended, for at one point he extolled the cumulative vote and later he read out passages from Mill's *Autobiography* in praise of Hare's scheme. The House decided that it was inexpedient to reopen the question of parliamentary reform.[69]

With the return to power of the Liberals in 1880, it seemed probable that a reform bill would soon be introduced. This stimulated Blennerhassett to raise the question again. He therefore moved a resolution in 1881 asking that 'a Select Committee be appointed to inquire into and report upon the system of election of members of this House best calculated to secure the just and complete representation of the whole electoral body'. He was still worried about the great increase in the size of the electorate which was impending, but he spoke in a less alarmist and melodramatic way than on previous occasions and put the case for getting full and accurate information about systems of election including proportional representation, the cumulative vote, and the restricted vote. He himself still favoured the Hare scheme, in praise of which he read out extracts from letters to Hare from eminent public men. The resolution was seconded by A. Elliot (Liberal), but he revealed in his speech how little he understood about the workings of electoral systems, as he recommended single-member constituencies as the best method of securing true representation. Three other members spoke in favour of an inquiry, but it was turned down by the government spokesman, Sir William Harcourt, who was himself clearly

[69] *HC Deb.* 244 (4 Mar. 1879), 216–56.

against any change.[70] Blennerhassett's motion was lost by 102 votes to 40.[71]

The next year (1882) Blennerhassett tried once more, unsuccessfully, to get an inquiry set .up to collect full and accurate information about various systems of election before it was too late. He was supported by Albert Grey,[72] who stressed that the public were completely uninstructed and uninformed on the matter. Grey was also concerned lest manual labourers should carry every constituency in the kingdom, but he reproved Blennerhassett for not coming out clearly in favour of extending the franchise.[73] This was the last attempt made in parliament to raise the issue of proportional or minority representation before the débâcle of 1884–5.

During the first fifteen years of the campaign (1859–74), its main supporters had by and large agreed on what they wanted— namely the Hare scheme or a modified form of it on the lines of that proposed by Walter Morrison. They had managed to get these ideas widely talked and written about and had secured the adhesion of many thoughtful people to the cause. They had also formed a society in conjunction with representatives of the working classes to work for a change in the electoral system.

But during the next nine years (1874–83) there was less unity among the campaigners as to what scheme was the best, and some of them changed their views for no obviously good reason. No organization to advocate the cause existed after the Representative Reform Assocation collapsed in 1874. This also resulted in the lapse of links with the working classes. Mill had died in 1873, as had James G. Marshall, one of the early influential thinkers about the defects of the existing system, and an advocate of some form of proportional representation.

---

[70] William G. G. V. V. Harcourt, 1827–1904. MP, Liberal, 1868–1904. Held various offices in Liberal governments from 1873 to 1895. For a good picture of Harcourt's attitude to proportional representation, see *HC Deb*. 207 (12 July 1871), 1535–6.

[71] *HC Deb*. 261 (27 May 1881), 1524–35.

[72] Albert Henry George Grey, 1851–1917. Nephew of third Earl. MP, Liberal, 1880–6. Became Liberal Unionist in 1886, and fourth Earl in 1894. Governor-General of Canada, 1904–11. President of the Proportional Representation Society, 1913–17.

[73] *HC Deb*. 267 (21 Mar. 1882), 1475–89.

Thomas Hughes was no longer in parliament after 1874; Thomas Collins was out from 1874 to 1881, and Morrison from 1874 to 1886. The cause also suffered from the premature death in 1875 of the very able professor of Political Economy, J. E. Cairnes, who had been a close friend of Mill and Fawcett and a keen supporter of proportional representation. Most of the Radicals at this period were concentrating on an extension of the franchise in rural areas and on a more rational distribution of seats—large and important reforms to which they gave priority over minority or proportional representation. This was particularly true of Trevelyan and to some extent of Sir Charles Dilke. Early on Dilke had looked like a possible supporter of the cause. He had got to know Fawcett at Cambridge in 1862, but they were never close, and later on, in 1880, Dilke described Fawcett as '*a little* better than a windbag—but only a little better'.[74] Though Dilke became a friend and great admirer of Mill from 1869 onwards, he did not share Mill's enthusiasm for Hare's scheme. He had gone as far as expressing general approval of proportional representation during the debate on Morrison's bill in 1872, even acting as a teller for it, but it seems doubtful whether he had thought much about or really understood the subject. This became even more evident later when he argued in 1885 that the general adoption by the government of single-member constituencies would secure a fair representation of minorities.

A few new figures were coming forward to assist the campaign, for instance Courtney and Blennerhassett, though the latter was of doubtful value; and the journals still carried many articles on the subject. Moreover the growth of the Home Rule movement in Ireland in the 1870s stimulated thought about the existing representative system, as it enabled Home Rulers to be greatly over-represented in the United Kingdom parliament. But by the early 1880s the campaign, if such it can be called, was not in a strong state, and it had to contend with formidable opponents in the two front benches in parliament and a mounting volume of objections from many quarters to any form of minority or proportional representation.

[74] Roy Jenkins, *Sir Charles Dilke* (1958), 149.

# IV

# Early Objections

'Hare's book proves itself. As you read it you can no more resist the conclusions than you can resist a proposition in Euclid', Professor Cairnes remarked to Leonard Courtney;[1] but the reception of Hare's ideas revealed that the grounding of most Englishmen in Euclidean geometry was imperfect. Objections abounded during the twenty-five years following the publication of the *Treatise* in 1859. Some were specific to Hare's scheme, and some developed into opposition to proportional representation generally.

One of the most common criticisms of Hare's plan was that it was far too complicated, and therefore difficult to understand, indeed unintelligible. This came mainly from MPs, on both the front and back benches, many of whom did not even try to understand it or indeed the concepts of minority or proportional representation. 'Englishmen understood a stand-up fight and a victory', one MP said, referring to Lord John Russell's proposal for the limited vote, 'but they did not understand the principle of the representation of a minority.'[2] 'The mind of an Englishman is a very straightforward piece of machinery', declared the Earl of Malmesbury, objecting to the limited vote on the ground that it was a novel plan, 'and I may say he generally puts the question in black and white. Upon the subject under discussion he is accustomed, and has been accustomed, ever to obey majorities, to be ruled by majorities, and to be obedient to the decisions and verdicts of majorities.'[3] Another MP was sure that those who argued for minority representation were as much in the dark as he was; it was impossible to say why minority

---

[1] G. P. Gooch, *Life of Leonard Courtney* (1920) 84, n. 1. The date of the remark is not given, but it must have been before 1875 when Cairnes died.

[2] *HC Deb.* 157 (22 Mar. 1860), 1073. William Massey, Liberal.

[3] *HC Deb.* 189 (30 July 1867), 442. Malmesbury (Conservative) was at that time Lord Privy Seal in Derby's government.

representation could not be right and equally impossible for anybody to prove that it was right.[4] John Bright constantly declared that he could never understand Hare's or similar schemes. As late as 1884 John Morley considered that the advocates of proportional representation did not say what they meant by it (though in fact they had often done so), and it is clear from his remarks that he too was in the dark.[5]

Lord Aberdeen, when Prime Minister, called the limited vote 'a conundrum' when it was proposed in 1854 by Russell who was a member of his cabinet. Gladstone recalled this in 1867, when he was arguing against its inclusion in the Reform Bill, and complaining of the short time (nine days) available for consideration of the proposal, adding, 'and a conundrum in many points of view it is'. Gladstone explained that he himself had been much engaged on other matters when Russell's proposal was being considered by the government of which he was a member and that he then failed to understand it properly.[6] In 1884 Gladstone admitted that he had not studied the electoral systems of other countries, though he then proceeded to add to his arguments for single-member constituencies the fact that they existed in many parts of the rest of the world.[7] It also seems clear from what Gladstone said then that he did not understand the working of the single transferable vote which had just been explained to the House of Commons by Courtney. 'My impression', Gladstone said, 'was that the proposition presented to us, which he (Courtney) said was of so simple a character, was, in truth, a *pons asinorum*, which very few of us indeed, if a record of consciences and understandings could at this moment be taken, would have been enabled to pass.'[8] (A *pons asinorum* is a bridge of asses and is the humorous name for the fifth proposition in the first book of Euclid, because of the difficulty which beginners or dull-witted persons find in 'getting over' or mastering it.) Sir William Harcourt too found the subject difficult, for when as Home Secretary he opposed a request for an inquiry into the various systems of election which had been

[4] *HC Deb.* 217 (16 July 1873), 487. John Locke, Liberal.
[5] *HC Deb.* 286 (1 Apr. 1884), 1566.
[6] *HC Deb.* 189 (8 Aug. 1867), 1163.
[7] *HC Deb.* 294 (4 Dec. 1884), 685.
[8] Ibid. 681–2.

proposed, he referred to them as 'a sort of Chinese puzzle'; he did not favour selecting MPs by 'a sort of double acrostic'.[9]

In contrast to the politicians, most serious commentators, even if critical of Hare's scheme, did usually make an effort to understand it,[10] but they pointed out with some justification that it was generally found incomprehensible. Thus Bagehot wrote that Hare 'was so anxious to prove what could be done, that he had confused most people as to what it is. I have heard a man say, "He never could remember it two days running".'[11] Nor was it only Hare's scheme which was found puzzling: the editor of the *Spectator* in 1883 declared himself incapable of understanding the single transferable vote or any other plan of proportional representation that had been suggested.[12]

Another common objection to the Hare scheme was that it abolished entirely representation by localities. This was in fact not so, as electors could group themselves on a territorial basis and return an MP for their locality if they so wished. But Hare undoubtedly emphasized the disadvantages of a system in which electoral divisions were founded solely on geographical areas, and stressed the advantages of a system in which electors could vote for any candidate in whatever part of the country he might offer himself; and his scheme would most probably have resulted in the election of many MPs representing 'constituencies' other than localities, though Hare himself thought it probable that many if not most voters would 'add their votes to those of their townsmen and neighbours' as 'contiguity of place produces a tendency to union'.[13]

Many critics of this feature of Hare's scheme and indeed of the other proposed changes in the electoral system often sought to strengthen their case by saying that the proposals ran counter to the history, traditions, and habits of the nation and were unknown to the constitution.[14] This was an argument which naturally appealed to Disraeli. As early as 1859 he had con-

[9] *HC Deb.* 261 (27 May 1881), 1535.
[10] See, e.g., *Saturday Review*, 26 Feb. 1859, 244–6, 'Mr Hare on Representation'. Author not identified.
[11] Walter Bagehot, *The English Constitution* (1867), 164 in Fontana edn. (1963).
[12] Charles Seymour, *Electoral Reform in England and Wales* (1915), 502.
[13] *Treatise* (1859), 87.
[14] See, e.g., the *Economist*, 11 June 1859, 649; and Sir R. Collier, *HC Deb.* 188 (5 July 1867), 1082.

demned minority representation as 'alien to the spirit of the constitution'.[15] He made the same point in 1867 saying that the cumulative vote was 'alien to the customs, manners and traditions of the people of this country'.[16] Gladstone too made a similar point when arguing against any form of minority or proportional representation, though he wrapped it up in more words. Each constituency, he said, was in itself an integer, a community. What should be represented in the House of Commons was 'the sense of the majority, which represents the whole community; because the community is, in the spirit and sense of the Constitution, recognised as being in itself an integral quantity'. Most schemes for minority representation, he said, were not known to our usages and history.[17] Other Liberal politicians took the same line; for instance Russell in 1865, and William Harcourt who said in 1871 that our ancestors had been content with the old, though he admitted clumsy, system of representation by majorities and that 'proportional representation was contrary to the habits and sentiments of the people'.[18]

Closely linked to this objection was the notion that the means proposed to secure minority representation were 'artificial' and therefore undesirable; one should not invent devices or mechanisms with this aim; one should be guided by prescription not theory. These views were expressed by both intellectuals and politicians of the two main parties: for instance among Liberals, Russell (in 1865), Gladstone, and G. J. Shaw-Lefevre, and among Conservatives, Stafford Northcote and Spencer Walpole.[19] Some of Burke's arguments were naturally used in support of this objection, particularly by Walpole. He was critical of the clause in Russell's 1854 bill which gave some minorities a potential voice. He was also critical of plans

[15] *HC Deb.* 154 (7 June 1859), 131.
[16] *HC Deb.* 188 (5 July 1867), 1111.
[17] *HC Deb.* 202 (15 June 1870), 147; and 294 (1 Dec. 1884), 381.
[18] *HC Deb.* 207 (12 July 1871), 1536.
[19] George John Shaw-Lefevre, 1831–1928. MP, Liberal, 1863–85 and 1886–95. Held office in various governments between 1866 and 1895. Created Baron Eversley in 1906. Objected to proportional representation on numerous grounds. Stafford Northcote, 1818–87. MP, Conservative, 1855–85. Held office in various governments from 1866 to 1887. Spencer Horatio Walpole, 1806–98. MP, Conservative, 1846–82. Home Secretary, 1852, 1858–9, and 1866–7.

'worked out in the closets of political philosophers'. These were in his view not based on experience or long usage. If we were to make any further alterations in our repesentative system, they should always be based 'as it were upon the same principles, as those by which we have hitherto been guided'. The science of constructing or reforming a government could not be taught by a priori arguments however ingenious or by abstract reasoning however plausible. We should make constitutions 'by reference to all those agencies, habitudes, and associations by which man is necessarily governed, not by reference to the first four rules of arithmetic with a partial smattering in the rules of proportion'.[20]

The intellectuals who put forward similar views included individualists like Herbert Spencer and G. C. Brodrick as well as anti-individualists like Frederic Harrison, the positivist.[21] Harrison admitted that the representation of minorities had in logic 'a tremendous case', but he considered that 'in politics, we must ever distrust logic, and look at results organically and always as a whole'. 'The capable man will appear when society is ripe for his work', but not through ballot boxes. What was needed were new tones of feeling, not new mechanisms. At times he wrote with great vehemence: faith in personal representation rested on a profound, but ruinous political and social theory, the theory of individualism, 'the pedant's paradise, the millenium of ideologues, the zero of politics, the *reductio ad absurdum* of representation'. The scheme for personal representation was 'a monument of the length to which inveterate habits of syllogising in the air can carry acutely argumentative minds, parading with drums and colours along the broad and trampled highway that leads to the great region of—Nowhere'.[22] Leslie Stephen took the same line, arguing against the importance of political machinery. He emphasized that society was a complex

---

[20] *Quarterly Review*, 106 (Oct. 1859), 541–62, and 107 (Jan. 1860), 220–66.

[21] Herbert Spencer, 1820–1903. Philosopher and sociologist. See his review of Hare's *Treatise* in *Westminster Review*, 17 NS (Apr. 1860), 486–507. George Charles Brodrick, 1831–1903. Political journalist and writer. Later Warden of Merton College, Oxford. See his review of Mill's *Thoughts on Parliamentary Reform*, in *The Times*, 1859, reprinted in his *Political Studies* (1879). Frederic Harrison, 1831–1923.

[22] Frederic Harrison, *Thoughts on the Theory of Government* (1875); *Parliament before Reform, 1867* (1867); *The Revival of Authority* (1873).

structure, which must be slowly developed, not spasmodically transformed; the road to political virtue was slow and trouble-some; there was no self-acting machinery which would some-how spontaneously purify political life. One could not make men wise or virtuous by sleight-of-hand tricks or arithmetical dodges; government would not become better by changing the system of voting; one should not rely on mere contrivances and clever manipulations of machinery to improve the security of the social order.[23]

A great deal was said by the opposition about the encourage-ment that proportional representation and Hare's scheme in particular would give to the advocates of various 'crotchets', by which was meant what would now be called single-issue pres-sure groups. It so happened that there was in the second half of the nineteenth century a proliferation of such groups each formed for a specific, limited purpose. The most prominent of these were the Liberation Society which aimed at the disesta-blishment and partial disendowment of the Church of England, the United Kingdom Alliance which advocated temperance, and the campaign against the Contagious Diseases Acts which provided for the regulation and control of prostitution in certain towns. Other causes dubbed 'crotchets' by their opponents included female suffrage, local option for the sale of intoxicating liquor, the right for a man to marry his deceased wife's sister, and even Home Rule for Ireland. 'Crotcheteers' and 'crotchet-mongers' were denounced constantly by opponents of propor-tional representation as people with peculiar views or pet schemes, with strong opinions on small issues, eccentrics with remarkable crazes, fanatics, faddists, fad-mongers, prigs, and hobby-riders. The case against enabling supporters of crotchets to get greater representation in parliament was that they would not understand national or imperial questions, and that they would promote only sectional interests, not the common good. It was even said that many MPs would under the Hare scheme have no political opinions at all. Frederic Harrison declared that

[23] Leslie Stephen, 1832–1904. Man of letters and philosopher. *Macmillan's Magazine*, 15 (Apr. 1867), 529–36, and *Fortnightly Review*, 18 NS (Dec. 1875), 836–52. Stephen expressed the same view years later in his book *The English Utilitarians* (1900) where he asks, referring to Hare's scheme, 'Is not the "water-mill" here expected to work the river?' (iii. 279).

representatives such as Contagious Diseases Acts abolitionists might be buffoons or busybodies on every topic of national interest.

This argument gained support from the fact that at that time some Liberal leaders saw pressure groups as a problem for their party and as something that needed suppressing or at least combating. Gladstone in particular disliked them passionately. 'What we want in this House is to have the prevailing sense of the community', he declared in 1870. 'We do not want to have represented in miniature particular shades of opinion that may at the moment prevail in it.'[24] The sects sacrifice 'the whole mass of the general public interests' for the sake of the particular and isolated questions they believe in, he wrote in 1878.[25] This was an issue on which Joseph Chamberlain agreed with Gladstone. 'What is the object of a representative system?', he asked in a speech on 7 October 1884. 'Surely it is to secure that the majority shall rule . . . Minority voting in every form . . . secures an over-representation of crotchets, which misrepresents great principles, which tempts the exhibition of personal ambition and personal vanity, which confuses the great issues we are called upon to decide, which divides the point of progress, and by all these means plays into the hands of the party of privilege . . . The majority has the right to enjoy the fruits of victory.'[26] Chamberlain suspected that the supporters of proportional representation wanted to undermine or neutralize the large extension of the franchise which was about to take place. 'Your proposals', he wrote to Lubbock, the president of the Proportional Representation Society, 'seem to me to proceed from a settled distrust of the people. You want to trammel their decisions by checks and devices. . . . The most open Tory opposition is less dangerous to Liberal progress than the theories to which you have given your influential support.'[27]

The anti-faddists included Conservatives as well as Liberals. Thus Disraeli characterized schemes to represent minorities as

---

[24] *HC Deb.* 202 (15 June 1870), 147.
[25] 'Electoral Facts', *Nineteenth Century*, 4 (Nov. 1878), 961.
[26] Quoted in Peter Fraser, *Joseph Chamberlain* (1966), 56.
[27] Chamberlain to Lubbock, 14 Oct. 1884. Avebury papers. British Library, Add. MS 49647.

'admirable schemes for bringing crotchety men into this house—an inconvenience which we have hitherto avoided, though it appears that we have now [in 1867] some few exceptions to the general state of things; but we do not think we ought to legislate to increase the number of specimens'.[28] And a pamphlet by an obviously Conservative author forecast in 1868 that if minorities were represented, people with peculiar views would be elected, 'absorbed in the contemplation of their own crotchets', with poor judgement on other matters, as it would be warped by any real or fancied bearing of a measure on their pet scheme.[29]

As a result of this general climate of hostile feeling against pressure groups advocating various reforms, the case against proportional representation based on the encouragement it would give to crotcheteers no doubt acquired considerable weight, for on the face of it the maxim that an MP should not represent sectional interests but should work for the public or common good is an excellent one. But it is not a good answer to those who advocate minority representation, because it may well be that in considering what is in the common good one should take into account the interests or good of everyone in the community including minorities, and to do this properly they must be represented.

Some objectors made a similar point to the 'anti-crotchet' one but in wider terms, arguing that one should not aim at making parliament an accurate mirror of public opinion. Different considerations were advanced in support of this view. Those who feared increasing democracy thought that the more the electoral system approximated to mathematical exactness, the greater scope it would give to the mass of poorer voters to submerge the wealthier minority; power would go to the most numerous class who would use it to their advantage. Others thought that the exact representation of the views of minorities would lead to inaction. Bagehot took this line as early as 1859 when discussing minority representation, by which he meant the limited vote. He granted that every active and intelligent minority should have adequate spokesmen in the legislature,

[28] *HC Deb.* 188 (5 July 1867), 1112.
[29] *The Representation of Minorities*, by R. C., 1868. Author unidentified.

but thought it was often undesirable that it should be represented there in exact proportion to its national support. The
judgement of parliament ought always to be coincident with
the opinion of the nation, but there was no objection to it being
more decided. There was a risk of indecision if every minority
had exactly as much weight in parliament as it had in the
nation. He even made the astonishing statement that it was
very frequently more important that the course selected should
be consistently adhered to and energetically carried through
than which of two courses was selected. Thus it was right in
Bagehot's opinion that the views of the persons who disap-
proved of the Crimean war had been very inadequately represented in the votes in parliament, though he does not seem to
have objected to the voicing of their sentiments by a few men.
'A strong conviction in the ruling power will give it strength of
volition. The House of Commons should think as the nation
thinks, but it should think it so rather more strongly, and with
somewhat less wavering.'[30] When reviewing Mill's *Representative Government* in 1861, Bagehot touched briefly on the same
point, forecasting that under the Hare scheme no government
would have security against repeated and continuous defeats,
because of the existence of a knot of small interests with
undefined party-relations;[31] but curiously enough this particular
argument against proportional representation is not repeated in
his famous book, *The English Constitution*, which was published
in 1867, though one of his criticisms of Hare's scheme in this
work is that it would lead to short-lived parliaments. However
Bagehot's fear that proportional representation would lead to
weak government became a commonly accepted view among
its opponents, and was voiced often during the debates of
1884–5. Thus Shaw-Lefevre considered that with proportional
representation governments would be liable to defeat at any
moment, whereas with single-member constituencies parliaments would have force and vigour to support the policy of the
executive. He and others, such as Dilke, therefore argued that
it was good to have a system which over-represented in parliament the majority of votes in the country, and which enabled

[30] *National Review*, 8 (Jan. 1859), 228–73.
[31] *Economist*, 18 May 1861, 540–1.

even a very small swing in votes to cause a large change in the representation of the House of Commons.[32]

Leslie Stephen too feared that the representation of minorities would lead to inaction, a worse tyranny than the tyranny of majorities; it was right to give a bare majority in the country an overwhelming majority in the legislature as this would be a valuable source of strength. Moreover he considered that the theory held by Hare and his disciples involved a palpable absurdity: parliament could not be at once an accurate mirror of public opinion and a collection of the wisest men; on the contrary, if elected by the system proposed, nine-tenths of the MPs would be fools; the Hare scheme went along with the mistaken idea that one man's opinions were as good as another's.[33] This was not in fact true of Hare or Mill, who both believed, with no doubt undue optimism, that the electorate, if properly constituted, would vote for the wisest and best men.

Some critics went to extreme lengths in their objections to representing minorities and even contended that there was no point in representing them at all if decisions were made by majority votes in parliament. This view was voiced by various MPs whose thoughts about representative government were rather superficial, but it received some support from a more weighty source, namely the prominent Radical politician Richard Cobden. Thus he considered in 1865 that 'What is wanted is to slay and bury those delusive projects which have of late owed their existence to men who wish to mystify the simple question of principle, and lead the public astray after crotchety details of their own . . . The idea of giving representation to minorities is an absurdity. It strikes at the very foundations of representative government by majorities.'[34]

In recent years one of the main arguments used by opponents of proportional representation has been that it would lead to coalition governments. This objection does not appear to have been made in the nineteenth century or in the early twentieth.

---

[32] For Shaw-Lefevre, see his articles in *Contemporary Review*, 45 (May 1884), 714–33, and *Fortnightly Review*, 37 NS (Feb. 1885), 202–15. Also *HC Deb.* 294 (2 Mar. 1885), 1832–7. Dilke's remarks are in ibid. 1817.

[33] *Fortnightly Review*, 17 NS (June 1875), 820–34, and 18 NS (Dec. 1875), 836–52.

[34] Letter to Bright, 16 Jan. 1865. Quoted in John Morley, *Life of Richard Cobden* (1908) ii. 466–7.

Disraeli's famous remark of 1852, 'England does not love coalitions',[35] had no reference to the effects of proportional representation.

Other objectors to electoral reform schemes claimed that parliament did in fact reflect most if not all facets of public opinion and that minorities were adequately represented already. They argued that the so-called anomalies in the existing arrangements—for example, the unequal size of electorates in different constituencies and diversities of franchise—enabled a variety of interests and views to be represented and that in two-member constituencies the two parties quite often divided the representation between them. These views were expressed from all sides of the political spectrum, namely by Conservatives, Whigs, Liberals, and even Radicals such as G. O. Trevelyan, but they carried less weight as pressure mounted for more equal electoral districts and rationalization of the franchise.

Amongst objections specifically to Hare's scheme, and not to proportional representation generally, was his commitment to voluntary constituencies, that is constituencies formed by voluntary association as contrasted with the existing compulsory ones which in Hare's view restricted electors by artificial bonds. Bagehot objected to voluntary constituencies not so much on the usual and reasonable ground that the system would be complicated and impracticable, but because they would, he thought, result in the election of MPs who would be subservient to their constituents. MPs would be either 'party politicians selected by a party committee, chained to that committee and pledged to party violence', or 'immoderate representatives, for every "ism" in all England'. He had in mind here 'associations of persons leagued on certain principles, and looking to those principles only', what now would be called pressure groups. They too would be violent, by which Bagehot meant not men of moderate and judicious sentiments. 'A voluntary constituency will nearly always be a despotic constituency' whose representatives would be 'hopelessly enslaved'. It would be a church with tenets, and the MP would be a delegate of its determinations. Party fetters would be worse even than they were already (in 1867) and caucuses would be far worse even than in

[35] *HC Deb*. 154 (16 Dec. 1852), 1666.

America. At present MPs were free because constituencies were not 'in earnest', but voluntary constituencies would be in earnest with eager opinions; this would lead to frequent, even annual, elections.[36].

One may well ask how a scheme devised partly with the aim of weakening the power of parties and increasing the independence of MPs both in and out of parliament came to be seen by Bagehot as doing exactly the opposite. The answer is that Bagehot thought that under Hare's plan there was a great risk of votes being wasted, 'thrown away', unless the voter knew how other people were going to vote. He had in mind here two sorts of situation: one where a popular candidate, like Mr Gladstone, would have far more votes than the quota, i.e. than he needed to get elected, and the other where a candidate had too few votes and was therefore eliminated. In either case, Bagehot thought, election managers would play a big part in guiding electors as to how to vote. In contrast to Bagehot, both Hare and Mill thought that very few votes would be wasted under the Hare scheme, or at least that many fewer would be wasted than under the existing system, because the voter would be able to indicate a large, indeed very large, number of alternative choices. Hare made this much clearer in the later editions of the *Treatise* than in the earlier ones, stating that 'an unrepresented voter would be a rare exception' and that a vote 'when given cannot be without effect'.[37] Though this was to claim too much, it is not possible to say which prediction, Hare's or Bagehot's, was the more correct. Much would depend on the number of candidates who offered themselves for election: the greater the number, the more chance there would be of an elector not including on his voting paper any candidate who achieved the quota or who came near enough to it to be elected. The chance of votes being wasted would also depend on how far voters availed themselves of the power of providing for successive contingencies.

Bagehot was not alone in thinking that Hare's scheme or any scheme which involved the transfer of votes, far from weakening the power of parties, as Hare and others confidently predicted,

---

[36] *The English Constitution*, 166–70.
[37] *Treatise*, 4th edn. (1873), 191 and 93.

would give an impetus to party organization and wire-pullers: several other commentators too thought that the voter, bemused by the large number of candidates, would want advice on how to order his preferences on the voting paper and would get it from party agents; but they did not usually go as far as Bagehot in fearing the despotism of autocratic constituency-makers.

Another objection to Hare's scheme, and indeed to any scheme involving the transfer of later preferences from a candidate who received more votes than the quota, was the alleged element of chance involved in the selection of votes to be transferred, though this objection disappeared later on when a system was devised solving the problem. Hare himself suggested a number of criteria for selecting votes for transfer, sometimes combining several of them, namely the time at which the elector had gone to the poll, the number of alternatives on his voting paper, and the more or less remote connection of the candidate with the local constituency from which the voting paper emanated. Others proposed selecting votes for transfer at random, drawing them by lot from among all the voting papers which had given a candidate the quota, these having been mixed thoroughly together. This was the system proposed by the Danish mathematician and statesman Andrae, and adopted in Denmark in 1855. Although Andrae demonstrated that the element of chance involved in this method was insignificant, it was rejected by Hare in favour of what he described as 'a series of simple rules', which of course were not at all simple. After much discussion the British Proportional Representation Society settled in 1884 on the lottery system, but later adopted the superior device of transferring votes to continuing candidates in proportion to the next preferences expressed by all electors who had voted for the successful first candidate. Thus if a candidate has 50 first-choice votes and only needs a quota of 20, he can spare 30, that is three-fifths of his total poll. Ballot papers on which he is marked 'one' are examined, and votes are transferred to candidates marked 'two' on them, each second-choice candidate getting three-fifths of the number of votes given for him on these ballot papers. Obviously different methods of selection might have an effect on the fate of candidates, but the emphasis put on this question by some objectors was curious and unwarranted, considering that the element of chance under existing electoral conditions due to the large number of variables at play was very great and far greater than that likely to result under the Hare or similar schemes.

Some objectors to proportional representation maintained that it was incompatible with the secret ballot. This suggestion was entirely erroneous, but as it was made by no less a prominent Radical politician than Sir Charles Dilke, it carried some weight particularly with working men.

Whatever one thinks about the desirability of proportional representation, it is clear that some of the criticisms of Hare's ideas and some of the objections made in the nineteenth century to forms of minority or proportional representation were far more valid than others. For instance Hare's scheme was undoubtedly over-elaborate and impracticable, but this was not a fair criticism of the single transferable vote system as proposed by Walter Morrison and others, which maintained compulsory constituencies based on geographical districts returning several MPs each. Moreover many of the critics misrepresented the advocates of proportional representation, alleging that they wanted minorities to be over-represented and actually to rule instead of the majority; but certainly Hare and others at times laid themselves open to this suspicion, stressing as they did the danger of 'mere numerical majorities'. As regards the objection that proportional representation would lead to weak government, the critics were wrong in supposing that the existing electoral system ensured strong government through an alleged built-in tendency to over-represent in parliament the majority in the country: sometimes the majority was over-represented, sometimes not. Nor can any weight be attached to their belief that changes in machinery are not able to have any effect on the political system. However they were justified in being sceptical of the forecasts made by some of the reformers that radical improvements in the political mores would result from the adoption of their proposals, for instance the moral regeneration of the voters and particularly the reduction or even elimination of bribery and corruption. The extent to which some of the advocates of proportional representation weakened their case by making exaggerated claims about its merits will be considered later when the reasons for their failure are being discussed.

# V

# The First Campaign: Part II, 1884–1885

ALTHOUGH many Liberal candidates at the general election in the spring of 1880 had pledged themselves to franchise reform, three-and-a-half years elapsed before the government decided to introduce a reform bill. It was no doubt intimations in the late autumn of 1883 that this was at last about to happen, combined with the increasingly obvious antagonism of Joseph Chamberlain to proportional representation, which made a few people—Sir John Lubbock and others—realize the need for concerted action to promote the cause. So, early in January 1884, Lubbock convened a group of sympathizers who decided to form an association. A provisional committee and a secretary were appointed. A notice was sent to the press on 16 January announcing the decision and inviting the adhesion of anyone in favour of proportional representation. This was the start of the (British) Proportional Representation Society (PRS).

Sir John Lubbock[1] was an amazing phenomenon. Influenced by Charles Darwin from the age of 8, he became a keen naturalist and in due course an eminent scientist. At the age of 14 in 1849, he left Eton partly because of the school's deficient curriculum, went into his father's bank, and rose to be a leading banker. He stood for parliament as a Liberal unsuccessfully in 1865 and 1868. He was at that time interested in Hare's scheme which he thought worthy of consideration, but he was not yet ready to support it. In 1870 he became MP for Maidstone, holding this seat until 1880 when he lost it. He was however immediately returned unopposed for London University of which he was Vice-Chancellor, and which he represented until 1900 when he went to the House of Lords as Baron Avebury.

---

[1] Sir John Lubbock, 1834–1913. Fourth Baronet.

During his first thirteen years in the House of Commons (1870–83), he introduced no less than thirteen bills which became law. These included the first Bank Holidays Act, bills for the protection of wild birds and ancient monuments, and many other useful measures covering a wide variety of subjects, specially financial and scientific. During his subsequent parliamentary career he was responsible for seventeen more Acts of parliament including several very necessary measures designed to improve the conditions of labour in shops. His record of success as a back-bencher is unique. He does not seem to have spoken in parliament on electoral matters before 1884, and it is not clear who or what kindled or rekindled his interest in the subject. Maybe, assisted by his remarkable capacity for engaging in a great many activities concurrently—due partly to his ingenious devices for saving time[2]—he was reading and thinking about the electoral system for years before he took the issue up and launched the campaign of 1884–5. Certainly his book, *Representation*, which came out in 1885, reveals considerable knowledge of proposals made on the subject both at home and abroad since 1832.

The most recent account of the events of 1884–5—the book *The Politics of Reform 1884* (1972) by Andrew Jones—portrays the PRS as irrelevant, supine, and inept. Jones considers that its members were fundamentally at variance with one another, that Lubbock was 'a political dabbler', and that he, Leonard Courtney, and Albert Grey were all absurd. How far these judgements are warranted will emerge from the narrative that follows. It will bring out both the difficulties faced by supporters of proportional representation during these years and weaknesses in the presentation of their case.

Immediately after the founding of the PRS, of which Lubbock became president, letters were sent to all MPs and to many other people announcing the formation of the society and explaining its aims in general terms. Anyone interested was asked to join; this could be done without paying a subscription, though financial support was welcomed. The society tried

---

[2] For instance, contrary to fashion and in the face of an indignant family, he insisted on wearing elastic-sided boots, remarking that one could easily learn a language in the time saved from doing up laces.

without success to get Walter Morrison to act as treasurer, and in due course appointed Albert Grey to the post. Largely through Lubbock's efforts the response from MPs was considerable: after six weeks, by the end of February 1884, 110 MPs had joined. A few months later this figure had risen to 184, of whom 93 were Liberals and 91 Conservatives. Indeed every section of the House of Commons was represented in the society except the Parnellites. It was, Lubbock pointed out, a remarkable assemblage of members who probably agreed on no other single question of practical politics. Thirty peers also joined. The records do not show the size of the non-parliamentary membership, but they reveal eighty-two subscribers other than MPs during the first year. Foreign proportional representation societies were at once asked for information, as were colonial authorities. Office premises were secured and a clerk was taken on to assist the honorary secretary, A. Cromwell White. A library of books and pamphlets was built up assisted in particular by gifts from Droop and Hare, who presented the society with fifty copies of his *Treatise*, curiously admonishing the secretary to distribute them with discrimination, i.e. only to those who would use them 'for our cause'.[3] The society also produced and distributed free of charge many pamphlets—160,000 in the first year—and much other propaganda material for which constant requests were made. A strong branch of the society was formed in Manchester in March 1884, mainly through the initiative of C. P. Scott, the editor of the *Manchester Guardian*.

Early on the PRS saw the need to spread information about proportional representation among the working classes and to get their support for the cause. So working men's Liberal clubs were approached, and George Holyoake was persuaded to join (which he did for a time) and to write something suitable for popular digestion.[4] These efforts were however not very successful until the campaign was taken to the north of England later in the year. Moreover they soon showed up one of the problems

---

[3] T. Hare to Cromwell White, 1 Apr. 1884. PRS Misc. Correspondence.
[4] George Jacob Holyoake, 1817–1906. He had been a Chartist and Owenite and remained radical in his views all his life. He was a suitable choice for the PRS to make in that he had written many books, pamphlets, and educational manuals, but his understanding of proportional representation and commitment to the cause were, as it turned out, rather weak.

confronting the society: it was pleased to have got so much support from Conservative MPs and drew attention to this in its literature; but this, as one supporter pointed out, alienated the class of person who went to workmen's Liberal clubs. Moreover the more radical of the working classes who were keen, as the Chartists had been, on equal electoral districts, were suspicious of the fact that most supporters of proportional representation did not see equal electoral districts as a remedy by themselves for the existing defects in the electoral system. Indeed advocates of proportional representation considered that in the absence of other changes equal electoral districts would probably make things worse, since variations in the size of constituencies enabled some minorities to get represented.

From its start many members of the society saw the need to decide which was the best scheme of proportional representation to advocate, but the executive committee of twenty-four members failed to agree on this for nearly a year. Droop, who had been clear about what was best since the 1860s, pressed his view on Lubbock as early as 4 January 1884, but with no success; for two months later the first general meeting of the society on 5 March passed a timid and unspecific resolution, namely that if a constituency returned more than two members some form of proportional representation should be adopted. Droop died in March 1884, and though others pressed for a decision, the committee was unable to come to one until 3 December 1884, getting bogged down considering different list systems, which many of them favoured, and the comparatively unimportant question of which votes should be transferred if the single transferable vote was adopted. The secretary, Cromwell White, gave the committee no lead on the matter, admitting as late as November 1884 that his acquaintance with the subject was but recent. This was undoubtedly true as he had for months been writing to all and sundry asking them which was the best plan to carry out proportional representation, and collecting information about the different systems which had been invented, probably getting more and more confused as he tried to assimilate them.[5] Hare had not been invited by Lubbock to the

[5] Albert Grey considered White was 'an ass' and utterly unfit for the job of secretary. Grey to Lubbock, 10 Dec. 1884. Avebury papers, BL Add. MS 49647.

foundation meeting in January and was not on the committee, but he was often in communication with the secretary and attended general meetings of the society. He was by this time recommending a rather simpler version of his original scheme, but it was still too complicated to be easily understood.

Parliament did not reassemble after 25 August 1883 until 5 February 1884, on which date the government announced that it would bring in a bill to extend the franchise. At the end of February the society asked Gladstone, the Prime Minister, to receive a deputation to urge in particular the inclusion of proportional representation in larger constituencies, but he refused to do so, telling them to wait for his statement on the franchise bill the next day. In this Gladstone explained that it was not practical to deal with the franchise and the redistribution of seats in the same bill, for redistribution would raise a host of questions including proportional representation; a redistribution bill would be introduced next session; that would be the proper time for considering all the propositions with regard to minority representation and other modes of voting; he himself had not changed the opinion he had always held on them, but they should be fully and impartially considered.[6]

This policy had been agreed by the cabinet though only after considerable discussion, as several of its members thought, understandably, that the two questions were closely interrelated and that they should therefore be dealt with together. This was in particular the view of those such as Earl Spencer and the Marquess of Hartington who were concerned with the effect a simple extension of the franchise would have in Ireland: they feared that the loyal Irish minority would be grossly under-represented. Spencer indeed favoured some form of minority representation at least for Ireland.[7] But Gladstone from the start emphasized that redistribution was a vast and difficult subject, involving tiresome minutiae and herculean labour, and that he was incapable of dealing with a complicated bill. This was no doubt how he felt in late 1883 and early 1884, but his unwilling-

---

[6] *HC Deb.* 285 (28 Feb. 1884), 122–31.

[7] Earl Spencer was at this time Viceroy of Ireland, a post he had held also from 1868 to 1874. The Marquess of Hartington (later Duke of Devonshire) was Secretary for War.

ness to get involved with redistribution and questions concerning the electoral system was partly due to his deep-rooted dislike of any scheme for minority or proportional representation. It was in his view a 'most unfortunate and annoying subject'; he 'utterly disbelieved in minority clauses' and 'believed we should never have them'.[8] The cabinet contained no supporters of proportional representation, though Spencer sympathized with the principle; so although there were two supporters of it in the government (Fawcett and Courtney), Gladstone got agreement to his strategy.

In these circumstances it was not easy for advocates of proportional representation to decide what were their best tactics. Immediately after Gladstone's statement of 28 February, the PRS issued a circular to all MPs calling attention to the grave objections to the present system of voting, and pointing out that the extension of the franchise, making it as the government proposed uniform in counties and boroughs, would tend to diminish the variety of representation. The circular also pointed out that the existing system did not in all cases obtain for majorities their due preponderance in the legislature, or secure for minorities proper representation according to their numbers; proportional representation was particularly necessary in Ireland; the results of general elections were to a large extent a matter of chance, leading to violent fluctuations in the balance of political power and thus of policy. The circular resulted in a substantial increase in support of the PRS amongst MPs and others, which was given considerable publicity in the press. It was suggested in some newspapers that the government was alarmed and that they put pressure on prominent Liberals who favoured proportional representation not to endanger the franchise bill and to leave the question to come up when redistribution was considered.

The PRS decided not to propose an amendment to the franchise bill; this was probably the right decision partly because a straightforward amendment in favour of proportional representation would no doubt have been ruled out of order. In any case they relied on the government's repeated assurances that

---

[8] Letter of 6 Dec. 1883 to Spencer, and Cabinet Minutes of 4 Jan. 1884. Quoted in Andrew Jones, *The Politics of Reform 1884* (1972), 45.

the question would be thoroughly examined as part of any new settlement.[9] Nevertheless supporters of proportional representation kept the subject alive in the House of Commons by raising it on several occasions during the long-drawn-out debates on the bill. Thus on 3 March 1884 Blennerhassett referred to the remarkable progress during the last few weeks in public opinion in favour of proportional representation. Wisely he did not on that occasion show his accustomed nervousness at the extension of the franchise, but confined himself to saying that the majority should not monopolize representation. After two other MPs, Edward Clarke (Conservative) and Goschen (Liberal), had spoken briefly in favour of minority representation, Lubbock made a substantial speech detailing the defects of the present system, emphasizing its chancy nature, and basing his case for a change not, as was so often argued, on the need to represent small minorities, but on the desirability of adequately representing the great parties in the state.[10] On 1 April Albert Grey urged the need for personal or proportional representation if the right to vote was to be of value, and proposed that the franchise bill should not take effect until a redistribution bill had been passed.[11] On 26 May when the abolition of the limited vote in 'three-cornered constituencies' was proposed, James Lowther, though a staunch Conservative, reminded the House that the greatest exponents of liberal opinions throughout the world had in a large number of instances pronounced in favour of some adequate system for the representation of minorities. He thought the Hare scheme unworkable, but there were many other systems which recommended themselves to those who took an intelligent interest in the subject.[12] Lowther returned to the issue on 17 June, backed up by C. B. Stuart-Wortley, also a Conservative, who agreed that the existing system 'most successfully secured what he might call the misrepresentation of the people'. A. J. Balfour also urged that proportional representation should be discussed currently and not put off until the next year, and another

---

[9] *HC Deb.* 285 (28 Feb. 1884), 123; and 288 (26 May 1884), 1328–9, statements by Gladstone; and 286 (24 Mar. 1884), 704, statement by Hartington.

[10] For the whole debate, see *HC Deb.* 285 (3 Mar. 1884), 396–456.

[11] *HC Deb.* 286 (1 Apr. 1884), 1315–30.

[12] *HC Deb.* 288 (26 May 1884), 1331–4.

Conservative, C. E. Lewis, foretold, rightly as it turned out, that the redistribution bill would be presented to them for acceptance as a whole 'as a pistol might be'. Lubbock however still believed the government's promise that the whole question of proportional representation would be fully and fairly considered next session.[13]

The position of Liberal advocates of proportional representation was tricky, as they did not wish to expose themselves to the criticism that they were hindering the extension of the franchise. It was suspected by some people that schemes for proportional representation were, as John Morley put it, 'but new disguises for the old Tory distrust of the people'.[14] On the other hand the Liberals did not wish to alienate their Conservative friends. Lubbock in particular was aware of this dilemma.

The franchise bill finally emerged from the House of Commons on 26 June 1884, and went to the House of Lords where, on its second reading on 7 July, Earl Cairns moved that it should not be passed unless 'accompanied by provisions for so apportioning the right to return members of parliament as to insure a true and fair representation of the people'.[15] This was the same Cairns who had sponsored the limited vote in 1867. He pointed out that redistribution raised many problems, mentioning among other things that there was a large body of men in the House of Commons who attached great importance to the subject of proportional representation. Cairns's motion was passed by 205 to 146 votes on 8 July. No doubt many of the peers who voted for the postponement of the bill did so because they were against a large extension of the franchise whether or not accompanied by redistribution (it was predicted that the bill would nearly double the number of voters); but some of them, even if not supporters of proportional representation, could reasonably argue, as they did, that there was a very good case for dealing with the two issues together, as had been urged constantly whilst the bill was in the Lower House.

During the debates on the bill in the House of Lords in July

---

[13] For the whole debate, see *HC Deb.* 289 (17 June 1884), 611–20.
[14] *HC Deb.* 286 (1 Apr. 1884), 1566.
[15] *HL Deb.* 290 (7 July 1884), 112.

and August 1884 there were occasional references to minority and proportional representation. Thus Lord Dunraven said that 'minorities . . . individuals, human beings should be represented in parliament', though the policy of legislation should in the main be governed by the wishes of the majority of the people. The Earl of Carnarvon pointed out that in a constituency of 30,000 electors returning two MPs, 14,900 of them might be misrepresented; he regarded this as 'flagrant and indefensible injustice'. Lord Colchester expressed the hope that the government, when it introduced a redistribution bill, as it had promised to do, would recognize the necessity of providing for the representation of minorities, adding perhaps rather unfairly that the secretary to the Treasury, Courtney, appeared to have forgotten what he had declared some years ago, in 1879, namely that to introduce a franchise bill without minority representation would be a proposal which showed neither foresight nor insight.[16]

But it was Lord Salisbury who put the case for proportional representation most fully. He said he wanted a true mirror of the actual numerical condition of opinions in the country to be produced in the House of Commons, in order that minorities might be able to express their views, which was essential to the just protection of their interests; this was 'the first idea of true and genuine representation'. The bill, he feared, by neglecting the representation of minorities would have a particularly disastrous effect in Ireland: the loyal minority of about a million and a half people would not secure more than 5 per cent of the representation. (The total population of Ireland at this date was about five million.) On another occasion Salisbury complained that the government was proposing that it alone would decide the grave issues which redistribution raised, above all 'the most vital question of proportional representation—that question which concerns the defence of minorities, a question that in all democratic forms of government is of supreme importance'.[17]

[16] *HL Deb.* 290 (7 July 1884), 175, and (8 July 1884), 381; 292 (11 Aug. 1884), 409.
[17] *HL Deb.* 290 (8 July 1884), 456–60, and (17 July 1884), 1369. Lord Salisbury, 1830–1903. Was Lord Robert Cecil. Became Viscount Cranborne in 1865 and Marquess of Salisbury in 1868. MP, Conservative, 1853–68. Held office in various Conservative governments. Prime Minister, 1885–6, 1886–92, and 1895–1902.

Salisbury's thinking about the electoral system is interesting. Admittedly his main concerns in the 1880s were why the Conservatives had been defeated at the general election of 1880, and how to ensure after the franchise was extended that they were represented in proportion to their numerical strength, which he assumed would always be smaller than that of their opponents. But unlike many other politicians he at least tried to understand how the electoral system worked or might work. He realized that if the two main parties were spread in the same proportions in each constituency all over the country, one party could get all the seats in parliament. He also saw that a modest swing in votes could produce a large change in seats; he was critical of a system which distorted the wishes of the electorate and whose results depended in his view on pure chance. Salisbury had, as Viscount Cranborne, listened to John Stuart Mill's exposition of the Hare scheme in parliament in 1867 and, whilst thinking it impracticable, had urged the House to give it respectful treatment. It seems possible that Salisbury's 'education' on electoral matters was also partly assisted by his acquaintance with C. L. Dodgson ('Lewis Carroll') whom he met in 1870 and who became a close friend of the whole Cecil family. Dodgson was keenly interested in voting theory: he had been writing about it for ten years both in general terms and in connection with university affairs; and in 1884 he became actively involved in the public controversy over proportional representation, publishing in November 1884 a substantial pamphlet entitled *The Principles of Parliamentary Representation*.

Dodgson was wholly in favour of parliament being a true index of the state of opinions in the nation it professes to represent. He considered that the proportions of political parties in the House should be, as nearly as possible, the same as in the whole body of electors. In order to ensure this he devised a scheme which was in some respects similar to the single transferable vote as recommended by others, but which he appears to have thought out on his own. He proposed multi-member constituencies of varying sizes with a minimum of three seats each, every elector having a single vote, but with no second or subsequent preferences. Any candidate who received the quota of votes, worked out in the usual way, was returned. If he had surplus votes, he transferred them to other candidates as he wished and these other candidates could assign their votes to one another. Dodgson's analysis of the existing system was acute: he saw that in some circumstances the House of Commons could consist wholly of one party, and that in other circumstances a majority, even a large majority, of the electors might not secure a majority in the House. He also pointed out that it was fallacious and absurd to give electors as many votes as there were seats to be filled in their constituency. Being a mathematician he was particularly interested in how votes should be transferred: this was unfortunate for the fortunes of the cause he upheld, as the resulting rather technical discussion of the merits of rival transfer schemes which he and others conducted in the press must have bemused the general public.

Whilst the debate on the franchise bill was taking place in the House of Lords, Dodgson sent Salisbury on 8 July a copy of an article in which he developed his scheme for parliamentary elections. In a covering letter he urged that some such scheme was much more needed than the mere redistribution of electoral districts. Salisbury in his reply on 9 July acknowledged the need for a scheme of electoral reform, but stressed the difficulty of getting a patient hearing for 'anything . . . absolutely new . . . however Conservative its object . . .'. Dodgson replied indignantly: '*please* dont call my scheme for Proportionate Representation a "Conservative" one! ("Give a dog a bad name, etc."). Most sincerely, *all* I aim is to secure that, *whatever* be the proportions of opinions among the Electors, the *same* shall exist among the Members. Such a scheme may at one time favour one party, at one time another: just as it happens. But really it has *no* political bias of its own.'[18]

In spite of Salisbury's passionate commitment to Conservatism, Dodgson may have been wrong in assuming that he was looking for a scheme which would be biased in favour of the Conservatives; for Salisbury purported at any rate to be aiming at an electoral system which would give the Conservative party the representation in parliament which was its due and only its due in the light of the support it had in the country. It is not clear what electoral system Salisbury favoured in order to achieve this objective, and it may be misleading to pose the

---

[18] *The Letters of Lewis Carroll*, ed. Morton N. Cohen (1979), 544–5.

issue in such terms. One historian goes so far as to say that it is wrong 'to think it worthwhile to inquire for which of all these various courses a "free" Salisbury would have settled' in the autumn of 1884.[19] It is no doubt true that Salisbury was above all concerned to secure the unity of the party under his lead, but nevertheless it is equally misleading to overlook such evidence as exists on the issue. Thus several contemporaries thought that he had leanings towards proportional representation,[20] even to a very radical scheme disregarding territorial divisions, for which he had shown some sympathy as far back as 1867 during the debate on Mill's motion. In his negotiations with the government in November 1884 Salisbury certainly tried to preserve the limited vote in some towns, and indeed to extend it to the whole of London, proposing that electors there were to have only one vote in four-member constituencies. Nor is there any reason to doubt the truth of his statement on 3 December 1884 that he would have been 'heartily glad' if it had been possible to maintain the three-cornered system, i.e. the limited vote, in large boroughs.[21]

Parliament was prorogued from 14 August to 23 October 1884. During this period there was a vehement campaign in the country against the Lords' refusal to pass the franchise bill before a redistribution bill had been enacted. This was understandably seen as a manœuvre by the Lords to kill the franchise bill, and gave rise to the slogans 'The Peers against the People' and 'Mend them or end them'. The PRS wisely kept out of this constitutional conflict. Indeed it seems to have been generally inactive until the autumn, though some individuals, particularly Albert Grey in Northumberland, were making speeches and organizing propaganda in their areas. Some members of the society criticized it for not doing more to popularize the cause, but it seems unlikely that they would have secured a hearing

---

[19] Jones, *Politics of Reform*, 194.

[20] For example, Albert Grey and Hartington. See also *The Times*, 25 Sept. 1884, 9. All referred to by Jones, *Politics of Reform*, 173–4, 194, and 193. The *Manchester Guardian* on 5 Mar. 1885 considered that 'there can be little doubt that Proportional Representation rather than single member seats would have been Lord Salisbury's condition for striking a bargain'.

[21] Salisbury to Freston, 3 Dec. 1884. Quoted in Jones, *Politics of Reform*, 218.

whilst the more momentous issue of the powers of the House of Lords was being fiercely debated. The agitation against the Upper House inevitably obscured the issue of proportional representation.

However, the day before parliament met, the PRS decided to bring the matter up at once in the House of Commons. So on 23 October Lubbock gave notice that on 4 November he would move that no redistribution bill would be satisfactory which did not recognize the principle of proportional representation, and on 27 October he asked for a separate day to be devoted to a discussion of the mode of voting to be adopted under the franchise bill before it was passed. Gladstone refused his request, saying that the time had not yet arisen for the discussion of this subject and that there was already sufficient business before the House. Nor was Lubbock able to introduce his motion on 4 November. Courtney, who was at that time Secretary to the Treasury, saw clearly that it was essential to get the principle of proportional representation and its various forms discussed before the Redistribution bill was published. So he wrote a long private letter to Gladstone on 8 November 1884, two days after his friend and colleague Fawcett had died, pleading for a consideration of the whole subject whilst this could still be fruitful. At the centre of his case for proportional representation, Courtney stressed in the Hare tradition the injury done to our national life by the deleterious 'training' received by most politicians and the exclusion from politics of those who refuse to submit to this training. Parliament is derived, he wrote, 'I will not say from contaminated, but from imperfect sources'. The struggles of parliament's 'degraded factions are in peril of becoming a by-word' and it was impossible to improve the situation with the present processes of election. He also detailed the many other points which had attracted its numerous supporters to proportional representation.[22] Courtney's letter had no effect on Gladstone except presumably to supply him with material which he could use later as a basis for ridicule. The franchise bill passed through the Lower House rapidly and went to the Lords on 13 November from where it emerged as an Act of parliament on 5 December.

---

[22] PP 1910 XXVI. Royal Commission on Systems of Election, Evidence, 11–13.

Meanwhile the government had been getting on with its plans for redistribution. These were being worked out in the summer and early autumn of 1884, but members of the PRS were not in a position to influence them. The only supporters of proportional representation in the government, Fawcett and Courtney, played no part in the preparation of the Redistribution Bill, whose main architect was Dilke, the President of the Local Government Board. Indeed Courtney seems to have been completely in the dark about the government's activities, for he said later that the question of redistribution was as far as he knew not considered by the cabinet or even by any member of it before he wrote to Gladstone on the matter on 8 November,[23] whereas in fact the cabinet had been discussing it since early August. Nor apart from Salisbury were there any sympathizers with minority or proportional representation among those members of the opposition whom the government consulted. The executive committee of the PRS decided on 21 November to urge Salisbury to leave open the question of proportional representation in any arrangement that might be come to between him and the government, but this was of no avail; indeed the next day Salisbury was forced to abandon any demand for even minority representation through the limited vote and to settle for single-member constituencies with election by simple majority, no doubt thinking that if all went well this would work in the Conservative interest.

The Redistribution of Seats Bill was introduced into the House of Commons on 1 December 1884. Besides producing greater equality in the size of electoral districts, it introduced single-member constituencies nearly everywhere in place of the plural-member system under which over two-thirds of the House of Commons was then elected; only twenty-seven constituencies (23 boroughs, the City of London, and three universities) were allocated two members by the bill, with voters having two votes each. The experiment of minority representation in the form of the limited vote introduced for certain constituencies in 1867 was ended. The bill embodied the agreement which had been reached with the opposition leaders. In announcing that one-member districts would be the general and prevailing rule,

---

[23] Ibid. Q. 145.

Gladstone justified the arrangement as the best on the ground that it was very economical, very simple, and went a long way towards 'what is roughly termed the representation of minorities'. Indeed it might be termed the representation of minorities, he said, for it would secure a large diversity of representation. He knew some gentlemen on both sides had wished to go further, but they were not agreed on the means to be adopted, and any scheme was open to the gravest objections, as being artificial, not known to our usages and history, and approved of by only a handful of people.[24]

The government's proposals were naturally a tremendous blow to advocates of proportional representation who in spite of previous rumours had hoped for something better. The PRS reacted at once with a strategy for resistance. A. J. Balfour later reproached Courtney and his friends for not beginning the agitation sooner, but at least after the franchise and House of Lords issues were disposed of, not a day was lost. Thus the society's committee decided on 2 December to draw up an amendment to the Redistribution Bill; a general meeting of members was held on 3 December, and an appeal for £5,000 was launched to enable the society to bring the subject before the country in the coming recess. People were asked to send in their names if they were willing to organize meetings or to speak on the subject.

In the meantime on 1 December Courtney had resigned from the government, explaining why in parliament on 4 December during the second reading of the Redistribution Bill. He devoted most of his long and passionate speech to an attack on single-member constituencies. In this he put some emphasis on what most supporters of proportional representation regard as the main objection to single-member constituencies, namely that they do not guarantee the proportionate representation in parliament of opinions in the country; but he berated them chiefly on other and less central grounds. Thus he said they would have a bad effect on the character of MPs, which was already deteriorating; that many electors would be alienated, and that decay and atrophy would set in. To support his case Courtney cited at some length the views of the recently assassi-

---

[24] *HC Deb.* 294 (1 Dec. 1884), 380–1.

nated President of the USA—Garfield—and reminisced about how he must have sat beside him under the gallery of the House of Commons in 1867. He then explained how the single transferable vote worked and recommended it as 'a new gospel' which would ensure the resurrection and liberation of the people and prevent them 'dying of inanity'.[25]

It was easy for Gladstone to ridicule parts of Courtney's speech and he did not miss the opportunity. It was on this occasion that he introduced the analogy of a *pons asinorum*. He also pointed out that as President Garfield was a keen protectionist as regards trade, his authority could not be considered superior to that of (the free trader) Cobden who had recommended dividing constituencies into wards, each returning one member, and that the 'degenerate individuals' chosen by single-member constituencies included Gladstone himself, as well as Courtney, Trevelyan, and Dilke.[26]

However other supporters of proportional representation did what they could in the short time at a late hour at their disposal to put the case against the government's proposals. Viscount Folkestone reproached Gladstone for treating the question in a joking kind of way[27] and for not dealing with the central arguments on the subject; and Viscount Crichton referred to the disastrous effect single-member constituencies would have in Ireland.[28] But the main speech against the government was made by Lubbock. In this he laid considerable emphasis on a report produced by a committee of the United States Senate in 1869 which condemned the single-district system and even considered that proportional representation might have prevented the American Civil War. This was because the electoral system deprived the people in the south, who were in favour of

---

[25] *HC Deb.* 294 (4 Dec. 1884), 658–80.

[26] *HC Deb.* 294 (4 Dec. 1884), 680–87. Cobden's views on this issue were often referred to and seem to have carried extra authority because they were expressed just before his death.

[27] Folkestone may well have been referring here to Gladstone's facetious and tasteless references (when talking about Garfield), to 'those disturbances' which on voyages across the Atlantic 'are fatal to all continuous thought in the case of many of us', meaning presumably seasickness. *HC Deb.* 294 (4 Dec. 1884), 682.

[28] Viscount Folkestone, 1841–1900. MP, Conservative, 1874–89, when he succeeded his father as Earl of Radnor. On executive committee of PRS. Viscount Crichton, 1839–1914. MP, Conservative, 1868–Oct. 1885. Then fourth Earl of Erne. A member of the PRS.

the Union, of representation in Congress and in the electoral colleges. Though this suggestion was not wholly absurd, it is doubtful whether it carried much weight in the British parliament, even though Lubbock pointed out the similarity between events in the USA and the likely effect of the bill in Ireland. The rest of his speech made the standard case for proportional representation, emphasising that the existing system was very chancy, as was shown by the results of the general elections of 1874 and 1880, whereas the chance of a wrong result with the single transferable vote was infinitesimal; both parties should be represented approximately according to their strength in the country; proportional representation offered the only way of securing a hearing for the minority and power to the majority.[29] Both Lubbock and others expressed the hope and belief that the government was not absolutely committed against proportional representation; it was this hope which made them feel it was worthwhile to put their case before the country in the coming recess. The Redistribution of Seats Bill passed its second reading that day, 4 December 1884, without a division.

The recess lasted from 6 December 1884 to 19 February 1885. During those ten weeks the PRS was extremely active. The executive committee met weekly with an average attendance of six members. The most assiduous were Lubbock, Westlake, Folkestone, and Courtney who had joined the committee on his resignation from the government. A pamphlet was immediately produced to show that the single transferable vote was not unintelligible or difficult to work: it explained in just three pages very clearly what the voter and the returning officer do. Extra staff were taken on by the PRS. A stream of letters was sent out from the office arranging meetings and distributing literature, on one occasion 10,000 handbills. Albert Grey took offices in Newcastle-upon-Tyne for three months and engaged a secretary. Many, often large, public meetings (at least forty of them) were held in several parts of the country, mainly in London, the Midlands, and the North; resolutions for fair representation were adopted at all of them except two. Various societies and clubs were also addressed by members of the PRS. At most of

---

[29] *HC Deb.* 294 (4 Dec. 1884), 731–41.

these meetings illustrative elections were held, nearly 50,000 voting papers in all being distributed.

Several periodicals carried articles criticizing the Redistribution Bill and putting the case for proportional representation. These included one by Courtney which listed and meticulously answered twenty-four objections to the single transferable vote,[30] and one by Hare in which he made some fair points against Gladstone and against an article by G. T. Shaw-Lefevre who was a member of the cabinet.[31]

But all was of no avail. On the first day of the committee stage of the Redistribution of Seats Bill (2 March 1885), in order to get the subject discussed, Lubbock moved:

that the committee be instructed that they have power in all cases where an elector is entitled to one vote only, to enable the elector to nominate more than one candidate to whom under certain circumstances that vote might be transferred in the manner indicated by the elector.

The debate on Lubbock's motion was spread over two days in spite of the government's attempt to confine it to one day, but only eight MPs spoke for the motion whereas fourteen spoke against it. On the first night many supporters of proportional representation were absent because they had not known the subject was to be discussed, but they seem to have been absent on the second night (3 March) too, partly because the debate was held during the dinner hour. The main speeches for the motion were made by Lubbock and Albert Grey on the first night and by Folkestone and Courtney on the second. Lubbock demonstrated that the bill would not, as many people assumed, necessarily represent the country fairly, backing up his case with some elaborate figures from Switzerland. He explained the working of the single transferable vote and answered the standard objections to it, particularly those concerned with the alleged element of chance in the transfer of votes, on which issue he asserted three members of the government (Shaw-Lefevre, Sir H. James, and Trevelyan) were mistaken. Grey put

---

[30] *Nineteenth Century*, 17 (Feb. 1885), 312–20.

[31] 'Representation and Misrepresentation: II. The Coming Steps in Representation', *Fortnightly Review*, 43 (Feb. 1885), 216–22. Shaw-Lefevre's article was in the *Contemporary Review*, 45 (May 1884), 714–33.

considerable emphasis on the fact that resolutions in favour of proportional representation had been carried by overwhelming majorities wherever they had had the chance of hearing it explained; with more time the process would continue. Folkestone found it strange that MPs had difficulty in understanding the proposal, because at all the public meetings where test elections had been held, uneducated people understood what they were required to do both as voters and in counting the votes. Courtney spoke as usual at considerable length, reiterating many of the points he had made before, for example about the threat the bill posed to the union with Ireland, and the distortion of votes at the 1874 election. In listing the benefits to be anticipated from proportional representation he forecast that it would enable MPs to be more independent of their parties, and (a curious point) maintain the return of political economists to the House, so ensuring that the arguments for free trade would be put.[32]

The vote on Lubbock's motion on 3 March was catastrophic, only thirty-one MPs supporting it against 134 'Noes'. This was only five more votes than Morrison had secured for his bill in 1872. Those in favour consisted about equally of Liberals and Conservatives. Twenty-five of the thirty-one were members of the PRS. What had happened to the remainder of the 184 MPs who had joined the society? Even allowing for the fact that some of them had no doubt joined simply to find out more about the subject, the turnout was very poor. Moreover six members of the society actually voted against the motion. There is no one explanation of what was little less than a fiasco. Probably the most important factor was that many MPs thought that if a major amendment of this kind were passed, the whole bill would be in danger, resulting in another serious constitutional crisis like the recent one. Others no doubt felt they must simply support the main lines of the arrangement made by their leaders, any further advocacy of alternative plans being impolitic, useless, or even disloyal. The attitude of A. J. Balfour, Salisbury's nephew, must have been influential here. He was a member of the PRS and announced that he believed a system of proportional representation like the single transferable vote was

---

[32] *HC Deb.* 294 (2 Mar. 1885), 1806–61; (3 Mar. 1885), 1917–35.

the best form of representation. He was particularly concerned about the gross under-representation of Scottish Conservatives. But he would not support Lubbock, one of his reasons being that all the trouble they had gone through in the last six months would have to be gone through again.[33] Some of those who voted against the motion had an inadequate grasp of the subject although they were members of the PRS; they were convinced by the government's assertion that single-member constituencies would protect minorities and generally work satisfactorily from their point of view.

No further debates on proportional representation took place in parliament during the passage of the Redistribution Bill which finally became law on 25 June 1885. Lubbock saw that any further struggle in the House of Commons would be useless, but Courtney took the opportunity at the end of the third reading of the bill to enter a last desperate protest against it: he repeated some of his arguments against single-member constituencies and forecast, amidst laughter and scoffing, that they augured badly for the character and independence of the House of Commons.[34]

One feature of the debates on the Redistribution Bill was the small amount of discussion engendered by the abolition of the limited vote which had been in operation in thirteen constituencies since 1867. These places returned three members each (four in the City of London), but a voter could cast only two votes (three in London). This lack of discussion may at first sight seem strange, particularly because the working of the limited vote had been only briefly discussed during the passage of the Franchise Bill when its abolition was proposed;[35] but the explanation is that the experiment had such a bad reputation by 1885 that few people pressed for its retention or extension to more constituencies. It was generally thought that it did not help the representation of minorities, or that if it did, this was undesirable; and that it encouraged caucuses and nefarious party organization. What is the truth? As regards helping the

[33] *HC Deb.* 294 (2 Mar. 1885), 1840.
[34] *HC Deb.* 294 (11 May 1885), 289–91.
[35] *HC Deb.* 288 (26 May 1884), 1319–37.

minority party in a constituency to get representation, provided of course that it was of the requisite size, the evidence suggests that it did help. This can be shown by comparing results of elections before and after 1867, and by considering what would probably have happened if the limited vote had not been introduced. Thus the Conservatives got some representation in Manchester—one MP in 1868 and 1880 and two MPs in 1874—whereas they had had none from 1832 to 1867. Similarly Glasgow elected a Conservative MP in 1874 for the first time since 1832. The Conservatives were also helped by the limited vote in the City of London, getting in three candidates in 1874 and 1880, whereas the Liberals had won all four seats at most elections since 1832. Equally in the seven counties which had the limited vote, the minority party, the Liberals, did rather better after 1867 than they had since 1832 when these counties were given three representatives each, but without the limited vote.

*Parties of MPs elected in constituencies where limited vote operated*

|  | 1868 | | 1874 | | 1880 | |
|---|---|---|---|---|---|---|
| Results | Actual | Probable | Actual | Probable | Actual | Probable |
|  | Lib.   22 | Lib.   19 | Lib.   16 | Lib.   9 | Lib.   20 | Lib.   15 |
|  | Cons. 18 | Cons. 21 | Cons. 24 | Cons. 31 | Cons. 20 | Cons. 25 |

*Source*: John H. Humphreys, *Proportional Representation* (1911), 65.
Humphreys explains how he estimated the probable results. He assumed that, as each voter could give one vote to each of three candidates (or, in the case of the City of London, four), each of the parties would have nominated three candidates (four in London), and that most electors would have voted on party lines. The larger body would thus have secured three (or four) seats.

The table compares what actually happened with what would probably have happened without the limited vote, assuming voters had had three votes where three MPs were to be elected, and four votes where four MPs were to be elected. It can be seen that the limited vote had an effect on the outcome of the three general elections at which it operated and that on balance it helped the Liberals rather than the Conservatives. However, full figures were not collected at the time and many people thought it had mainly helped the Conservatives; this was because they focused more on the towns than the counties.

What was uppermost in many people's minds when evaluating this experiment was the impression that it led to the dragooning of voters by party workers. This was certainly true of Birmingham where the Liberals saw from the start how to defeat the purpose of the limited vote, 'driving a coach and six through the law in O'Connell's spirit' as J. L. Garvin later put it.[36] By careful planning the Liberals throughout the city were drilled so as to secure an ingenious allocation of votes at the general election of 1868. Some were directed to vote for candidates A and B, others for candidates A and C, and others for candidates B and C, in such a way that the total votes cast for each of the three Liberal candidates should be as nearly as possible the same. The great mass of Liberal voters voted as they were told, and all three Liberal candidates were elected. At the general election of 1874 the Conservatives in Birmingham did not even bother to put up any candidates, so three Liberals were returned unopposed. In 1880 the Liberal party machine was in operation again and secured all three seats for its candidates. The only other constituency in which this kind of manipulation of the electorate took place was Glasgow. Otherwise, that is in the eleven other constituencies where the limited vote operated, the Birmingham model was not copied, partly because party organization was not as effective as at Birmingham, but also because the parties do not seem to have tried to influence elections by the Birmingham device. If they did try, they certainly were not successful, because the seats in these constituencies were divided between the parties in all three general elections. So the bad reputation acquired by this experiment in minority representation was by no means wholly deserved.

It is in general not the job of the historian to speculate whether the outcome of the events he has related could have been different if this or that factor had not obtained. Nevertheless one cannot help wondering whether proportional representation could have been introduced in 1884–5 if the PRS had been founded earlier, if it had had more money, if it had been more active, more efficiently run, more astute politically. So it may be

---

[36] J. L. Garvin, *Life of Joseph Chamberlain* (1932), i. 95.

permissible to attempt answers to these questions. There can be no doubt that advocates of proportional representation faced a very difficult political situation from 1880 to 1885: they had no supporters in the cabinet, and Gladstone's distaste for the whole subject and inveterate opposition to any form of proportionality, combined with his dominant position in the party, were tremendous obstacles. Even if the PRS had staged a massive propaganda effort right from its foundation in early 1884 and converted hundreds of thousands of electors to the cause, it seems very doubtful whether this would have made any difference to the outcome. Certainly once the leaders of the two parties had agreed in November 1884 on the main lines of the Redistribution Bill, providing for single-member constituencies with the first-past-the-post system almost everywhere, the battle was lost. No doubt the PRS would have been more effective if it had had larger funds: it raised only £1,300 between January 1884 and March 1885 and spent £1,000, but its policy of not requiring a subscription from supporters and supplying propaganda material free was probably correct at this time when one-third of the members contributed something.

The PRS displayed some of the common weaknesses of organizations run almost wholly by volunteers advocating a cause, such as unrealistic optimism amongst some of them combined with defeatism amongst others; but it also displayed some of the common strengths of such bodies, namely an immense amount of devoted labour performed by its supporters and largely voluntary staff. Its main mistake was probably not to settle on the form of proportional representation it recommended until very late (December 1884). This left many people confused about the subject, though discussion about the means of obtaining proportionality should not have prevented them from understanding the principle.

Were the main protagonists of the cause inept in their advocacy of it? This could not be said of Lubbock who in general put the case for proportional representation in sensible and moderate terms. Nor is it true of Grey who managed to explain the system in simple language and to make it comprehensible to working men. But this criticism could be made of Courtney whether one is considering his effect in or out of parliament.

That Courtney would be 'a dead failure' in the House of Commons was predicted by an experienced MP when he was first elected to parliament in December 1876.[37] This proved to be a correct prediction, for from the outset of his parliamentary career Courtney often irritated and alienated the House of Commons; it resented being counselled on a variety of subjects by a new member who, rising with a portentous sheaf of notes in his hand, spoke frequently and at considerable length. It was said by the *Pall Mall Gazette* in 1885 that he 'lectured the house as a master does a backward pupil'. Courtney however was usually well pleased with his performance. His general style of advocacy was probably due to his extensive experience from 1864 to 1880 as a leader writer on *The Times*, 'a position from which the most modest-mannered man learns to regard his fellow-kind with a certain air of superiority', as the parliamentary journalist, H. W. Lucy, commented.[38] Moreover as professor of Political Economy at University College, London, from 1872 to 1875, Courtney was used to lecturing to a captive audience.

The fullest and most vivid contemporary picture of Courtney is to be found in the diaries of Beatrice Webb who became his sister-in-law in 1883, though one must allow for her severely critical mind when evaluating her judgements. Her view of him is captured in some entries of her diary. Thus:

*15 October 1882*: Leonard Courtney is no doubt an excellent and an able man, but not companionable to an ignorant young woman. His conversation bores me. It is made up of a certain amount of facts, given out in an assertive tone, and quotations from English poets, which from his ugly pronunciation are difficult to catch. He never argues (with his inferiors, i.e. with us) [the Potter family] but denies and quotes. . . . On general subjects he is wonderfully well informed but surely neither original nor powerful. . . . He is a theorist without being a reasoner; his conversation and his speeches are coarse (not in the bad sense) in matter and manner, lacking in subtlety and depth of thought. It may be that we shall learn to appreciate him and that the fault lies with us and not with him.

*10 September 1883*: I am now quite fond of him because I have ceased to expect to be interested by him.

[37] Justin McCarthy, *Reminiscences* (1899) ii. 369.
[38] Henry W. Lucy, *Memories of Eight Parliaments* (1908), 240.

*6 November 1884*: A character you learn to admire and reverence for its high integrity of purpose and honesty of means. Wanting in sympathy and the humility which sympathy brings. A man who believes firmly in his mission as *teacher*—perhaps ignoring too completely the wisdom of learning from others and through others. And as this deficiency is not supplemented by any adaptability through worldly motive, he seems likely to fail in political life. His intellectual faculty does not show itself in conversation, except in the rugged integrity of his judgment. Faculty he *must* have had to have risen to his present position. But in his views there is a curious want of coherence . . . He pleases no party, is representative of no class *interest* or school of *thought*. Unless of great value as an official, he will be spurned off the battlefield of politics.

Later Beatrice Webb came to think better of Courtney, appreciating his integrity and courage, but she still considered that he had 'bad manners (in which include his supercilious depreciation of other people's claims and his lack of graciousness)' (19 March 1895). When Courtney died she summed up her views of him in her diary on 13 May 1918:

Leonard combined moral genius and a good mechanical intellect with considerable artistic faculties . . . What he lacked was any distinction in the quality of his intellect. He had no subtlety, no originality—he thought in the grooves made by other minds and by minds of the plainer sort . . . He was, to all who disagreed with him, *an impossible person to talk to* except on the trivialities of daily life. Unless you agreed, he refused to discuss, for the sufficient reason that he had not the mental equipment to carry on an argument on any other premises but his own.

Beatrice Webb also recorded that her father originally thought Courtney 'an intolerable doctrinaire prig with little knowledge of human nature or practical affairs', though later he became proud of his son-in-law.[39]

Some of the poor opinions held of Courtney were based on social snobbery. His origins were fairly humble: his father worked in a bank earning only £230 p.a. by the 1850s; his mother had been a shop assistant. The family with nine children lived in the western tip of Cornwall, cut off from the main currents of national life and thought. After attending a local

---

[39] *The Diary of Beatrice Webb*, ed. Norman and Jeanne MacKenzie (1982–4).

school until the age of 13, Leonard worked as a bank clerk for six years, but he had the good fortune to receive evening education chiefly in classics and mathematics from a local doctor. This enabled him to get to St John's College, Cambridge in 1851, where he did well as a mathematical scholar, and became a Fellow. But it was a hard life of unremitting labour, followed by six years (1858–64) of struggle and disappointment in London as a briefless barrister and freelance journalist, until he was taken on to the staff of *The Times*. It is true that in due course he got to know Mill, Cairnes, Fawcett, and other radical intellectuals, but he does not seem at this time to have had many friends and he retained marks of his provincial origins. Dilke for instance thought he would be unsuitable as Speaker of the House of Commons in 1883 because he dropped his h's, 'which more than neutralised his radicalism'.[40]

This biographical sketch explains, but does not excuse, the somewhat frosty welcome Courtney received when he entered London politics in 1877 as MP for the small Cornish borough of Liskeard. However his uncouthness and humble origin would probably not have mattered much if he had simply made the case for proportional representation by emphasizing as its objective that electors who have common political sympathies or interests should be represented in parliament in rough proportion to their numerical strength in the country; but instead he excited resentment by tactlessly recommending it as a method of improving the calibre of MPs, and describing the good effects which would result from a reformed system in extravagant terms reminiscent of the wilder Utopian claims of Hare and Mill. He secured, it seems, a rather better reception outside parliament, when addressing clubs and public meetings after he resigned from the government in December 1884. Audiences at that time had a remarkable capacity to listen to long and involved speeches by politicians; even so, some of them were clearly mystified by Courtney's exposition of the more intricate workings of the single transferable vote. However this was not a problem during the next twenty years when, as we shall see, the effort to influence public opinion was in abeyance.

[40] Roy Jenkins, *Sir Charles Dilke* (1958), 172.

# VI

# School Boards, Local Government, and Home Rule, 1885–1904

IT is sometimes supposed that, after the failure in 1885 to get proportional representation adopted for elections to parliament, the electoral reform movement petered out for twenty years. It is true that from April 1885 the Proportional Representation Society (PRS) cut down its work and expenditure substantially and that, without being formally dissolved, it became less and less active; but this did not mean that the main leaders of the campaign, in particular Lubbock and Courtney, ceased their activities. On the contrary, as if invigorated at first by the defeat of 1885, they seized every available occasion to explain and advocate their case. Opportunities to do this in parliament arose in connection with three main subjects: school boards, local government, and home rule for Ireland.

Only three weeks after the hostile vote of 3 March 1885, Lubbock proposed that a select committee should be set up to inquire into the mode of voting in school board elections.[1] The government agreed and a committee was duly appointed. In July 1885 it submitted the evidence it had received in reply to the 5,000 questions it had asked of witnesses, but made no recommendations.[2] Both Lubbock and Courtney were members of the committee and played an active part in questioning witnesses. Courtney also gave extensive evidence himself. They brought out again and again the main disadvantage of the

[1] *HC Deb.* 296 (24 Mar. 1885), 517–18.
[2] PP 1884–5 XI. Select Committee on School Board Elections (Voting), Report and Evidence, 389–728.

cumulative vote, by which school boards were elected, namely that it often wasted votes, citing *inter alia* the example of Millicent Fawcett's 48,000 votes at Marylebone in 1870 when about 8,000 votes would have sufficed to get her elected. They also mentioned that the cumulative vote could result in the under-representation of a party because it ran either too many or too few candidates. They showed how the single transferable vote avoided both these difficulties, and that it involved only a small element of chance.

The main problem encountered by Lubbock and Courtney during the proceedings of the select committee was in getting the previous and existing Permanent Secretaries to the Education Department (Sir Francis Sandford and Patrick Cummin) to address their minds to a system embodying the transfer of votes. Both said they had not studied and did not understand systems of minority representation other than the cumulative vote. The transfer system, the 'movable vote', declared Cummin, was a conundrum, an arithmetical question, 'a very confusing subject'. Courtney poured scorn on him for being unwilling to consider any other methods for securing the desired results or for doing so 'in a very sluggish manner'. Other witnesses, including clerks to school boards and the editor of the *School Board Chronicle*, also showed lack of comprehension of the whole subject, even after their protracted, dogged examination by members of the committee and exhortations from Courtney such as 'Now just fasten your attention . . .'.[3]

Nevertheless the work of the select committee resulted in some progress for the cause, because the Royal Commission on the Elementary Education Acts (the Cross Commission) reported in 1888 that they were on the whole in favour of retaining some form of proportional representation in school board elections and that they would be glad to see the adoption of the single transferable vote, as it possessed the advantages of the cumulative vote without the inconvenience which sometimes arose in its operation: the single transferable vote obviated the waste of voting power, diminished the opportunity for wire-pulling, and was regarded as simpler than the present system.[4]

---

[3] Ibid. Qs. 584, 616, 619, and 3075.
[4] PP 1888 XXXV. Royal Commission on Elementary Education Acts, Report, 226.

This recommendation was gratifying to the PRS, especially as only one member of the Commission, J. G. Talbot, was a member of the society; this contrasted with the membership of the 1885 select committee, one-third of whose members were members of the PRS. However, the recommendation of the Royal Commission was not implemented.

The next opportunity to make the case for proportional representation in connection with school boards arose in 1897 when an attempt was made in parliament by a Conservative back-bencher, Sir J. B. Maple, to reduce the size of electoral areas for school board elections in London, replacing them by single-member constituencies, thus substituting the simple majority system for the cumulative vote. The proposal was opposed by Lubbock and Courtney who argued that the existing system secured the representation on school boards of members of different classes, and minorities such as Roman Catholics, which they approved of even though Lubbock thought that 'it would be a great advantage if every one in this country were a Protestant'. They also gave examples from elections in Ireland and for the London County Council to show how the simple majority system often misrepresented voters' choices. The government opposed the bill and it was not passed.[5]

Soon after this, in 1898, Courtney took the initiative and introduced a bill—the School Board Voting Bill—which would have allowed school boards to adopt by a two-thirds majority the method of the single transferable vote instead of the cumulative vote as an experiment which could be reversed. He argued that the main drawback to the cumulative vote was that voters could not tell whether they were over-rating or under-rating their strength. Joseph Chamberlain was suspicious of the proposal, wanting to know whether it was 'a development of the minority voting system', meaning the limited vote, which he had always been against. Another MP brought up the often rejected objection that it would reduce an election to a pure game of chance. The bill was dropped at the end of the parliamentary session.[6]

The proposals contained in the 1902 Education Bill did not

---

[5] *HC Deb*. 48 (28 Apr. 1897), 1205–19. Lubbock's remark is at 1206–7.
[6] *HC Deb*. 57 (10 May 1898), 955; and 58 (7 June 1898), 977–80.

offer much scope for the advocacy of proportional representation, although by abolishing school boards in England and Wales it ended the use of the cumulative vote. Moreover neither Lubbock nor Courtney were in the House of Commons then: Lubbock had gone to the Lords and Courtney had lost his seat at the general election of 1900. The bill transferred the powers of school boards to the councils of counties, boroughs, and larger urban districts, all of whom were elected under the simple majority system. During the interminable and acrimonious debates on the bill some speakers feared that the change would involve the loss of the services of men and women who, with their special knowledge of educational problems, were doing valuable work on school boards. To meet this objection the bill contained provisions regarding the composition of the local education committees through which the councils were to work. Though some MPs criticized the effects of the cumulative vote, the argument turned less on this issue than on the anomaly of keeping 2,500 *ad hoc* bodies which could levy a rate, and on the need to get all spending in a locality under one authority. The 1902 Education Act abolished school boards in England and Wales and thus the use of the cumulative vote, but they were both retained in Scotland.

The government's proposal to create democratically elected local authorities in rural areas gave greater scope for raising questions about electoral procedure. In November 1887 Courtney wrote a long letter to Goschen, the Chancellor of the Exchequer, pressing the case for the representation of minorities in local government. Then early in 1888 the PRS held a general meeting of members and decided to send a deputation to ministers to urge that some form of proportional representation should be adopted for elections to county councils which the pending Local Government (England and Wales) Bill was about to create. The deputation of thirty-seven people included Hare, who perhaps fortunately did not speak. It was received on 2 March by Lord Salisbury, the Prime Minister, and Ritchie, the President of the Local Government Board.[7] Lubbock argued that

[7] Charles T. Ritchie, 1838–1906. MP, Conservative, 1874–92, and 1895–1905. Held several offices in Conservative governments.

whilst it might not matter if in a general election the minority in a town elected the majority of its MPs, as had happened at Leeds in 1885,[8] because this could be counterbalanced by what happened elsewhere, this did not apply in local government. Courtney pointed out that as a county might well be more homogeneous than the whole country, a minority in a county could, with single-member constituencies, be totally unrepresented on the county council. The PRS followed up the deputation by holding a test ballot among MPs to illustrate the working of the single transferable vote. The response was good: 454 papers were returned of which only six were defective.

On the second reading of the bill which created county councils Courtney made in April 1888 a long, rather pompous speech, criticizing the method of election proposed, which was the election by simple majority of one councillor per district every three years. It was not altogether clear what he proposed in its place, as he mentioned both the cumulative and the limited vote, but Joseph Chamberlain's remark that Courtney wished 'to introduce a system by which the views of the majority shall not be put into practice' was not fair. Ritchie saw 'undoubted merits' in Courtney's scheme, but considered it could not be adopted by the government as public opinion in the country was not ready for it.[9]

Undeterred by the government's attitude, Lubbock raised the issue at the committee stage of the bill in June 1888, by moving an amendment to enlarge the electoral areas, so that they would each return several councillors instead of only one as proposed in the bill. He did not spell out the mode of voting which he thought should be adopted in these larger constituencies, but it is clear from his speech that he had in mind some form of proportional representation, for he gave the main argument in its favour, namely a more accurate representation of the views of voters, and he answered some of the common objections which had been made to it. Courtney was in the chair so could not speak, but several MPs from both sides of the House supported Lubbock's proposal, reinforcing some of the points

[8] Liberal voters were in a substantial majority, but the Conservatives got three seats as against the Liberals' two.

[9] *HC Deb.* 324 (16 Apr. 1888); Courtney's speech is at 1331–53, Chamberlain's at 1354, and Ritchie's at 1427–9.

he had made and adding new ones. The main opposition speakers were Harcourt, Chamberlain, and Ritchie. Harcourt as usual showed how little he understood the subject, saying that 'he adhered to the doctrine that majorities should prevail'. Chamberlain ridiculed supporters of proportional representation, exaggerating the differences between them: each one, he said, had a favourite system of his own 'which he could not get a single other person to support when he brought it forward'. Ritchie as before was more sympathetic to the reformers' cause, but stood by the view that the government should not reopen the controversy, especially as the advocates of proportional representation had not made 'the smallest impression on the public mind'. He also added that it would be difficult to have one method of voting in parliamentary elections and another in elections to county councils. Lubbock's amendment was turned down by 372 votes to 94.[10]

Two days later Lubbock proposed another amendment instituting the alternative vote in single-member elections. Under the alternative vote an elector is able to indicate how he would vote if his favourite candidate is defeated and he has to choose between the remaining candidates. If no candidate receives an absolute majority, i.e. more than 50 per cent of the votes, the second preferences on the ballot papers for the bottom candidate are transferred, the process being repeated if necessary, until some candidate achieves an absolute majority. Lubbock pointed out that in almost every country where the single-member system was in operation, it had been found necessary to adopt a system of second ballot; his scheme of the alternative vote would enable the two elections to be taken together. However in the face of government opposition he withdrew his amendment.[11]

An attempt was also made during the passage of the Local Government Bill to introduce an amendment aimed at preventing a bare majority of county councillors electing all the aldermen. It provided that any six councillors could join together and elect one alderman, each councillor having only one vote.

[10] *HC Deb.* 326 (12 June 1888), 1859–89. Harcourt's remark is at 1869, Chamberlain's at 1881, and Ritchie's at 1870.
[11] *HC Deb.* 327 (14 June 1888), 211–12.

This, it may be recalled, was not a novel idea, being similar to the scheme devised fifty years before by Rowland Hill and put into operation in Adelaide. The amendment was introduced by Henry Hobhouse[12] and supported by Courtney not only on the ground that it would protect the interests of minorities, but also because it would, he thought, eliminate party spirit in the election of aldermen, and avoid the sharp antagonism which arose from the existence of two conflicting factions on councils. It would also, he said, result in the election of the best men as aldermen. The President of the Local Government Board (Ritchie) said he sympathized with Courtney's objectives, but that there were strong practical objections to the proposal. The amendment was lost by 232 votes to 113.[13] This could have been regarded as a fairly substantial majority against the proposal, but Courtney interpreted the figures differently: he considered the House of Commons was very largely converted on the election of aldermen and that many more MPs would have voted for the amendment if they had not thought wrongly that the government was inflexibly against it. So, ever persistent, he urged Lubbock to press Lord Derby, the leader of the Unionist peers in the House of Lords, to get the Commons' decision reversed in the Upper House; but Derby refused to act.[14]

The next initiative came (unusually) from the government, in connection with local government in Ireland. Many people had in recent years felt that the case for some form of proportional or minority representation was clearer and stronger in Ireland than in Great Britain, for under a simple majority system probably neither Protestants in the south nor Catholics in the north would secure any representation on elected bodies. So the government's bill of 1892 creating county and district councils in Ireland provided for multi-membered constituencies elected by the cumulative vote. In introducing the bill A. J. Balfour admitted that the cumulative vote was not the best system, but argued that experience showed it was very easily worked and understood in school board elections in England.

---

[12] Henry Hobhouse, 1854–1937. MP, Liberal, 1885, Liberal Unionist, 1886–1906. Expert on local government. Cousin of L. T. Hobhouse.

[13] *HC Deb.* 329 (26 July 1888), 594–8.

[14] Courtney to Lubbock, 5 Aug. 1888, and Derby to Lubbock, 7 Aug. 1888. Avebury papers, BL Add. MS 49651.

The proposal attracted little support in parliament except from Courtney who thought the cumulative vote would have the good effect of dissipating and destroying party strife. The London school board (on which he sat) was, he said, better than the London County Council, because the board contained an independent section which moderated the hostility between the extreme parties. Most objectors to the government's proposal focused on the likelihood that it would not help minorities to secure representation, but a different objection was made by Gladstone in his characteristically tortuous style.

What is the meaning of a Government when they say that minorities ought to be represented? The meaning of the Government is that minorities ought to be protected by having the majorities delivered into their hands. By providing for that minority you set up a standing majority on behalf of that minority to put down the majority, to whom you profess to be giving this emancipating Bill. That is not what we mean by protecting the minority.

The bill was withdrawn in June 1892 shortly before parliament was dissolved; the government fell in August.[15]

When the Conservatives next introduced legislation concerning local government in Ireland (in 1898), they had given up their efforts to protect minorities and reverted to the English model of single-member constituencies with election by simple majority. This scheme was defended by the Chief Secretary for Ireland, Gerald Balfour, who clearly did not share his brother's penchant for proportional representation. One strange feature of the debate on the bill was that Courtney did not try to amend it, taking the (for him unusual) line that as he had failed to realize his ideal for England and Scotland, he could not propose to make Ireland the basis of an experiment which had not been applied to other parts of the United Kingdom. (The Scottish Local Government Act of 1889 had followed the English Act of 1888 in regard to the mode of election of the new councils.) Lubbock on the other hand was less faint-hearted, pointing out that even if, as some MPs proposed, constituencies were to elect two members instead of one each, this would not guaran-

[15] *HC Deb.* 4th ser. 1 (18 Feb. 1892), 700–98. Balfour's case for the cumulative vote is at 711–13. Courtney's remarks are at 780–7. See also *HC Deb.* 4 (19 May 1892), 1320–1707. Gladstone's remark is at 1707.

tee the representation of minorities; it was the system of voting and not the number of members per constituency which determined whether electors, whether in the minority or the majority, were represented in proportion to their votes; he added that in the last election for the London County Council a minority of voters secured a majority of representatives, which could not have happened with proportional representation. The bill became a statute with no form of proportional or minority representation incorporated in it.[16]

Meanwhile in 1893–4 critics of existing electoral systems had attempted to amend the method proposed for the election of parish councils, which were to be created in Great Britain by the government's Local Government Bills, one for England and Wales and one for Scotland. The bills allowed electors to give as many votes as there were parish councillors to be elected, but only one vote to each candidate, a system confusingly known at the time as *scrutin de liste*, but better called the 'block vote'. Courtney pointed out that this would allow a majority of the electors, however small, to return all the members of the council. He did not propose full proportional representation in its place, because 'politicians were not familiar with it', but confined himself to recommending the cumulative vote. He was supported by several MPs including prominent Conservatives such as Walter Long, George Wyndham, and A. J. Balfour, who all feared that parish councils would be swamped by agricultural labourers and employees unless some provision were made for minority representation. But Harcourt, the Chancellor of the Exchequer, thought the cumulative vote was 'a conundrum not easily understood by the peasantry', and he ridiculed the proposal, saying 'that a man is to vote for a candidate whom he does not prefer in order that he may secure a majority for some purpose which he does not understand—that seems to be the *ne plus ultra* of the cumulative vote!' This elicited a rebuke from Lubbock who complained that Courtney's arguments had not been answered; he admitted that the cumulative vote was not the best method, but it was better than *scrutin de liste* which had been described by W. E. Forster in 1885 as the very worst

---

[16] *HC Deb.* 53 (21 Feb. 1898), 1235, 1275; and 57 (12 May 1898), 1106–7.

method that could possibly be devised.[17] One interesting feature of the debate was the intervention made by the Radical MP W. R. Cremer who had been one of the working men co-operating with Hare and Mill in the Representative Reform Association of the late 1860s. He said he preferred a scheme modelled on the lines of Hare's proposals to the 'sort of bastard system' of the cumulative vote. Courtney's amendment was defeated by 186 votes to 114.[18] Undeterred he also tried to get the cumulative vote adopted for the election of Boards of Guardians who administered the Poor Law, but this too was turned down.[19]

When the Scottish Local Government Bill creating parish councils was being considered in 1894, another attempt was made to alter the electoral method proposed by the government. This was initiated by J. Parker Smith who was a member of the PRS.[20] He was bolder than Courtney and proposed the single transferable vote instead of *scrutin de liste* which he said had proved very unsatisfactory when used in foreign countries. Sir G. O. Trevelyan, the Secretary for Scotland, said that he would not support the principle of 'compulsory plumping', thus showing that he did not understand Parker Smith's proposal; but not wishing to argue about the question (which he was clearly incapable of doing) he fell back on the fact that he had voted on every possible occasion against the principle contended for. This defence of his position was criticized by a Conservative MP (Bethell), but Parker Smith did not pursue the matter and the bill passed unamended in this respect.[21]

The final attempt made by supporters of proportional representation in connection with local government during this period occurred in 1899 during the passage of the government's bill which created borough councils in London. These councils

---

[17] Evidence by Forster to Select Committee on School Board Elections. Forster said that *scrutin de liste* 'gives the greatest possible inducement and opportunity to a majority to exclude the minority altogether' (above, n. 2, Qs. 430 and 492). Forster had been Vice-President of the Committee of Council on Education, 1868–74.

[18] *HC Deb.* 18 (21 Nov. 1893), 1432–61. Courtney's remarks are at 1432–8, Harcourt's at 1441–3, and Cremer's at 1461.

[19] *HC Deb.* 20 (28 Dec. 1893), 394–402.

[20] James Parker Smith, 1854–1929. Fellow of Trinity College, Cambridge; barrister; MP, Liberal Unionist, 1890–1906.

[21] *HC Deb.* 28 (9 Aug. 1894), 500–2.

were to be elected under the block-vote system triennially from wards returning three, six, or nine members. Each voter had as many votes as there were members to be elected in his ward, but could give only one vote to any candidate. Courtney and Lubbock pointed out once again that the existing system of municipal and parliamentary elections did not ensure that a majority of the votes secured a majority of the representatives, but they confined their proposed amendment to the method of electing aldermen, reviving the scheme suggested in 1888 for the election of aldermen to County Councils. In order to prevent the party in the majority on the council electing all the aldermen, Courtney suggested that they should be elected by groups of councillors: thus if sixty councillors were to elect five aldermen, any group of twelve councillors could elect one alderman. A. J. Balfour in answering for the government showed that he at least understood the proposal and its purpose, but thought that it might result in the election of unsuitable people as aldermen and undermine party responsibility; he did not wish any rash experiments to be tried on these nascent boroughs, though he would not object to trying the system out on more mature bodies and extending it if satisfactory. The amendment fell without a division.[22]

The third subject offering scope for the advocacy of proportional representation was Home Rule for Ireland. The bill introduced by Gladstone's government in 1893 provided for predominantly single-member constituencies and election by simple majority, both for members of the Irish legislature which was to be created and for the representatives from Ireland who were to sit in the UK parliament at Westminster. In August 1893 J. Parker Smith moved that constituencies for both elections should return three or five representatives each, and that no elector should vote for more than one candidate. He conceded that the existing system did not work too badly in England and Scotland, but said that in Wales and Ireland it distorted the wishes of the electors. He did not mention the transfer of votes, but he was presumably intending to incorporate it in his proposal in due

[22] *HC Deb.* 69 (23 Mar. 1899), 194; (24 Mar. 1899), 400; 70 (4 May 1899), 1355–62; and 72 (6 June 1899), 487–9.

course. Parker Smith's amendment was supported by several MPs, including Courtney, Lubbock, and A. J. Balfour, who were all against Home Rule but who thought that if it were introduced proportional representation was necessary.

The debate is chiefly interesting for the further light it throws on Gladstone's turn of mind, for he condemned the proposal chiefly on the ground that it was 'scientific'. Its supporters, he said, are 'merely airing those scientific ideas for the benefit of I know not whom and I know not what'; opposed to 'these scientific schemes' are 'the universal tradition of the world, and the long, and, on the whole, the satisfactory experience of this country'; it was an attempt at 'speculative legislation'. Gladstone also referred to the fact that a similar plan for England had been rejected recently, an argument which was weakened when an MP pointed out that the House of Commons had also rejected Home Rule for Ireland a few years ago. Chamberlain recalled his objections to the limited and cumulative methods of voting and forecast that Parker Smith's proposal would also probably over-represent the minority and under-represent the majority; fairer representation, he said, could be secured by single-member constituencies and a redistribution of seats according to population. The amendment secured as many as 148 votes, but was lost by a majority of 49.[23]

This account of the efforts of supporters of proportional representation to keep their case alive in parliament illustrates vividly the three main obstacles they faced, namely: the very limited understanding of the effect, or possible effect, of the electoral systems which prevailed in this country for parliamentary and local elections; distortion of the aims of the reformers; and misrepresentation of the likely results of the electoral systems which the reformers proposed. These difficulties were largely due to the unwillingness of opponents to think seriously about a subject which they were convinced was incomprehensible.

Most of the objections made against proportional representation at this period were similar to some of those made earlier; for instance, that the single transferable vote would be a pure game of chance; that it would result in weak governments; that

---

[23] *HC Deb.* 15 (7 Aug. 1893), 1503–23. Gladstone's remarks are at 1506–9.

electors would be confused; and that party machines would be strengthened. But occasionally a new objection was introduced. The most interesting of these is that made by the political psychologist Graham Wallas in 1903, foreshadowing the thesis developed later in his influential book, *Human Nature in Politics* (1908). Wallas thought far too much attention had been given to the process by which opinions were ascertained, ignoring the process by which they were created. It was no use trying to reform the machinery of democracy on the assumption that voters were rational, because they were not. He admitted that proportional representation made citizens more free, because they had greater liberty of choice, but he doubted whether they would be more likely to be right. What was needed was to create right opinions, not to collect free opinions, which might well be based on inadequate information.[24] This comes near to being an objection to democracy itself, not just to proportional representation.

One problem faced by the reformers was to know which tactics would be most successful: sometimes, afraid of being too ambitious, they were willing to settle for what they saw as the second-best method such as the cumulative vote, or limited experiments with proportional representation such as its use only in some areas; at other times they stuck firmly to recommending the general adoption of the single transferable vote, thus perhaps giving opponents an excuse for confusion as to what they wanted. But though none of the reformers' activities in parliament had any effect on the legislation which was passed, they may have helped to prevent the subject of proportional representation being wholly forgotten.

Other factors contributed to a continuing interest in electoral systems. One of these was the traditional fear of increasing democracy. This was well exemplified in a substantial book, *Democracy and Liberty* (1896), by the well-known historian W. E. Lecky, who was by the mid-1890s convinced that liberty was in great danger from the spread of democracy. He deplored the existing tendency to place property and liberty under the

---

[24] Graham Wallas, 1858–1932. 'The American Analogy', *Independent Review*, 1 (Dec. 1903), 505–16. Wallas was reviewing Ostrogorski's book, *Democracy and the Organisation of Political Parties* (1902).

complete dominion of the most ignorant and unintelligent people. So he was keen that the better-educated classes who valued constitutional and economic liberty should be properly represented, which he thought the existing electoral system did not always secure: the Hare scheme would in his view effect this. Amazingly he thought there would be no great difficulty in working it, but he was realistic enough to be sceptical about the chances of its being adopted in Britain. This was because he doubted whether democratic public opinion would ever demand the representation of minorities with sufficient persistence, and because the nation as a whole would be reluctant to deviate from traditional forms and habits.[25]

Another factor helping to focus interest on electoral systems was the current criticism of party machines and in particular of the 'caucus'. This criticism was not new, but having originally been mainly directed at American politics, it now embraced, as indeed it had since the 1870s, British political practice as well. Some of these critics thought proportional representation inevitably meant the party list system, which tends to strengthen party machines, and so they were of course hostile to proportional representation; but others realized there were alternative means for obtaining fairer representation and thought these would also help to reduce the power of parties in and out of parliament. The most notorious exposition of this view was contained in a book which came out in 1902, M. Y. Ostrogorski's *Democracy and the Organisation of Political Parties*, the result of fifteen years' labour during which the author studied with great thoroughness the working of parties in the USA and Britain. Ostrogorski admired the 'grandeur' of Hare's scheme, of which he gave an excellent account, but he also saw serious drawbacks to it. To obviate these he recommended its adoption in a modified form, i.e. geographical constituencies, combined with other devices such as temporary associations for definite ends and preliminary polls before the election proper; but Ostrogorski's views on electoral matters attracted less attention than his strictures on political machines.

There was also at this time some interest in the working of political institutions in countries which were experimenting

---

[25] W. E. Lecky, 1838–1903. MP, Unionist, 1895–1902.

with different electoral systems, viz. in Europe, Switzerland, Belgium, France, and Italy, and, in the colonies, the Australian state of Tasmania. None of these European countries used the single transferable vote method, so they only helped supporters of this device by illustrating the alleged disadvantages of other systems, especially those involving party lists. The system of proportional representation introduced in Tasmania was derived from Hare, though it was much simpler than his scheme, having constituencies of four to six members.

Advocates of proportional representation did not confine their exertions to parliament, though the level of extra-parliamentary activity during the years 1885 to 1904 was very much lower than in the previous and following decades. Thus the PRS, although inevitably much less active than in 1884 and early 1885, continued to comply with requests for literature and arranged an occasional lecture or debate with an illustrative election. Early in 1886 it sent copies of Lubbock's book, *Representation*, and a letter of his to *The Times* to all MPs (except Parnellites) and to PRS members, and in 1888 it circulated 1,000 copies of Courtney's speech on the second reading of the Local Government (England and Wales) Bill. The level of the society's work can be gauged from the fact that it spent £316 between April 1885 and July 1888, but almost nothing thereafter until it was revived in 1905. In 1894 Catherine Spence, one of the main Australian advocates of fair representation, came to Britain and spoke at meetings in Glasgow, Edinburgh, and London.

There was during these years some analysis of election results under the single-member constituency system which had been made almost universal for the UK parliament in 1885. Thus it was argued by H. F. Amedroz, one of the earliest advocates of proportional representation, that at the general election of 1885 the Liberals secured in Great Britain 24 seats too many, though under a more accurate system of representation they would, he calculated, still have had a majority, of 26 instead of 74. Amedroz also showed how in certain places in 1885 (for example, Kent and Glasgow) one party was entirely unrepresented although it had received a high proportion of the votes. Thus in Kent 44 per cent of the vote went in its fifteen constituencies to the Liberals, but they won no seats, and in

Glasgow's seven constituencies the Conservatives with 45 per cent of the vote won no seats. Amedroz considered Irish statistics to be of little value because of intimidation and coercion, but nevertheless he was sure that results would have been different with a proportional system of representation.[26]

The general elections of 1892 and 1895 were analysed in a paper read to the Royal Statistical Society in 1896. The author, J. A. Baines, confining himself to England, showed that in 1892 the Unionists obtained 27 more seats than they should have had in relation to the votes they received, and in 1895 92 too many seats. During the discussion several speakers argued for proportional representation.[27]

Lubbock and Courtney referred often to the results of elections to the London County Council, which illustrated clearly the capricious working of the electoral system. They also showed how in certain towns the wrong party had returned the majority of MPs at some general elections.

But in spite of these efforts the work done on election results at this period was fragmentary and inadequate; much more could have been made of the random relationship between votes and seats over the whole country at general elections. There were admittedly problems in such an undertaking due mainly to the large number of uncontested seats which still prevailed (sometimes as high as one-third of all UK seats), but this difficulty could have been overcome if someone had set their mind to it, as a member of the Manchester Statistical Society (Rooke Corbett) did in 1906. Allowing for uncontested seats, he calculated that the Liberal majority in 1885 should have been 92, not 158; that in 1886 the Liberals should have won with a majority of 18 seats instead of the Conservatives winning with a majority of 104; that the Conservative majority in 1895 should have been only 2, not 150, and in 1900 also 2 instead of 184. Thus the election of 1892 was, according to Corbett, the only one to have produced in the UK a result reasonably close to the popular vote during the period 1885 to 1900. His figures were accepted by the 1910 Royal Commission on Systems of Election

[26] Henry Frederick Amedroz, *The Reform Measure of 1885, and subsequent General Election, with its bearing on Proportional Representation* (1886). His previous pamphlet on electoral matters came out as early as 1858.

[27] *Journal of the Royal Statistical Society*, 59 (Mar. 1896), 38–124.

as probably representing the truth as correctly as circumstances would permit, even though they were questioned by several witnesses.[28]

Among other extra-parliamentary activities was the reissue in 1890 of Lubbock's book, *Representation*, after 6,000 copies had been sold or distributed. He also wrote many letters to the press on various electoral matters, particularly in the early part of this period.

Courtney's activities included lecturing on proportional representation in Belfast in October 1900, and the production of a substantial book in 1901 dealing with the working of the constitution generally, but including criticism of the existing electoral system and the case for its reform. In an article in 1904 he deplored what he saw as decline in the quality of candidates for parliament, which was, he considered, partly due to the single-member constituency system; he contrasted this with the virtues of parliamentary life during the fifty years following 1832, when minorities were heard with growing success and the advocates of progressive change converted ministers to their view by rational argument. It is not altogether absurd to think that there is some truth in this account of mid-nineteenth-century politics, but it is much more difficult to accept Courtney's view that 'a comparatively simple change holds the promise of a complete transformation', the change being six-member constituencies with the single transferable vote which would at once 'emancipate' electors and candidates. Courtney was still writing in the language and idiom of Hare.[29]

The period 1885 to 1904 thus saw continuing advocacy of proportional representation both in and out of parliament, but with very little success of either a specific or more general nature. One of the factors which detracted from support for proportional representation was the enthusiasm displayed in

[28] Corbett's paper was read to the Manchester Statistical Society on 12 Dec. 1906. His table of figures is reproduced in the report of the Royal Commission on Systems of Election, PP 1910 XXVI, p. 10, §31. The method adopted by Corbett to allow for uncontested seats was to assume that the strength of each party varied in uncontested seats from one election to another in the same ratio as in the contested constituencies in the same county.

[29] Leonard Courtney, *The Working Constitution and its Outgrowths*, 338 pp. (1901); and *Monthly Review*, 17 (Dec. 1904), 13–21.

some quarters for the referendum as the solution to the alleged defects in the existing electoral system. If parliament did not, as the electoral reformers maintained, always represent the views of the majority of voters, the solution surely was to ask the people directly what they thought on specific issues; so the introduction of the referendum on the Swiss or American model was advocated, to 'counteract the accidents and eccentricities of representation'.[30]

Others were partial to the referendum on rather different grounds, seeing it as a tool for safeguarding the constitution against sudden change. The most famous expositor of this view was Professor A. V. Dicey who in 1890, after studying the working of the Swiss referendum, felt confident that a referendum held in England (he may have meant Great Britain) would turn down Home Rule for Ireland to which he was passionately opposed. One must ensure, he wrote, that a temporary or factitious majority in parliament does not override the will of the nation.[31] Dicey was also critical of the party system because it enabled the control of legislation to be in the hands not just of a party but of a part of a party, which was probably a mere fraction of the nation. But he did not recommend the remedy advocated by other critics of the party system such as Hare, Mill, and Courtney. Indeed later he came out clearly against proportional representation and in favour of the referendum in order to diminish the most patent defects of party government. He admitted that elected legislatures often misrepresented the will of the nation, but he thought this was because MPs were subjected to party discipline: they were loyal to their party and put its interests above the welfare of the nation. The remedy was therefore not a reform of the electoral system, but to confer on the people a veto to restrict the unbounded, absolute power of a party majority.[32]

---

[30] J. St Loe Strachey, 'The Referendum', *National Review*, 23 (Apr. 1894), 196–200. See also his article 'A Poll of the People', in *Cosmopolis*, 6 (Apr. 1897), 48–63. Strachey was a Liberal Unionist, and editor and proprietor of the *Spectator*, 1898–1925.

[31] A. V. Dicey, 'Ought the Referendum to be Introduced into England?' *Contemporary Review*, 57 (Apr. 1890), 489–511. See also his article 'The Referendum', in *National Review*, 23 (Mar. 1894), 65–72.

[32] *Quarterly Review*, 212 (Apr. 1910), 538–562; and *Introduction to the Study of the Law of the Constitution*, Introd. to 8th edn. (1915), pp. lxvi–lxxiii and xci–c.

Lack of interest in the working of our electoral system is well exemplified by contemporary, and indeed later, explanations of the large Conservative and Unionist parliamentary majorities obtained at the general elections of 1895 and 1900. Why was Liberalism declining so dramatically? it was asked; but the questions whether it was really declining and if so to what extent should have first been posed. For if the figures of votes cast, instead of only the figures of seats gained in parliament had been considered, it would have been apparent that the decline of Liberalism was much less pronounced than was generally thought. Thus the Liberals received 45 per cent of the votes cast in contested seats in the United Kingdom at all four general elections between 1886 and 1900 (included); this was only 2 per cent less than they received in 1885. If the votes given to the Nationalists and others (including left-wing parties) are added in, the anti-Conservative/anti-Unionist percentage of the poll was as high as 51 per cent in 1895 and 50 per cent in 1900.

Pressure was put on Courtney from 1900 onwards to revive the campaign for proportional representation, but he was unwilling to do so until 1905. One of his reasons for refusal was that, because he had been defeated at the general election of 1900, he thought any pleading of his on the subject would be tainted with a suspicion of personal interest. Moreover he was deeply involved in opposing the Boer war. But even after the war had ended in May 1902, he was reluctant to speak on proportional representation or to try to revive the PRS, realizing how difficult this would be, given the uphill task he and others had faced during the last twenty years with little result.[33]

[33] Letters to J. H. Humphreys in Courtney box at Electoral Reform Society, previously Proportional Representation Society.

# VII

# The Second Campaign, 1905–1914

THE revival of the Proportional Representation Society came about in a curious way. It was largely due to the initiative and persistence of a clerk in the Post Office, John H. Humphreys, who was disturbed by the results of elections to London Borough Councils.[1] Right from the first elections in 1900, there was in many places no rational or consistent relationship between votes and seats. Thus in some boroughs one party got no representation at all on the council in spite of having a substantial number of votes, sometimes as many as one-third of the total; in other places the minority party was grossly under-represented; and sometimes the party with least votes obtained the majority of seats. So, although apparently unacquainted with Courtney, Humphreys wrote to him several times between 1900 and 1904 pressing him to reopen the campaign. For some time Courtney was doubtful about trying to revive the PRS, but, stimulated by the announcement in February 1905 that the government intended to introduce proposals for a redistribution of seats, he finally decided to do so. A few members of the old Executive Committee of the PRS met together several times in the spring of 1905, appointed Humphreys as honorary secretary, and arranged a public meeting which was presided over by Lord Avebury (formerly Sir John Lubbock) and addressed by Courtney on 'Real Representation'. In May 1905 the society announced that it was resurrecting itself.

From then onwards the PRS engaged in many activities directed at awakening public interest in the subject. It produced

---

[1] John Henry Humphreys, 1869–1946. He entered the Savings Bank department of the Post Office in 1890 as a second division clerk. For the method of election to London Borough Councils, see Ch. VI.

and distributed propaganda literature, organized meetings, and wrote or stimulated articles and letters to the press. It also set about trying to build up its membership and funds. A new treasurer was appointed in the place of the previous one, Albert (the fourth earl) Grey who had become Governor-General of Canada.[2]

The revived PRS worked through the same structure as before. There was an executive committee of nominally twelve to eighteen people, but only three or four of these usually attended meetings, which took place once a month from 1905 to 1914. The society was therefore in effect run by a small group, consisting of Courtney and his wife, Professor Westlake and his wife (daughter of Hare), Aneurin Williams MP, the secretary, and treasurer, joined occasionally by others such as C. P. Scott, J. M. Robertson MP, Blennerhassett, and Courtney's old school-friend and brother-in-law, Richard Oliver. There was also a general committee, numbering about eighty people, on which sympathetic MPs, peers, trade unionists, and public figures were invited to sit. It met only occasionally, to discuss specific matters of policy. Annual meetings open to all members of the society were held regularly. In April 1912 a parliamentary committee was set up numbering nearly seventy MPs and peers. The chairman was Sir William Anson, the constitutional lawyer.[3] The PRS hoped that a local branch would be formed in every large town, but this was fully successful at this time in only two places—Glasgow and Manchester.

The staff of the PRS was exiguous. Apart from one typist, none of them were paid until 1910 when a part-time secretary (Alfred Gray) and another typist were appointed. Humphreys no doubt did most of the work, at first as honorary secretary in his spare time from the Post Office, and from 1912 onwards as full-time paid secretary on leave from the Civil Service until he resigned from it in 1913. He was compensated for the loss of pension rights by an anonymous donor, but he undoubtedly

---

[2] The new treasurer was John Fischer Williams, a barrister with a keen interest in proportional representation. His articles and brief books on the subject are some of the best things written about it, but he was not so adept at raising money for the PRS.

[3] Sir William Anson, 1843–1914. MP, Liberal Unionist, for Oxford University, 1899–1914.

took considerable risks in sacrificing a secure career for a precarious post to work for a cause he had at heart.

The society resumed the issue of annual reports which had ceased in 1888, and in 1908 launched a journal, *Representation*, which came out at first monthly and then at longer intervals. Thousands of copies were normally printed and circulated.

There are problems connected with estimating the size of the society's home membership. Subscribers to the funds numbered 97 in 1906 and had increased to 648 by 1913, but the membership can be regarded as larger because many members paid no subscriptions, although from 1907 onwards they were expected to subscribe a minimum of 2s. 6d. per annum. Moreover the figure of 648 does not apparently include any members of the provincial branches of the society who subscribed locally. It does however include members who were not United Kingdom residents, several of whom were Rhodesians or from the Cape. The society continually made desperate pleas for more members, being particularly concerned about its precarious financial position. From 1906 to 1910 the average annual income from subscriptions was £417, but as a result of special efforts the situation improved during the next four years, the annual average for 1911–14 being £1,545. A fairly substantial proportion of the society's funds was from the start contributed by a small number of generous donors, such as Walter Morrison, Lord Avebury, Mr and Mrs Oliver, Lady Farrer, the Courtneys, and Sir Henry Kimber.

One of the society's first targets was Labour men. For several years Courtney, though critical of socialism or at least of collectivism, had urged what he called 'the claims of labour' to fair representation. So the revived PRS at once made several attempts to talk with Keir Hardie and other representatives of Labour, and to get the subject brought up at their meetings. (The response from the Labour side is discussed beneath.)

The other main target of the PRS was naturally MPs, who were invited to a conference in May 1906, to explain to them the case for proportional representation and to get them to join the society. One of the first fruits of this activity was to secure an address from the House of Commons in June 1906 asking the government to get reports from foreign countries to show what progress proportional representation had made abroad.

The results of the government's inquiries were published in 1907 as a White Paper.[4] This contained some useful information, but its value was limited by the fact that several of the British representatives abroad on whose answers the report was based had no idea what was meant by 'the principle of proportional representation'.

The general election of 1906 was for supporters of proportional representation an object lesson in this country's defective system of election, for it resulted in the Liberals and their supporters getting many more seats than the votes for them warranted. Their majority in parliament was 356, whereas their voting strength entitled them to a majority of only 114, according to the most reliable contemporary calculation (Rooke Corbett's). By contrast the Conservatives who got 44 per cent of the total vote secured only 23 per cent of the seats. But the PRS wisely realized that it was too soon to propose legislation dealing with the electoral system for parliament. Apart from the fact that the Liberal government had a full legislative programme, there were several other matters connected with representation and elections which were thought by many people to require attention, some of them urgently. These included a redistribution of seats to relate them more closely to population, the abolition of plural voting, votes for women, and reform of the electoral registration system which excluded many people from voting. This meant that a bill dealing only with proportional representation would stand little chance of success.

So the PRS decided to concentrate its parliamentary activities at first on municipal elections. It produced a bill which enabled the councils of boroughs in England and Wales to decide, if they so wished, that they should be elected by the method of the single transferable vote. The bill contained safeguards to ensure that the decision was not made by a snap majority, and it allowed the decision to be reversed after a trial period of three years. The purpose of the bill was to enable councils to reflect

---

[4] PP 1907 LXXXVII. Reports from His Majesty's Representatives in foreign countries and in British Colonies respecting the application of the principle of proportional representation to public elections, 315–462.

accurately the opinions of their electorates, but in introducing it into the House of Lords in April 1907 Courtney, as so often, did not focus on the misrepresentation on councils of voters' opinions, due to the method used for their election, but on peripheral issues. Thus he criticized the system operating in provincial boroughs (since 1835) by which elections were staggered with one-third of the council being elected every year, on the ground that it had not prevented the introduction of party politics into municipal life. But he also criticized the system in use in London (since 1899) by which elections were held every three years, resulting often in substantial changes in the composition of the council, which meant lack of continuity, and control going to the permanent officials. He said he would not put the case for proportional representation for parliament though he wanted it, but he then talked at some length about the 'revivification' and regeneration of our political life by 'the new birth' which was promised by the right form of voting. He also outlined some of the developments taking place abroad. After a brief debate Lord Rippon said the government did not support the bill: a party system was necessary in parliament, and the system was too complicated for ladies, many of whom would be voters for borough councils.[5]

Nevertheless the Municipal Representation Bill was referred to a select committee of the House of Lords which sat for two months in 1907 hearing evidence. Their discussions with witnesses reveal once again the difficulties faced by supporters of proportional representation and the mistakes some of them made in presenting their case. For instance it was obviously unfortunate that the bill contained detailed rules setting out how votes were to be transferred in order to calculate the result of an election, and even a five-page appendix giving (unusually in a statute) an example of an election conducted under the prescribed system. The result was that the representatives of the PRS were questioned by the committee at great length about exactly what returning officers would have to do, and about how votes had been transferred at the test election recently run by the society in which 13,000 people took part. Some members of the committee naturally got confused by the welter of figures

---

[5] *HL Deb.* 173 (30 Apr. 1907), 632–57.

which their questions elicited. They focused on how the quota was calculated and on the alleged complications of transferring votes, rather than on the central issues, namely the results of existing methods of electing municipal councils and on whether there was any harm in giving them an opportunity to experiment with a proportional method if they so wished. But had the bill not spelt out how the single transferable vote system worked, its promoters would probably have been criticized for not making clear what they were proposing.

Moreover the question of proportionality at times became submerged in the relative merits of annual and triennial elections. In the provinces elections were held annually for one-third of the seats in each ward, which in some places meant electing only one member every year. In London elections were triennial for all the seats. This was thought to have the undesirable effect of often producing a clean sweep of the whole council, whereas in the provinces changes were more gradual. But if proportional representation was to be introduced, elections everywhere would have to be triennial, because the system required multi-membered constituencies.

The evidence given by one witness, the town clerk of Nottingham (Sir S. G. Johnson), revealed in a telling way the obstacles confronting the reformers and the gulf between them and their opponents. He said he was too busy to indulge in ideals; the present system was as perfect as anything you could have; he saw nothing wrong in two-thirds of the voters having all the representation; the majority should not be obstructed by minorities; in any case mathematical certainty could not be secured in elections any more than a butcher could be expected to weigh out meat on scales from the chemist's laboratory. It was also clear that the Associations of Municipal Corporations and of Metropolitan Borough Councils had given very little time or thought to the bill; according to one of their members the proportional element was too much for some of them: the mathematical calculations seemed to prey on their minds.

Some of the witnesses put more stress on the desirability of reducing party politics and the power of the machine in local government than on the need for a closer relationship between votes and seats, and thus distracted the committee from what most supporters of the bill saw as its central purpose. Nevertheless the committee reported that the machinery proposed would work properly and secure a more adequate representation of minorities, though they were worried that the system would not be understood by most of the electorate.[6]

The next year (1908), when the Municipal Representation Bill was reintroduced into the House of Lords, Courtney made a long speech on its first reading, contrary to the conventions of the House. He repeated much of what he had said before about keeping politics out of local government and avoiding sudden, huge changes in the composition of councils not warranted by the votes of the electorate; but he also emphasized that it was a matter of chance whether a council did or did not represent a majority of the electors.[7] On the second reading of the bill Courtney spoke only briefly. The government spokesman did not oppose the measure, but said this did not mean it favoured the plan for parliamentary elections. The bill's only critic was the old inveterate opponent of proportional representation, Lord Eversley (formerly G. T. Shaw-Lefevre), who produced some calculations purporting to show that with the single transferable vote minorities would be over-represented and majorities under-represented. His mathematics were condemned by Avebury as very extraordinary.[8] In a later debate Eversley tried to get the bill confined to London on the ground that there was ample protection for the minority in the provinces, but he did not explain how this came about, given that, as Avebury pointed out, a majority could return its candidate every year and therefore, even if only small, could secure the whole of the representation on a council.[9]

The bill was passed by the Lords in April 1908 and sent to the Commons, but it was not debated there until March 1910. Then, as a prelude to introducing the bill, a resolution was moved by Aneurin Williams:[10]

---

[6] PP HL 1907 VII. Select Committee on Municipal Representation Bill, Report and Minutes of Evidence, pp. v–vii and 1–171.

[7] *HL Deb.* 184 (17 Feb. 1908), 384–90.

[8] *HL Deb.* 185 (3 Mar. 1908), 474–88.

[9] *HL Deb.* 186 (16 Mar. 1908), 104–9.

[10] Aneurin Williams, 1859–1924. MP, Liberal, Jan.–Dec. 1910 and 1914–22. An active member of the PRS committee from 1905 onwards. An advocate of copartnership, co-operatives, and profit sharing.

that inasmuch as the present systems of electing representatives, whether to parliament or municipal bodies, result in grave anomalies and injustices, it is expedient to test the system of proportional election, and for that purpose to empower municipal boroughs to apply that system in the election of their councils.

Most of those who spoke in support of the resolution focused on parliament rather than on municipal councils. This may have been thought the right tactic at a time when the large question of the relations between the Lords and Commons was at issue, raising as it did the unrepresentative composition of the Lords. It was certainly successful in that the case for proportional representation was supported from all sides of the house, by Conservatives, Liberals, and a Labour whip, George Roberts.[11]

The case against Aneurin Williams's resolution was put by John Burns, the President of the Local Government Board. Given his working-class origins and his background as a labour leader and trade unionist, it is understandable that he poured scorn on the notion that one wanted 'glorified superior persons' in parliament; but it is less easy to see why he thought that if the two-party system was weakened the Empire would be threatened, exposed as he put it 'to shocks and caprices'. He cited in his support the view of his Rt. Hon. friend on his right (perhaps Lewis Harcourt) that proportional representation was 'politically the eighth deadly sin . . . which should take the position of bi-metallism and perpetual motion' and that it was 'one of the most illusory problems that could disturb mankind'. His only reference to municipalities was to defend staggered annual elections against triennial ones.

It seems unlikely that Burns understood much or perhaps anything about proportional representation except that it might help the Labour party to whose existence he was opposed, although he described himself for many years as a socialist. At all general elections from 1892 to January 1910, standing as a Lib.-Lab., he had to fight only against a Conservative. His views were also influenced by the fact that he had from 1889 to 1907 worked closely on the London County Council with the Liberals

---

[11] George Henry Roberts, 1868–1928. MP, 1906–23; Labour until 1918, then a coalitionist. Held government posts, 1915–20. On Executive Committee of Labour Party, 1910–18. Whip, 1907–14.

as a 'progressive'. The only support for Burns came from the staunch conservative MP for the City of London, Sir Frederick Banbury.[12]

In spite of the government's opposition, Williams's resolution was passed, but the Municipal Representation Bill got no further than a first reading in 1910 and 1911. Further unsuccessful efforts were made in 1912 and 1913 to persuade the government to introduce or at least favour the measure. It was pointed out in the debates that at the London Borough Council elections of 1912 one party won all the seats in four boroughs in spite of considerable support for the other party amounting in one case (Fulham) to 43 per cent of the electorate. Effective criticism, it was argued, was the breath of life of representative government; without it, triumphant and unexposed majorities had every inducement to domineer over their opponents; corruption too was a danger when the publicity secured by opposition was lacking; moreover the existing system led to much apathy which was a foe to good government; proportional representation was in operation in several foreign countries for municipal and parliamentary elections, and the proposal was supported by some metropolitan and provincial borough councils.[13]

Whilst Burns remained at the Local Government Board, the Municipal Representation Bill had no hope of progress. After he left it in February 1914, the bill was immediately reintroduced by Courtney into the House of Lords who passed it in all its stages, but it was blocked in the Commons by Sir Frederick Banbury.[14] Ever persistent, the supporters of the bill persuaded Burns's successor at the Local Government Board, Herbert Samuel, in June 1914 to agree to set up a select committee to inquire into London municipal elections, but the outbreak of war prevented further action. The issue was not revived until 1919.

\*

[12] *HC Deb.* 15 (30 Mar. 1910), 1387–1430. Burns's remarks are at 1414–21. John Burns, 1858–1943. MP, 1892–1918. Lib.-Lab. until 1910, then Liberal. Held government offices, 1905–14. Sir Frederick Banbury, 1850–1936. MP, Conservative, 1892–1924, when he went to the Lords.

[13] *HC Deb.* 45 (12 Dec. 1912), 765, and 56 (5 Aug. 1913), 1289–92.

[14] *HL Deb.* 15 (23 Mar. 1914), 654–6 for second reading. And *HC Deb.* 61 (20 Apr. 1914), 726.

The government's attitude to electoral systems had also been revealed a few years before in connection with elections to Scottish school boards. For in 1908 it proposed to abolish the cumulative vote in the elections of school boards in Scotland, substituting for it the block vote, each voter having one vote for each seat that was to be filled. Under this system the whole board could be of one colour. Some MPs argued for the retention of the cumulative vote in spite of its defects, particularly because it helped Roman Catholics, who formed 10 per cent of the Scottish population, to get representation. Others took the opportunity to propose once again the election of the boards by the single transferable vote. This received considerable support in the Commons and Lords, but the government spokesman objected to introducing the principle of proportional representation 'by a side wind', and thought the question should await the inquiry into the whole subject which had been promised by the Prime Minister. They wished however to shorten the discussion and withdrew the proposal to abolish the cumulative vote, which was therefore retained.[15] The PRS was active on this question, sending out 10,000 letters to members of Scottish school boards. Success came finally in 1919 when the single transferable vote was introduced for Scottish education authorities, until they ceased to be elected separately in 1928.

Although the revived PRS focused its legislative proposals at first on municipal elections, it did not lose sight of its long-term objective—proportional representation for the election of the House of Commons. Thus Courtney took the opportunity of the debate on the Plural Voting Bill in the House of Lords in December 1906 to point out that the bill did not go far enough to implement the desire of its backers to equalize voting power. Even if plural voting was abolished, he said, so that no elector had more than one vote, and even if this was accompanied by equalizing the size of constituencies, voting power would still vary indefinitely and be dependent on the chance of the voter's place of residence; moreover the election of 1906 showed that

[15] *HC Deb.* 197 (24 Nov. 1908), 203–8; *HL Deb.* 198 (7 Dec. 1908), 20–1, 34–7; (9 Dec. 1908), 433–40.

inequality in one area was not balanced by inequality in another. Courtney voted for the Plural Voting Bill, but urged that, if it was rejected by the Lords, a true solution to the whole question of representation should be planned.[16]

The Plural Voting Bill was rejected in 1906, but Courtney was a year later realistic enough to see that there was little hope of the government introducing a bill based on the principle of proportional representation in the coming session or indeed in the existing parliament, because ministers had already enough on their hands. However the situation was changed by the Prime Minister's announcement in May 1908 that the government intended to introduce a large measure of electoral reform before the expiration of the present parliament.[17]

The PRS reacted at once by stepping up its efforts to arouse public interest in proportional representation. It distributed thousands of copies of the journal *Representation*; many people were invited to join the general committee; a lecturer was appointed and a large test election was organized. In August 1908 Courtney wrote to the Prime Minister suggesting a Royal Commission on proportional representation to educate people and prepare them for a Reform Bill which had to come in soon.[18] This was followed up in November 1908 with a huge deputation from the PRS to the Prime Minister asking for an inquiry into the whole subject of electoral methods. The Society was delighted when Asquith agreed that the present 'rough and ready' method of election was indefensible, and when the government in December 1908 appointed a Royal Commission on Systems of Election. Its terms of reference were:

to examine the various schemes which have been adopted or proposed, in order to secure a fully representative character for popularly elected legislative bodies; and to consider whether, and how far, they, or any of them, are capable of application to this country in regard to the existing electorate.

The composition of the Royal Commission was unusual because Asquith wanted to keep it small and confined to people who had not expressed any views on the subject. The chairman

[16] *HL Deb.* 166 (10 Dec. 1906), 1501–7.
[17] In fact this was never done.
[18] Courtney papers. Courtney to Asquith, 27 Aug. 1908.

was Lord Richard Cavendish who had been a Liberal Unionist MP from 1895 to 1906 when he fought the general election unsuccessfully as a Liberal.[19] The other members were Asquith's private secretary, Edwin Montagu, a Liberal MP; Sir Courtenay Ilbert, the Clerk to the House of Commons; Lord Lochee, who, as Edmund Robertson, had held minor jobs in Liberal governments; Sir Francis Hopwood, the Permanent Under-Secretary at the Colonial Office; William Pember Reeves, a New Zealand socialist and director of the London School of Economics; Sir Charles Eliot, an ex-diplomat and orientalist; and John W. Hills, a solicitor and back-bench Conservative MP.

The Commission did its work quite thoroughly. It took evidence between April and July 1909 from twenty-nine witnesses, who were asked over 3,000 questions. The case for proportional representation was put by the officials of the PRS (Courtney, Humphreys, and Fischer Williams, but not by Avebury), and by a wide assortment of others, including Conservatives, Liberals, and H. M. Hyndman for the Social Democratic Federation. He was the only witness representing labour interests, as the Labour party preferred not to air their disagreements on the subject in public. The case against proportional representation was put by amongst others four party agents, the elder statesman Lord Eversley, and Lewis Harcourt, Sir William Harcourt's loyal son. Lewis Harcourt was then a member of the cabinet but said he was expressing his personal views. Four witnesses from abroad were heard (from Belgium, Tasmania, Western Australia, and France), and evidence was given by local officials on the practicality of vote counting.

As so often in the past, many of the advocates of proportional representation based the case for it not so much or indeed at all on the frequent misrepresentation of parties in the House of Commons, but on what they saw as other defects in the existing political system. For instance they complained that the more extreme men of each party got over-represented; they wanted to see more thoughtful and sober-minded MPs, men with

[19] Richard Frederick Cavendish, 1871–1946. He was the nephew of the eighth Duke of Devonshire who had been an important politician for many years in Liberal and Conservative governments; but Cavendish seems to have played little part in politics, speaking only once briefly during his ten years in parliament. This was in 1905 against duties on manufactured goods.

sincere and single-minded convictions, 'real men', statesmen. Others said that the independent member was disappearing, and stressed the desirability of weakening the party system and party organization in and out of parliament, and the power of money. The chief exponents of these views were Sir William Anson, Lord Balfour of Burleigh, Lord Hugh Cecil, Courtney, and Earl Grey. However the relationship between votes and seats and the case for a more proportional system were emphasized by a few witnesses, and there was considerable discussion about the effect of the alternative vote, list systems, and the single transferable vote.

The main points made by the opposition witnesses were that it was good if majorities in parliament were larger than was warranted by their support among voters, and that under a proportional system a clear majority of one party would not be returned, which would lead to weak government; moreover cliques, fads, and cranks would be not just represented, but over-represented; minorities were 'born to suffer'; it was the duty of the minority to turn itself into a majority. Little was made of the alleged difficulties facing the elector and returning officer under a proportional system, though some witnesses may have had this in mind when they said that the idea was all right in theory but not in practice. This was not exactly Sir Charles Dilke's view though it approximated to it; for he accepted the theoretical argument in favour of proportional representation and said that he would in the abstract like to see realized many of the objectives of Courtney and others, but that it was no good dealing with abstract speculations. He added that although he himself did not believe in a two-party system, one could not go against the views of the leaders of the two great parties who considered proportional representation inconsistent with it. He seems here to have been thinking back to 1884–5 rather than reflecting on the existing situation.

One marked feature of the Commission's discussions with witnesses is the ignorance of the subject displayed by some of its members, including the chairman, in spite of their experience of public and political life. They also had difficulty in grasping the most elementary points, for instance that one cannot obtain the representation of several opinions in a constituency if there is only one seat to be filled, and that proportional representation would inevitably involve a redistribution of seats. Some thought that redistribution by itself would prevent a minority in the country returning a majority of MPs. One member, focusing on the word 'single' in the single transferable vote system, asked whether the abolition of plural voting would be the beginning of proportional representation. Another, the chairman, on being told that the Conservatives in Wales received 38 per cent of the vote in 1906 but no representation in parliament, asked whether it was conceivable that they would have done better under a scheme of proportional representation. (Wales sent thirty-four MPs to parliament.) It is only fair to add that members of the Commission admitted afterwards that they had learnt a lot from witnesses.

The Royal Commission took nine months to draw up its report, which suggests that agreement to its terms proved difficult. In its conclusions the Commission admitted, as indeed it could not help doing, that majorities in the House of Commons had since 1885, with one exception, shown a very great, and at the same time variable, disproportion to majorities in votes, and that there was nothing in the system to warrant the belief that such exaggerations would not recur. But the Commission did not consider that it was a fair argument against the existing system that it failed to represent parties according to their voting strength, 'because it does not profess to do so'; a general election was considered by a large portion of the electorate as practically a referendum on the question which of two governments should be returned to power; this view, whether right or wrong, had to be taken into account in any discussion which turned on the composition of the House of Commons. They were therefore unable to recommend the adoption of the (single) transferable vote in existing circumstances for elections to the House of Commons. They did however recommend the introduction of the alternative vote where more than two candidates stood for one seat.

One member of the Commission, Lord Lochee, put in a memorandum dissenting from his colleagues' conclusions regarding the single transferable vote. He considered that legislatures should have as fully representative a character as possible and that the cause of good government was not bound up with the maintenance of a distorted representation. He thought British statesmanship would be able to cope with the problems which a better system might bring in its train. It is curious that whilst holding these views Lochee signed the report.[20]

The advocates of proportional representation took a little comfort from some of the Commission's findings, guarded and timid though they were: for instance that the present system suffered from a certain brutality and roughness of justice besides other defects to which, perhaps, no virtues corresponded; that the varying size of constituencies (i.e. electorates) did not account for the exaggeration of majorities as far as they could see; that the Belgian and (proposed) French list systems would not be acceptable here; that at some future time the situation might change making proportional representation desirable; and that if it was to be introduced for parliamentary elections, the change would be facilitated if experience had been gained in municipal elections.

But the proportionalists were naturally disappointed with the Commission's final verdict and criticized the report. Courtney complained that the Commission had been told to find out how to improve the representative character of the House of Commons,[21] but that it came to the conclusion it did not want to improve the representative character at all because that was not the primary object of a general election. It was not in his view the duty of the Commission to express this opinion. Others complained that the Commission based its verdict on a theory of government held by those who desired to maintain the present electoral system. It was also pointed out that a general election could be an unreliable referendum as a majority of the voters could fail to return to power the government they wanted: these critics did not accept the Commission's view that the theoretical possibility of a minority of electors returning a majority of MPs could in practice be disregarded.

Other criticisms were also made, for example of the report's view that proportional systems only secured proportionality 'in a limited and generally unascertainable degree'; it was con-

---

[20] PP 1910 XXVI. Royal Commission on Systems of Elections, Report and Minutes of Evidence, 295–567.
[21] This was not in fact a correct account of the terms of reference.

tended that this was belied by the experience of foreign and Commonwealth countries where a proportional system operated. It was also pointed out that one of the Commission's criticisms of the single transferable vote, namely that it might give undue weight to late preferences in deciding the result of an election, applied much more to the alternative vote which the Commission recommended than to the single transferable vote. For under the latter the final transfer might determine the character of only one out of five or more members (assuming constituencies with a minimum of five members), whereas under the alternative vote it would affect the whole representation of the constituency. It was also thought odd that having given much greater space to the objections to the alternative vote than to its advantages, the report without further explanation suddenly came down in its favour.

The report received less extensive attention in the press than is usual in the case of Royal Commissions because it was issued three days after the nation had been stunned by the death of King Edward VII and in the middle of the constitutional crisis over the House of Lords, but it was commented on fully in a leading article in *The Times*. This found the report somewhat disappointing, because 'It is cautious to the verge of timidity. It says and unsays so much, leaves undecided so many things of interest and importance, and appends to almost every conclusion so much qualification, that it fails to give a clear lead where such a lead was wanted.' *The Times* acknowledged that the report stated the defects of the present system very frankly and emphatically, but complained that no corresponding decisiveness or clearness was shown in its conclusions. The difficulties and drawbacks of all solutions were stated forcefully, but little help was offered as to the choice of remedies. The article concluded by wishing that the Commission had recommended that the next Reform Bill should contain provisions for a genuine application of the principle of proportional representation on a considerable scale, as the present system produced very strange and unsatisfactory results.[22] Such comments as there were in other newspapers and journals also tended to be critical of the report, particularly of its view that it was not the purpose of a

---

[22] *The Times*, 16 May 1910, 9d–e.

representative system to represent the opinions of the electorate.

The Commission's support for the alternative vote encouraged the advocates of this electoral method. For many years some people had been recommending the introduction of a second ballot where no candidate received more than half of the votes in his constituency. Various forms of the second ballot were in operation abroad: these provided for a second election a week or so later at which usually only the two top candidates stood again. Other people thought that the alternative vote was a more satisfactory way of ensuring that no one was elected with fewer than half of the votes, for it enabled the two elections to be taken together. Under the alternative vote the elector could indicate on his ballot paper how he would vote if his favourite candidate was defeated.

There was a considerable revival of interest in the alternative vote from 1906 onwards due to a substantial increase in the number of three-cornered contests which were won by a candidate on a minority vote, namely less than half and sometimes much less than half of the total votes cast. Some notorious by-elections had highlighted this phenomenon. For instance at Jarrow in 1907 the successful candidate received as little as one-third of the votes polled, and at Attercliffe in 1909 only just over a quarter of the total vote. Between January 1911 and January 1914 thirteen by-elections out of eighteen three-cornered contests were won on a minority vote.

Advocates of the alternative vote can be divided into two categories: (1) those who saw it as an alternative to and a way of avoiding proportional representation, an improvement of the existing system securing the preservation of single-member constituencies; and (2) supporters of proportional representation who thought it would prepare the public mind for a really effective system by providing experience of preferential voting and vote transfer, and encouraging discussion about the representative system.

All the party agents who gave evidence to the Commission fell into the first category as they were hostile to proportional representation. The second category included some confirmed advocates of proportional representation; but most proportionalists condemned the alternative vote on several grounds. Thus they pointed out that in a three-cornered contest the candidate with least first votes who was eliminated might be the second preference of many of the voters for the two top candidates, and could therefore be considered to have greater support than either of them. Supporters of proportional representation therefore viewed with mixed feelings the many attempts made from 1906 onwards to get parliament to pass bills providing for the alternative vote. None of them obtained a second reading, though a motion was passed in its favour in the Commons in 1914 after a quite long debate.[23]

On balance it seems clear that the campaign for the alternative vote at this period, and indeed later, hindered rather than helped the campaign for proportional representation. It added to the difficulties of understanding the subject felt by many people; in particular the issue of how to apply the alternative vote in the two-member constituencies which still existed was very complicated, as the Royal Commission found. Moreover it appeared to offer a solution to the problem seen by the critics, whereas in fact it addressed itself only to the issue of three (or more) cornered contests in single-member constituencies—and that not satisfactorily. Indeed some advocates of proportional representation considered the alternative vote even worse than the existing system. Thus the statistician J. Rooke Corbett calculated in 1910 that if it had been in operation since 1885, it would have led to a more equitable result at only one general election (in 1895), and that at four general elections (in 1885, 1892, 1906, and January 1910) it would have increased an already exaggerated majority.[24]

Despite the discouragement of the Royal Commission's report, interest in proportional representation continued to increase during the years 1910–14. A number of different factors fostered this interest and resulted in the subject being treated far more seriously than it had been in the 1880s. Amongst Conservatives and Unionists was the realization that since 1906 the electoral

---

[23] *HC Deb.* 60 (7 Apr. 1914), 1897–1943. The voting was 145 votes to 23.
[24] PRS Pamphlet No. 14. This was a reprint of Corbett's paper of 1906 read to the Manchester Statistical Society, brought up to date in 1910.

system had not worked in their favour as it had so often previously, inflating their majorities much more than Liberal ones. Moreover Unionist free-traders found it difficult to get fair representation in the Commons because the party machine had since the split of 1903 remained under the control of tariff reformers. They saw that a proportional system based on multi-membered constituencies would leave electors free to choose between Unionists of various views without the risk of losing seats to the Liberals.

For a time after the general election of 1906 many Liberals were disposed to look more charitably on the existing electoral system than previously, but several of them, especially back-benchers, were keen advocates of proportional representation even if it did not appear to be in their party's immediate interests. These included Aneurin Williams, J. M. Robertson, H. G. Chancellor, John Gulland, Thomas Burt, Alfred Mond, Richard Holt, and E. T. John. Among ministers the only definite supporters seem to have been Sir John Simon and Lord Lore-burn.[25] Various Liberal intellectuals such as J. A. Hobson and L. T. Hobhouse also advocated proportional representation. Hobson thought Liberalism would be able to tackle social and economic issues in a new way if, amongst other political reforms, the House of Commons was made to represent the will of the people more accurately, and Hobhouse considered that Liberals would find themselves driven to the proportional system, whether against the grain or not, the more they insisted on the genuinely representative character of the House of Commons.[26]

Moreover Liberal interest in the subject generally was stimu-lated by the rise of the Labour party, and the problems this posed for them unless the 'Lib.–Lab.' electoral pact held. The pact originated in an agreement made in 1903 between Herbert Gladstone and Ramsay MacDonald; its purpose was to enable Liberal and Labour supporters to make common cause against the Conservatives without sacrificing their respective long-term aims. The 1910 Liberal victories were obviously precarious; for

[25] Robertson held a post in the government from 1911 to 1915.
[26] J. A. Hobson, *The Crisis of Liberalism: New Issues of Democracy* (1909), ch. 1; L. T. Hobhouse, *Liberalism* (1911), 243.

it was thought that the Conservatives would have been returned to office if Labour had not been contained through arrangements which restricted their candidates (to 78 and 56) in the two elections of that year.

But it was the Labour party which showed the greatest interest in the issue, being the first party to invite its members to make a thorough investigation of the question. It was discussed by the parliamentary party in 1910, and quite extensively at Labour party conferences in 1911, 1913, and 1914. The leading protagonists of proportional representation included George Roberts, W. C. Anderson, and Philip Snowden, both of the Independent Labour Party, Harry Quelch of the Social Democratic Federation and London Trades Council, and D. R. Campbell of the Belfast Trades Council;[27] but many others showed a good understanding of the subject and supported the reform with intelligent arguments. They saw that equalizing the size of constituencies would not secure the proper representation of minorities in parliament; also that the Lib.–Lab. pact would not last; in any event they disliked the fact that it was curbing the independence of Labour MPs. They were also much influenced by the strong support for proportional representation shown by socialist and labour parties in other countries. But they encountered opposition: from advocates of the alternative vote who thought it would help Labour candidates in three-cornered contests, and most importantly from Ramsay MacDonald.

MacDonald considered that under the existing system 'all the people' ruled, for the pressure of public opinion acted effectively on governments. Besides advancing most of the standard objections to proportional representation, he added a rather

[27] William Crawfurd Anderson, 1877–1919. Failed to get returned to parliament in 1910 (Jan.) and 1911, but succeeded in Nov. 1914. Defeated in Dec. 1918. Well thought of by a wide circle of Labour people: it is said that he might have become leader of the party after MacDonald if he had lived longer. Married to Mary Macarthur who was important in women's trade unionism.

Philip Snowden, 1864–1937. MP, 1906–18 and 1922–31. National Chairman of ILP, 1903–6 and 1917–20. In 1912 he calculated that if there were proportional representation at the next general election, Labour would certainly secure 110 MPs from Great Britain. See PRS Pamphlet No. 24, Jan. 1913.

Henry Quelch, 1858–1913. A Marxist. Failed to get returned to parliament in 1898, 1902, 1906, and Jan. 1910. Described in the *Dictionary of Labour Biography* as 'an outstanding working class intellectual'.

pretentious structure of organic metaphors when discussing electoral systems. The individual was naturally in a hurry, he said, 'but social evolution is in no hurry, and has an awkward way of resenting spurs . . . The organic evolution of political parties and legislation was secure'; the present system did not need mechanical readjustments. Opinions should not be coddled in their infancy; they should have to surmount reasonable obstacles. Every opinion which claimed parliamentary recognition should be asked to prove its staying power, lest it may have been favoured by temporary circumstances into a 'gourd-like growth'. Mathematical thoughts were misleading. Proportional representation would be a manipulation of the democratic machine. The socialist knows that democracy in government cannot be secured 'by an elaborate set of paper perfections of beautiful but intangible delicacy'.[28] As MacDonald held important posts in the party and was regarded as its leading intellectual, his views undoubtedly carried weight and contributed to the defeat of a resolution in favour of proportional representation at the Labour party conference of 1914;[29] but many did not share the assumptions which appeared to be at the back of MacDonald's mind, namely that the labour movement would be able to permeate, if not terrorize, the Liberal party and that then all would be well.

Other branches of the labour movement also evinced considerable interest in a reform of the electoral system, being acutely aware of the difficulties facing a new and relatively small party. Thus both the Trades Union Congress and the Social Democrats asked in 1908 for the subject to be investigated, and resolutions in favour of proportional representation were passed by many trades councils and trades organizations, by the English TUC in 1911 and 1913, the Scottish TUC in 1912, and by the Independent Labour Party and the British Socialist party in 1913. Will Thorne, general secretary of the General and Municipal Workers' Union, said at the TUC meeting of 1912 that it was difficult to understand why a proposal so pronouncedly democratic should ever have been regarded with

[28] These views were expressed in, *inter alia*, *Independent Review*, 5 (Feb. 1905), 18–26; *Socialism and Government* (1909); and *The Socialist Movement* (1911).

[29] The voting was 1,387,000 to 704,000, but it is difficult to know what significance to attach to these figures. The alternative vote was also defeated.

any coldness by members of the labour and socialist movements in this country. It seems that rank and file members of the labour movement had much less difficulty in understanding proportional electoral systems than many MPs and others. This may have been partly due to the fact that proportional systems were used by several trade unions and other labour organizations when electing their officers.

By contrast the Fabians as a group were hostile to proportional representation. Their early Tracts (1887–92) had advocated an extension of democracy and an improvement in the machinery of democratic government, but made no proposal to alter the electoral system apart from introducing the second ballot in order to prevent the anti-Conservative vote being split between Radicals and Liberals. These were the views of the two dominant Fabians Sidney Webb and Bernard Shaw and remained the approved policy of the Fabian Society, though not supported by some individual members such as Philip Snowden and W. C. Anderson. In 1911 the Fabian case against proportional representation was set out fully in their Tract no. 153 written by the lawyer Henry H. Schloesser.[30] This stressed the desirability of strong government and considered that a method of election which would accentuate the majority was preferable to one which accurately represented it.

In some ways it is strange that (with a few exceptions) the Fabians were not concerned about the vagaries of the electoral system, particularly as they stressed the importance of getting sympathizers elected to local authorities. The explanation is partly that for a time at least the Progressives were successful in local elections in London, and partly that Fabians thought they could work the system of the block vote to secure the election of the right people on to local councils. Thus a Fabian Tract of 1894 pointed out that as working men were always in a majority in the electorate, if they could elect one man on to a parish or district council, they could capture the whole council, assuming they put up exactly the right number of candidates and voted solidly. Clearly the idea that this was in some sense unfair carried no weight with the Fabians.[31]

---

[30] Later known as Slesser. MP, Labour, 1924–9. Solicitor-General in Labour government of 1924.

[31] The Tract of 1894, No. 53, on the Parish Councils Act was in fact written by

There was another and rather conflicting strand in Fabian thought which separated them from the proportionalists. Beatrice Webb spotted this early on when she noted in her diary:

> To do Leonard [Courtney] justice he is a democrat at heart, in that he honestly desires that the government of the country should be the reflection of the free desires and views of the whole body of the people. Possibly he is more of a democrat than we are ourselves; for we have little faith in the 'average sensual man' . . . (28 Dec. 1894)

So the Webbs and other Fabians became increasingly concerned with the problem of obtaining an efficient bureaucracy and with the need for expertise in government rather than with strengthening the democratic character of elections. This was neatly summed up by Beatrice Webb once again when she wrote in her diary, 'What the Courtneys have worked for, the Webbs have thought unimportant, and vice versa' (2 May 1922).

Several current issues besides those already mentioned stimulated interest in proportional representation, the main ones being the controversy over the powers and constitution of the House of Lords, the referendum, and devolution or Home Rule all round. Critics of the Lords had to face up to the fact that the Commons were often not, in Burke's much quoted but misused phrase, 'the express image of the feelings of the nation'. Moreover some of the schemes for a reformed Upper House involved the election of part of it by proportional representation. The device of the referendum, which received considerable support at this period, was shown by the proportionalists to be unnecessary if parliament reflected accurately the views of the country. Devolution of power to some regions such as Wales would have been out of the question unless accompanied by a proportional electoral system, for the Conservatives, numbering about a third of the electorate, would probably have obtained no representation in a Welsh legislature. This was realized by the sponsor of the Government of Wales Bill which was introduced into parliament in March 1914, but curiously enough not by the sponsors of the various Government of Scotland Bills.

---

Herbert Samuel who was not a Fabian, but the advice on how to exploit the electoral system was presumably put in by the Society's executive committee which approved it.

However it was the problem of how to constitute an Irish legislature if Home Rule were granted to Ireland which was the most important factor in stimulating discussion about electoral systems.[32]

In 1911 the government was preparing a Reform Bill designed to extend the franchise, but as it seemed certain that an amendment to it about the electoral system would not be admissible, the PRS decided to go ahead with its own bill. When the government finally introduced its Franchise and Registration Bill into parliament in June 1912, the minister in charge, J. A. Pease, made it clear that because of shortage of parliamentary time the bill did not deal with the redistribution of seats, nor with electoral reform, nor with the problem of the minority vote.[33] The omission of electoral reform from the bill was adversely commented on by J. R. P. Newman who drew attention in particular to the total disfranchisement of Unionists in the south, west, and east of Ireland during the last thirty years.[34] So, ever hopeful, the PRS sponsored a Proportional Representation Bill, which was backed by members of the Liberal, Labour, and Unionist parties, including F. E. Smith (the later Lord Birkenhead). The bill applied only to Great Britain. It contained a schedule of proposed constituencies, numbering 110 instead of the existing 514. They were to return between three and eleven members each, the average being five. In introducing the bill on 26 June 1912, R. D. Holt put the case for proportional representation on the central ground that the present system resulted in the misrepresentation of the views of electors, sometimes even giving a minority of voters the majority of seats.[35] The bill was given a first reading but got no further, and the government made it clear early in 1913 after its Franchise Bill was withdrawn (because of the problem of female

---

[32] Dealt with beneath.

[33] *HC Deb.* 39 (17 June 1912), 1332. Pease was then President of the Board of Education, and it seems strange that he was the government spokesman on parliamentary and electoral reform.

[34] *HC Deb.* 40 (12 July 1912), 2284–6. J. R. P. Newman, 1871–1947. MP, Conservative, 1910–23.

[35] *HC Deb.* 40 (26 June 1912), 333–5. Richard Durning Holt, 1868–1941. Shipowner. MP, Liberal, 1907–18. He failed to get elected to parliament in 1922, 1923, 1924, 1926, and 1929.

suffrage) that it was not contemplating any alteration in methods of election.[36] A private member's bill similar to Holt's was introduced again in March 1913, but its sponsor, L. S. Amery, did not get an opportunity to speak about it and it never secured a second reading. Snowden, who disagreed with Amery's views on most subjects, was one of its backers, which illustrates once again the cross-party support for proportional representation.[37]

In 1914 advocates of proportional representation had two opportunities to press their case in parliament. One was during a debate in March on the redistribution of seats, when H. J. MacKinder pointed out that even with more equal electoral districts single-member constituencies produced only rough justice and pleaded that if, as requested by the mover of the motion, a select committee was set up to consider redistribution, it should also consider proportional representation at least for certain localities like large towns. The President of the Local Government Board, Samuel, said the government would not rule this out. Once again the opponents of proportional representation, including the Conservative Walter Long, cited in support of their case the views expressed by Gladstone in 1884.[38]

The next occasion for raising proportional representation in parliament occurred during the debate in April 1914 on a Liberal MP's motion advocating the alternative vote. George Roberts admitted that the Labour party, like every other party in the house, was very sharply divided on electoral reform, but said he could not conceive any democratic principle other than one which secured to each party in the state a representation proportionate to its numerical strength in the country. He also took the opportunity to answer the MP who denied that a Labour party existed outside parliament. Aneurin Williams pointed out that the alternative vote would not prevent the misrepresentation of parties which occurred over the whole

---

[36] *HC Deb.* 47 (4 Feb. 1913), 1982–3.

[37] L. S. Amery, 1873–1955. MP, 1911–45. Liberal Unionist, then Conservative on the extreme right. He had been Courtney's private secretary for eight months in the 1890s. They disagreed fundamentally over almost the whole field of politics, but not on proportional representation, female suffrage, and bimetallism.

[38] *HC Deb.* 59 (4 Mar. 1914), 517–64. MacKinder was the eminent geographer. He was a Unionist MP from Jan. 1910–22.

country, but pleaded that the question should not be looked at from a party point of view. The government spokesman (Pease) revealed implicit faith in Gladstone's 'unrivalled insight' into the question and added that 'the great object of an electoral system is that it should be intelligible'.[39]

In contrast to these failures there was one field where the proportionalists achieved some success—Ireland. They had for many years argued that the case for proportional representation was even stronger in Ireland than it was in Great Britain, but the opportunity for effective action on this issue did not come until 1912 when a Home Rule Bill was introduced into parliament, protected from a House of Lords veto by the Parliament Act, 1911, which provided that a bill became law, even if the Lords did not agree to it, if it was passed three times by the Commons.

In fact for some time before 1912 Courtney had been preparing the ground for the inclusion of proportional representation in any legislation embodying Home Rule. Thus in January 1911 he wrote a substantial letter which was published in an Irish journal (*Freeman*'s) arguing the case for making a new national assembly as representative as possible. Courtney confessed he was still 'in wish and desire a Unionist', but he thought that one should be realistic and prepare for Home Rule.[40] The letter attracted considerable attention in the Irish press, with support coming mainly at this stage from the Nationalist side, as many Unionists did not wish to discuss 'with what sauce they are to be cooked'. Courtney was invited over and gave what was described as a rousing speech to a large and enthusiastic audience in Dublin on 20 April 1911. From then on events moved rapidly. It was decided at once to form an Irish society. A circular was issued by an organizing committee emphasizing the case for Unionist support; by mid-September 1911 an Irish PRS existed (called hereafter the IPRS). The President was Sir Horace Plunkett. He was well suited to this position, for although a Unionist, he was a moderate one whose aim was to

---

[39] *HC Deb.* 60 (7 Apr. 1914), 1897–1943. The sponsor of the motion was C. H. Lyell, MP 1904–17.

[40] The letter is reproduced in *Representation*, Feb. 1911, 4–7.

reconcile conflicting sections of opinion in Ireland, and who had had considerable success in doing this through his work for agricultural improvement.[41] Plunkett seems to have been the driving force in the Irish movement, but the IPRS was by no means a one-man show. On the contrary, with headquarters in Dublin and a branch in Belfast, it attracted support from a wide spectrum of people, Unionists and Nationalists, professional and farming, organized labour, and commercial and industrial interests. Its claim to have all the leading men in Ireland behind it seems to have been substantially justified. By December 1911, assisted by the press, it had organized a model election at which 9,000 people from all parts of Ireland voted with apparently no difficulties. In all its activities the IPRS was much helped by advice and support, some of it financial, from the PRS of Great Britain to which it considered itself allied.[42]

The British government, however, when preparing its Home Rule Bill was clearly not impressed by the case for proportional representation; it said it hoped to safeguard minorities by the device of a nominated Senate. The bill, introduced into parliament on 11 April 1912, thus contained no element of proportional representation. This was naturally a great disappointment to the IPRS, especially as the Chief Secretary for Ireland, Augustine Birrell, had told a deputation from the society that he was in favour of proportional representation and would put the case for it to the cabinet. The Irish House of Commons was to have 164 members; most of these were to be elected in single-member constituencies under the first-past-the-post system as in Great Britain, but thirty-one members were to be elected in multi-member constituencies by a method even more distasteful to proportionalists—namely the block vote; for in nine constituencies electors were to have as many votes as there were seats to be filled, which was three to five. The bill itself actually made no reference to the mode of election of members in multi-membered constituencies, which suggests either that the gov-

[41] Horace Curzon Plunkett, 1854–1932. Founded Agricultural Organisation Society, 1894. Vice-President, Department of Agriculture and Technical Instruction for Ireland, 1899–1907. MP, Unionist, 1892–1900; later converted to Home Rule but opposed partition; became a member of the British PRS in 1910.

[42] The IPRS received £575 from the PRS in the three years 1911–13. The records of the Irish society appear no longer to exist.

ernment wanted to conceal that it was to be the block vote, or more probably that they regarded methods of election as of little importance. The position on this point was not brought out into the open and acknowledged by the government until December 1912 when a parliamentary question was asked about it,[43] though Courtney had drawn attention to the issue earlier.[44]

The IPRS resolved at once to try to get the bill amended so as to provide that both Houses of the proposed Irish legislature should be elected by proportional representation. On 25 June 1912 they sent a large deputation to the Prime Minister, emphasizing their extensive and varied support. Asquith answered in a friendly way though he referred rather typically to 'what is called the system of proportional representation'. The next day the deputation waited on Bonar Law (the leader of the Unionist party) and Sir Edward Carson, both strong opponents of Home Rule. Law promised to allow a free vote on the issue. Carson later said he did not know anything about, and could not understand, proportional representation, in spite of having received the deputation. This was followed by a letter to the Prime Minister with a list of 1,600 supporters, claiming among other things that the Irish movement was more representative of the whole political thought of the country than in other countries. A deputation also waited on MPs, who had all been circularized and lobbied by *inter alia* Irish Trade Unionists.

The result of this campaign was an immediate success in regard to the Senate: for on 30 October 1912 Asquith announced that he had been much impressed by the facts and arguments put to him by the June deputation and that the government proposed that the Senate should be elected by the principle of proportional representation after a period of nomination. The IPRS was delighted, but the British society's pleasure was diluted by Asquith's simultaneous firm announcement, which seemed at odds with views he had expressed before on several occasions, that he was 'not an adherent of or even a convert to the principle of proportional representation as applied to popular elections in this country'; Ireland was different because of its peculiar social, political, and economic conditions.[45] Several

[43]  *HC Deb.* 45 (10 Dec. 1912), 239.
[44]  *Contemporary Review*, 102 (July 1912) 1–11, 'Home Rule'.
[45]  *HC Deb.* 43 (30 Oct. 1912), 507.

MPs, mostly Conservatives and Unionists, opposed the government's proposal, some on the rather strange ground that a nominated Senate was more democratic than an elected one, or at least one elected by proportional representation. Others raised the traditional objections that the system was complicated and incomprehensible—'a mysterious sausage machine'—and that it would encourage cranks. Amongst the opponents was James Craig, who later (in 1929) when Prime Minister of Northern Ireland as Viscount Craigavon secured the abolition of proportional representation for elections to the Northern Irish parliament. The opposition mustered 209 votes, but the government with the whips on secured a majority of 89; so the bill provided for the election of the Irish Senate by proportional representation after a period of nomination.[46]

The IPRS then turned its attention to a more important issue—getting proportional representation for the Irish House of Commons. J. R. P. Newman, an Irishman from Cork who sat as a Conservative for an English seat, moved an amendment to secure the election of the whole Lower House by proportional representation. The chief interest of the debate lies in the fact that the proposal was welcomed from many sides though on different grounds: supporters included prominent Conservatives such as A. J. Balfour and Bonar Law, many Liberals, and T. M. Healy who though a Catholic and Nationalist thought Protestants should be fairly represented. As usual some opponents poured ridicule on the idea. Thus Sir Frederick Banbury said:

I do not understand proportional representation. It is, as far as I can make out, a fad advocated by certain scientific people, who are under the impression that by putting forward something the electors do not understand they are certain to do something which is wrong, and that by doing something which is wrong right will accrue. That, as far as I can make out, will be the result of proportional representation.

The government opposed the amendment chiefly on the ground that the issue should be left for decision by the Irish House of Commons, and the amendment was defeated by 265 votes to 162.[47]

[46] *HC Deb.* 43 (31 Oct. 1912), 621–706.
[47] *HC Deb.* 43 (4 Nov. 1912), 903–95. Banbury's remarks are at 973.

However, the advocates of proportional representation did not give up and secured its inclusion in the bill for constituencies which were to return three or more members to the Irish House of Commons, in place of the block vote system proposed by the government. The amendment to effect this was sponsored at the report stage of the bill in January 1913 by Sir Alfred Mond.[48] It was accepted, though very reluctantly, by the government on the ground, as Asquith put it, that the circumstances in Ireland were 'absolutely special and exceptional'. In emphasizing how he was not in general in favour of proportional representation, he praised a previous speaker who had argued that the present system of election had never pretended to produce accurate representation, and that 'it does not want to do anything of the kind'. (This was, it will be recalled, the much criticized line taken by the Royal Commission.) After a brief debate during which most of the speeches were in favour of the amendment, it was passed by a very large majority, 311 votes to 81.[49] This provision affected, as things stood, only thirty-one members in nine constituencies, but the PRS regarded it as a milestone, because this was the first occasion on which the parliament of the United Kingdom approved the principle of proportional representation for elections to 'a popular elected assembly'.

The IPRS, however, was determined to go on fighting for 'the whole loaf': it regarded thirty-one members out of a total of 164 as 'a mere crust'. So they made a further effort in the summer of 1914 when the Government of Ireland (Amendment) Bill was being considered by the Lords to get proportional representation applied to all constituencies. This was proposed by Lord MacDonnell who produced a detailed scheme.[50] By then Ulster had been excluded by the Lords from the Home Rule Bill, so MacDonnell's amendment would not have assisted minorities in the North of Ireland. The need to help Unionists in the South

[48] Alfred Moritz Mond, 1868–1930. MP, 1906–28. Liberal until 1926, then Conservative. A member of the PRS from 1911, and a generous contributor to its funds.
[49] *HC Deb.* 46 (7 Jan. 1913), 1089–1130.
[50] Anthony Patrick MacDonnell, 1844–1925. Indian Civil Servant, 1865–1901. Permanent Under-Secretary, Ireland, 1902–8. Though a Roman Catholic and a Liberal, he was concerned that Protestants and Conservatives should be fairly represented in an Irish legislature.

was, however, felt to be stronger than ever: it was predicted that without proportional representation they would get no representation in the Irish House of Commons except for two members for Dublin University. This was thought to be particularly undesirable as it would allegedly have resulted in the non-representation of the more wealthy, educated, and active elements in the country, such as the commercial, industrial, and manufacturing classes; though with a proportional system they would be only a minority in the House, they would have an open forum in which to voice arguments and criticisms. Some of the supporters of proportional representation weakened their case by overstating it, in particular by suggesting that their proposal would make the exclusion of Ulster unnecessary and that it would even help to prevent civil war in Ireland—a very real threat at that moment; they recommended it as a solution to what Viscount Milner described as 'the greatest political muddle we have ever known'.

The government opposed MacDonnell's proposal: Lord Crewe considered proportional representation was unnecessary as the division between Home Rulers and Unionists would, he predicted, become blurred. Moreover he thought it wrong to impose the system on the Irish parliament treating it like a *corpus vile* upon which an experiment was to be made, apparently overlooking the fact that the Government of Ireland Bill already included some proportional representation. Lord Morley took the same line, adding that although he had been brought up by John Stuart Mill to regard proportional representation as the salvation of parliamentary government, he did not understand the single transferable vote, and that it was unfair to expect comparatively unpractised voters to work such a scheme. Nevertheless MacDonnell's revised, simpler proposal, which was that no constituency should return fewer than three members, was passed by the Lords without a division. This would have ensured that all elections were held under a proportional system.[51] However it was not considered by the Commons due to the outbreak of war, and so did not reach the statute book.

---

[51] *HL Deb.* 16 (1 July 1914), 580–1; (2 July 1914), 651; (6 July 1914), 714; (9 July 1914), 988–1018; (13 July 1914), 1073–91.

The net result of the Irish campaign was that the Government of Ireland Act, 1914, provided that the single transferable vote was to be the method of election for the Irish Senate after five years and for thirty-one members (about one-fifth) of the Irish House of Commons. But the Act never came into force as its operation was suspended until the end of the European war, by which time events in Ireland required a new settlement. This incorporated proportional representation as the method of election of the legislatures and local councils of both northern and southern Ireland, a result in large part due to the work of the IPRS. The society had operated on two main fronts, educating the people of Ireland generally on the need for proportional representation, and focusing specifically on the politicians who would be making the decisions. In some ways its task was easier than that of the British society because of the obvious need to protect minorities in Ireland; but in other ways it faced greater obstacles: higher rates of illiteracy and innumeracy, and passionately held political positions which often made co-operation between parties difficult if not impossible. But these problems were somehow overcome, with long-term success in the South where the electoral method established by the constitution of the Irish Free State in 1922 has been retained ever since.[52]

What had been achieved by 1914? There were some legislative successes: in the UK an element of proportional representation in a future Irish legislature, and in the Empire a proportional system for the election of the Senate in South Africa. Moreover, although none of the changes proposed for parliamentary or local elections in Great Britain had reached the statute book, there was during the period 1906–14 as compared with the previous twenty years a slightly improved understanding of the effects of different electoral methods and wider support for a proportional system. As Lord Crewe said rather patronizingly, Courtney's 'stock had gone up'.

This progress was due in large measure to the activities of the PRS. They concentrated their efforts mainly on the political class and on opinion formers rather than on the population

---

[52] See Ch. IX.

generally, apart from a manifesto to electors before the first 1910 general election. Thus they sent out their literature to delegates at party conferences as well as to MPs on many occasions; they circularized mayors and town clerks about the Municipal Representation Bill; they arranged lectures to political clubs and organizations; they secured attention to the subject in newspapers and journals; and to demonstrate how the single transferable vote worked, they organized several nation-wide model elections involving tens of thousands of electors.

Advocates of proportional representation during these years tended to base the case for it more narrowly on the distorted and haphazard relation between votes and seats than they had previously, when they had emphasized the iniquities of party government. But some of them continued to press for proportional representation as a cure for other alleged defects in the political system, such as the tight hold of party over candidates and MPs, the increase in the control of parliament by the executive, and disillusionment with the parliamentary system as shown in particular by support for syndicalist doctrines.[53] It was therefore still easy for opponents of proportional representation to ridicule the idea that it was a panacea for all political ills.

In spite of difficulties due to small membership and inadequate funds, the PRS, to judge by its annual reports, remained determinably optimistic about the ultimate success of the cause. This was due partly to the fact that the society was in effect a centre for movements for proportional representation all over the world. It watched these closely and felt that because the cause was progressing and succeeding in many foreign countries and in some outposts of the British Empire, it was bound to triumph at home. Subsequent history has shown this prediction to be wrong, but nevertheless there were by 1914 reasonable grounds for a measure of optimism.

---

[53] See, e.g., the writings and speeches of Courtney and Earl Grey, J. H. Humphreys' book *Proportional Representation* (1911), and H. G. Wells, *An Englishman Looks at the World* (1914). Wells was a keen advocate of proportional representation. He became a member of the General Committee of the PRS in 1908.

# VIII

# The Speaker's Conference and the Representation of the People Bill, 1916–1918

WITH the outbreak of war in 1914, the PRS had to curtail its propagandist activities, but it was kept in being despite cutbacks in staff and expenditure. The Executive Committee continued to meet, though less often than before, and even Annual General Meetings were held in 1915 and 1916 in spite of a decline in membership and funds. The Society was determined to be ready to act when a favourable opportunity presented itself, which it did with the appointment of the Speaker's Conference on Electoral Reform in 1916. By then the secretary of the PRS, Humphreys, had returned from the world tour on which he had been sent in May 1915, to visit New Zealand, Australia, and the USA. The purpose of the tour was to assist the progress of the cause in these countries, and to gain information about successful developments in other parts of the English-speaking world, knowledge of which was considered important for the movement at home.

By 1915 the government had to decide whether to prolong the life of the existing parliament which expired on 31 January 1916, or to hold a general election. The possibility of an election raised perplexing, indeed intractable, problems in relation to the register of electors. The existing register was stale, but a new one would also be unsatisfactory because of the absence from home of those members of the armed forces and others on war work who were, as the law stood, entitled to vote. This problem in turn raised larger issues, namely whether the franchise should not be extended to include at least all those who were fighting for their country with no present entitlement to vote, or perhaps all males, or even some females.

A general election was avoided by the passing of Acts to extend the life of parliament, and work on the electoral register was suspended. But the problems remained, and after extensive but abortive discussions in cabinet and lengthy and acrimonious debates in parliament, it was decided in August 1916 to set up a conference in the hope that it could resolve the issues. The government had in July proposed the appointment of a select committee of the Commons for this task, but withdrew the suggestion when it was vehemently criticized.[1]

The President of the Local Government Board, Walter Long, then suggested a conference. He seems to have been thinking of a body which would include others besides members of the two Houses of parliament, because he suggested 'a representative conference, not only of parties, but of groups . . . a conference of earnest men', and he asked for help from people in or outside the House to get the conference together.[2] The PRS was quick off the mark. They immediately pressed on Long the necessity of having their views represented at the conference and gave him a list of MPs favourable to proportional representation. Courtney also wrote at once to *The Times* pointing out that if, as the Prime Minister declared, parliament must possess moral authority, the extension of the franchise must be accompanied by redistribution of seats and proportional representation.[3] In fact Long had already proposed that the conference should deal with methods of election as well as with the franchise, redistribution, and registration, and although himself opposed to proportional representation, he recommended that the president and chairman of the PRS (Earl Grey and Aneurin Williams) should be members of the conference.

The idea of appointing the Speaker of the House of Commons, James Lowther, as chairman of the conference seems also to have been Long's when it proved impossible to find a

---

[1] *HC Deb.* 84 (12 July 1916), 843–4, and (19 July 1916), 1075.

[2] *HC Deb.* 85 (16 Aug. 1916), 1949. Walter Hume Long, 1854–1924. MP, Conservative, 1880–92 and 1893–1921. Created Viscount Long in 1921. Held office in Conservative and coalition governments from 1886 to 1921. The idea of a conference apparently originated with a Labour MP, G. J. Wardle.

[3] *The Times*, 26 Aug. 1916, 7c.

judge for the task.[4] The curious device of a Speaker's conference was entirely novel. It was thought (rightly) that it would carry more weight than a select committee of the Commons, both because it could include members of both Houses of Parliament and because the chairman, whilst having the experience and insight of a politician, would be seen as impartial. Lowther was in fact an inspired choice as he was, according to a clerk in the Commons, both very popular and 'a little formidable'.[5]

There was naturally considerable discussion with the whips and in the cabinet about the composition of the conference, the final decisions on which were made by the Speaker. In the end pressure groups and other outsiders such as local authority representatives were not included and the thirty-two members were confined to MPs and peers, representing all the parties in parliament. However the conference included two members of the PRS who had been actively engaged in the movement (Grey and Williams) and three others who were sympathetic to it—Sir John Simon, Lord Burnham, and Lord Salisbury who was later replaced by Lord Stuart of Wortley, also a sympathizer. (See Appendix B for membership.) The PRS may not have known that the secretary of the conference, Walter Jerred of the Local Government Board, was according to Lowther, 'a disbeliever in proportional representation'.[6]

No records of the work of the conference exist because its procedure was very informal. It met in private; there was no agenda; no minutes were taken, and no names were recorded when (the rare) divisions were held. Our knowledge of what went on has therefore to be culled from a few scattered remarks made subsequently by some of the participants who did not always agree about what had happened. The decisions of the conference were simply recorded in a brief letter from the Speaker to the Prime Minister. In this he paid tribute to the members, all of whom he said showed 'admirable temper and conciliatory disposition' in grappling with the difficulties. He

---

[4] James William Lowther, 1855–1949. MP, Conservative, 1883–5 and 1886–1921. Deputy Speaker, 1895–1905. Speaker, 1905–21. Became Viscount Ullswater in 1921. He is not the James Lowther, MP who spoke about electoral reform in the 1880s, mentioned in Ch. V.

[5] Campion in the *DNB*.

[6] J. W. Lowther, *A Speaker's Commentaries* (1925), ii. 205.

added that they wanted to equip the nation with 'a truly representative House of Commons'.[7]

The conference met between 12 October 1916 and 26 January 1917. Already by 28 October the PRS had submitted a memorandum to the members, demonstrating that redistribution of parliamentary seats, if it was to secure 'one vote, one value', required the abandonment of single-member constituencies and their replacement by multi-membered constituencies with a system of proportional representation. However it seems that the conference did not seriously consider the wholesale use of proportional representation, on the ground that it had not achieved widespread public interest and approval. A restricted measure of it was therefore the most that could be hoped for, and this was what the conference agreed unanimously: namely that elections in all boroughs which returned three or more members should be held on the principle of proportional representation with the single transferable vote. If a borough was big enough to return more than five members it was to be divided into two or more constituencies, each returning three to five members. The same arrangements were to apply to London: it was to be divided into constituencies of three to five members elected by proportional representation. The conference did not indicate how many seats they thought would be affected by their proposal. Indeed it would have been difficult for them to do this before the Boundary Commissioners had produced a redistribution scheme. When the Commissioners had done their work, it appeared that proportional representation would have applied to 211 seats in Great Britain out of a total of 569. The conference did not deal with redistribution of seats or methods of election in Ireland. The conference also recommended that the universities of Oxford and Cambridge should use the limited vote for the election of two members each, and that the other universities grouped into two constituencies of three members each should use the single transferable vote. It also recommended (though not unanimously) that the alternative vote should be used in all the remaining seats if more than two candidates were nominated.

---

[7] PP 1917–18 XXV. Conference on Electoral Reform, Letter from Mr Speaker to the Prime Minister, 27 Jan. 1917, 385–92.

The inclusion of a unanimous recommendation for proportional representation (in some constituencies) has been described by historians as 'astonishing' and as 'the most striking and novel feature of the Report'.[8] The explanation of how this happened appears to be as follows. A lead on the issue was given to the conference by Lowther, who according to one member (McCallum Scott) dominated the proceedings.[9] Lowther had at that time become a convert to proportional representation, at all events to the extent that he thought it should be tried; so in his original plan for redistribution which he submitted to members it occupied in his words 'a prominent place', probably involving a wider application of a proportional scheme than the one which eventually emerged in the report.[10] It seems that the willingness of members to recommend this change in the long-established electoral system of the country was mainly due to the fear of many of them that the substantial extension of the male suffrage making it virtually universal, which the conference was recommending, would prevent their parties from winning seats in the large towns, unless provision were made for the representation of the minority in these places.

Doubt about this explanation of how proportional representation in some constituencies came to be unanimously recommended arises partly because of the repercussions which it would have on the exercise of the plural vote; for an increase in the size of constituencies entailed by proportional representation meant a substantial reduction in opportunities to exercise the right to vote more than once, a right which at that time was possessed by about half a million voters. This was particularly worrying to some supporters of plural voting because the conference also proposed its limitation to one extra vote (other than the one for residence) which could be claimed in respect of business premises or as a university graduate. Further, the exercise of the second vote would be limited if, as proposed, all elections were held on the same day. Nevertheless it seems

[8] D. E. Butler, *The Electoral System in Britain since 1918* (1963), 7; and Martin Pugh, *Electoral Reform in War and Peace 1906–18* (1978), 82.

[9] *Manchester Dispatch*, 31 Jan. 1917.

[10] Lowther, *A Speaker's Commentaries*, ii. 205. He had previously shown an interest in the subject as he was a member of the PRS in its early days, 1884–5.

clear from what was said in parliament during discussions on the Reform Bill that fears of elections in populous boroughs being swamped by Labour voters were important in moving some members of the conference to support proportional representation in these constituencies. Moreover, huge constituencies, which opponents of proportional representation criticized, were not being suggested, as the maximum number of MPs to be returned by any constituency was to be five. It is also possible that some members of the conference who previously knew little about electoral systems were not simply thinking about the effects of proportional representation on their party's or their own fortunes, but were persuaded by the more general case put for it by its supporters. This was certainly true of one member, Sir R. Adkins. 'I approached this subject in the first instance with very little interest [he said] . . . I knew very little about proportional representation and I cared less.' But he became convinced that 'it was the only way in which this House would actually reflect the considered opinion of the country whose servant this House is proud to be'.[11] Finally there is considerable evidence that members of the conference were willing to accept proposals to which they were hostile, in order to achieve the inclusion of those for which they cared.

The cabinet took two months to decide to introduce legislation embodying the recommendations of the Speaker's conference. Several factors contributed to the delay, the most important of which was the desire to avoid controversy on domestic issues during a terrible war, for the recommendations of the conference covered a wide range of sweeping reforms. There was considerable opposition in Unionist circles in particular to the large increase in the male suffrage which the conference proposed and to giving votes to many women. Agreement to legislate was finally reached in the cabinet on 26 March 1917, though it wanted the Speaker's conference to reconsider the question of proportional representation. Nothing came of this idea, as presumably the Speaker was unwilling to comply with it, but it meant that the conference's proposal about proportional representation went into the bill without government

[11] *HC Deb.* 106 (13 May 1918), 112.

support and was left to a free vote in parliament. The cabinet's decision, which was criticized by some members of the government, such as F. E. Smith, the Attorney-General,[12] was probably due in the main to the attitude of Lloyd George, who had become Prime Minister in succession to Asquith in December 1916. Lloyd George had on his own admission never thought about the subject, and did not propose to study it during the war unless forced to do so. The result was that he did not regard it as an essential or integral part of the conference's scheme though the Speaker and many members of the conference were adamant that it was.[13] In fact he was not just indifferent but actually hostile to proportional representation. Thus he referred to it privately as 'a device for defeating democracy', the principle of which was that the majority should rule; it would bring faddists of all kinds into parliament, and cause parties to disintegrate.[14] Behind these standard objections to proportional representation there no doubt lay in Lloyd George's mind the obvious threat it would pose to the monopolistic position of Liberals in Wales, where thousands of Conservative and Labour voters were unrepresented. Later, in 1925, he felt he had made a great mistake, complaining to C. P. Scott that someone ought to have come to him in 1918 and gone into the whole matter, as he could have carried it then.[15] The cabinet's desire to omit proportional representation from their bill became known to the PRS, but Lloyd George refused to meet a deputation from them in April 1917.

The government's bill started its second reading in parliament on 22 May 1917 and finally emerged from the Commons on 7

[12] F. E. Smith, 1872–1930. MP, Conservative, 1906–19, when he went to the Lords as Birkenhead. He had advocated proportional representation in his 1906 election address.

[13] For Lloyd George's attitude, see *HC Deb.* 92 (28 Mar. 1917), 492. For the Speaker's views, see *The Political Diaries of Sir Robert Sanders, Lord Bayford, 1910–35*, ed. John Ramsden under the title *Real Old Tory Politics* (1984). The diary entry for 15 June 1917 records that 'the Speaker was very angry' when proportional representation was defeated in the Commons on 12 June.

[14] *Political Diaries of C. P. Scott 1911–28*, ed. Trevor Wilson (1970), 3 Apr. 1917, 274.

[15] Ibid. 13–14 Nov. 1925, 484–5. In fact Scott had explained to Lloyd George in 1917 that 'the single-member system might easily—as it had already been known to do—give a majority of seats to a minority of voters the country over', which Lloyd George had not realized. Ibid. 3 Apr. 1917, 274.

December 1917 with no provision for proportional representation in it except for some University seats. A majority of MPs had voted against proportional representation no less than three times, each time more decisively. The bill then went to the Lords, who reinstated proportional representation in it three times, but their proposals were always turned down in the Commons. (For details of the votes, see Appendix C.) A compromise was finally agreed, the result of which was that the Representation of the People Act, 1918, did not prescribe that elections in any constituencies except some University seats should be held under the principle of proportional representation, but provided that a Royal Commission was to prepare a limited scheme to apply it in one hundred seats. Any proposals emanating from the commission would only be implemented if approved by both Houses of parliament within twenty-one days. The commissioners with Lowther as chairman got to work at once, holding twenty-eight thorough local inquiries. As might have been expected, opinion was sharply divided in the great majority of the areas inquired into. The commissioners' final scheme, published on 13 April 1918, affected ninety-nine MPs who were to be elected in twenty-four constituencies of three to seven members each.[16]

The cabinet was fairly evenly divided over the commission's scheme and was not prepared to support it in parliament. It therefore decided that H. A. L. Fisher, the President of the Board of Education, should introduce the plan in his capacity as a private member. His speech on 13 May 1918 recommending the commissioners' scheme was typically terse and cogent. He did not, he said, favour proportional representation as a method of bringing into parliamentary prominence 'angularities and singularities of character and conduct—for which I think our present system satisfies all reasonable requirements—but as a more exact method of ascertaining the true feeling and judgment of the country'. He offered opponents 'the exquisite pleasure of verification'. In a brief debate he was supported by Asquith and a few others, but hotly opposed by *inter alia* Austen

---

[16] PP 1918 VIII. Report of the Royal Commission on Proportional Representation, appointed in pursuance of the Representation of the People Act, 1918, section 20(2), with the scheme prepared by the Commissioners, 603–10.

Chamberlain who was a member of the cabinet.[17] The Commons rejected the scheme, so even this minor experiment with proportional representation was not tried. It was perhaps fortunate for Courtney that he died two days before, and so did not live to witness this final defeat of his long campaign.

The Speaker's conference had recommended that the alternative vote should be used in all constituencies to which proportional representation did not apply if more than two candidates were nominated. According to Lowther this recommendation was approved by only eleven members of the thirty-two-strong conference with eight voting against it. Nevertheless it was included in the government's bill.[18] An effort was made in the Commons in August 1917 to get the alternative vote deleted from the bill, but they voted to retain it albeit by only one vote.[19] However it was approved by a larger majority in the Commons in November 1917. It was cut out by the Lords three times, as it was disliked by their Conservative majority, and twice reinstated by the Commons, on one occasion for boroughs only. But ultimately the Commons gave up the struggle for fear of losing the whole bill; so the alternative vote was not enacted. (For details of the votes, see Appendix D.)

As before the war, views on proportional representation cut across party lines. Thus in the Commons the Conservatives were divided, but with a substantial hostile majority. The Liberals too were divided, but with a majority in favour until faced with the Lords' amendments supporting proportional representation which they rejected by over two to one. Similarly Labour MPs were divided, though a majority of them voted for proportional representation until alienated by the Lords' decisions. This hostility to the action of the Lords was due not so much to a feeling that it was improper for the upper house to determine how the Lower House should be elected (though some MPs did think this), as to a suspicion that the Lords were trying to wreck the whole bill and were proposing proportional representation merely for tactical reasons. This suspicion was

---

[17] *HC Deb.* 106 (13 May 1918), 63–118.

[18] PP 1917–18, ii. 379. Representation of the People Bill, 15 May 1917, Clause 15(2). The alternative vote was defined most inadequately in Clause 28(6).

[19] *HC Deb.* 97 (9 Aug. 1917), 605–54.

largely unwarranted, for the House of Lords did not wish to provoke a constitutional crisis in 1918. Moreover the peers who were most active in the cause of proportional representation were keen on the Reform Bill.

In the Lords the Conservatives voted overwhelmingly (four to one) for proportional representation, and the Liberals split evenly.[20]

What explains the difference in attitudes on this issue between Conservative peers and MPs? Some peers found it difficult to understand the opposition of their party in the Lower House, particularly as the Speaker's conference had, they understood, assumed that proportional representation was a safeguard for Conservatives. One answer to this question is that, in so far as party interests were the dominant consideration, there was a difference of opinion as to whether or not the Conservatives could win the next general election—an anticipated 'khaki' election—with the existing electoral system. But more important is the probability that the peers were taking a longer-term view than the Commons and thought that even if the Conservatives could win the next election without proportional representation, their luck might not hold: there could be a repeat of the 1906 disaster resulting in what they considered extremist programmes. This consideration was particularly important at a time when the future of their own chamber was being discussed by the Bryce committee. Moreover it may well be that the attitude of some Unionist peers was not determined just by party interests, for several of them had been strong supporters of proportional representation on general grounds for many years. These included Balfour of Burleigh, Cromer, Parmoor, and Selborne. Parmoor's support went back as far as the early 1880s.

Among the Liberals, consistent support for proportional representation came mainly from the more radical members;[21] it also included Asquithians, though they tended to be less committed to the cause. Asquith himself admitted that it was not a matter which excited his passions, but in July 1917 he put

---

[20] For fuller details of the voting, see Pugh, *Electoral Reform*.

[21] For example, Richard Holt, A. J. Sherwell, Edward Hemmerde, H. G. Chancellor, Arthur Ponsonby, Joseph King, and H. B. Lees-Smith.

the case for it quite fully and fairly, and said he heartily supported the limited proposal which was then before the House, meaning apparently proportional representation in large boroughs but excluding London. He spoke again on three occasions in favour of a moderate experiment involving about 100 seats,[22] but he abstained from voting in all the six Commons divisions on the subject.

Herbert Samuel clearly had great difficulty in knowing what he thought about it. He said he subscribed to the view that 'the first object of a representative system is to be really representative', but he then listed very fully most of the arguments against proportional representation, making it clear that he agreed with them.[23] Nevertheless he sometimes voted for what he hoped would be a very limited experiment which he pointed out could always be reversed. Some years earlier Samuel had shown himself to be satisfied with the existing electoral system, for in his book on Liberalism he wrote that 'the task of making the House of Commons as fully representative of the people as laws can secure is nearly done', and the remaining reforms which he advocated did not include proportional representation, or even an extension of the franchise.[24]

Another Asquithian, Sir John Simon, also admitted that he was not a tremendous enthusiast for proportional representation, but he thought it very important to have it for the post-war parliament. His main argument was the rather unusual one that at that time cranks and faddists could determine the result in some constituencies and that it was the 'very object' of proportional representation to prevent that, thus enabling big, solid groups of considered opinion to be represented.[25] He voted for it twice, and abstained on four occasions.

---

[22] *HC Deb.* 95 (4 July 1917), 1168–76; 101 (30 Jan. 1918), 1635–7, (6 Feb. 1918), 2364–6; and 106 (13 May 1918), 70–2.

[23] *HC Deb.* (12 June 1917), 820–6. He also spoke on 23 May 1917 and on 6 Feb. 1918. Herbert L. Samuel, 1870–1963. MP, Liberal, 1902–18, and 1929–35. Created Viscount Samuel, 1937. Held many different offices in governments, 1905–Dec. 1916, and 1931–2. Graham Wallas thought Samuel was 'not very clever'. Letter to Halévy, 8 Oct. 1929, quoted by Peter Clarke in *Liberals and Social Democrats* (1978), 253.

[24] Herbert Samuel, *Liberalism: An Attempt to State the Principles and Proposals of Contemporary Liberalism in England* (1902), 254.

[25] *HC Deb.* 95 (4 July 1917), 1233–7.

In the Lords the leading Liberal figures (Crewe, Harcourt, Haldane, Gainford, Buckmaster) viewed proportional representation with varying degrees of distaste and voted against it.

Understandably perhaps, Liberals did not foresee that their party would benefit from proportional representation in the next decade and indeed thereafter. If even half of the Liberals who voted against it in 1917–18 had supported it, proportional representation would have been passed and the fate of the Liberal party would have been rather different, for Liberals have been seriously under-represented in parliament at all general elections except one since 1918. But pre-war conditions led Liberals to neglect proportional representation in favour of the alternative vote as an immediate solution to the electoral problems of the time.

Amongst Labour MPs, there was a solid group of supporters, but others changed their votes repeatedly, partly because they found it difficult to predict what would happen with proportional representation, and felt with Arthur Henderson that the Labour party would be better off with the alternative vote, which was in the bill until the very end. Whilst the bill was going through parliament, a Labour party conference passed a resolution without debate in January 1918 in favour of various electoral reforms including proportional representation through the mechanism of the single transferable vote. This may have affected some Labour votes in parliament, but many Labour MPs did not consider they were bound by the decisions of party conferences. A similar resolution was passed by the Labour party conference of June 1918 after the bill had become an Act in spite of an effort at the conference to delete support for proportional representation.

For some time support by the Irish Nationalists at parliamentary divisions on proportional representation was feeble for a number of different reasons, though the situation had changed by November 1917 when they gave it full support.

Division of opinion on the alternative vote followed party lines very closely, in contrast to views on proportional representation; for the alternative vote was seen by most Liberal and all Labour members as a device to help them in three-cornered contests, whereas Conservatives thought they would suffer from it. These predictions may have been correct at the time, but not necessarily in the long term, as it should not have been assumed that the majority of Liberals would always put Labour rather than Conservative as their second choice.

The proposal on methods of election which was put to parliament by the Speaker's conference was not a revolutionary one (A. J. Balfour considered it 'relatively innocuous'), and not anywhere near as radical as the other recommendations it made which were all accepted. Why then had the advocates of proportional representation failed again? Part of the answer is to be found in the poor quality of many of the arguments they used in putting their case in numerous parliamentary debates on the subject. Some of them indeed pointed out the main defect of the existing first-past-the-post system, namely that it was haphazard and chancy and that it frequently misrepresented the electorate's opinions; but as examples of distortion they usually cited the results in certain areas such as Scotland and Wales, and in some particular towns such as Birmingham and Leeds where one party monopolized the representation. Only a few speakers referred to the national figures to show the lack of proportionality between the votes and seats obtained overall by the political parties, though there were several allusions to exaggerated party majorities, in particular at the general election of 1906. Similarly there were few references to the need to prevent votes being wasted, which many advocates of proportional representation regarded as an important consideration.

A great deal of emphasis was placed on the dangerous situation which would result from the extension of the franchise if 'the minority' were not protected from the proletariat and the passions of the populace. The minority which most speakers had in mind was the propertied classes, employers, the wealthy, the upper layer of society. Proportional representation, they said, would prevent the proletariat, the irrational majority, getting power and would avoid the tyranny of the mob; it would ensure the security of property and the stability of our institutions; it would produce the co-operation of classes instead of conflict. These fears were fanned by the occurrence of the Bolshevik revolution in Russia in November 1917; they were mainly expressed in the Lords, but they were also heard in the

Commons. Thus Lord Hugh Cecil said in June 1917 that he viewed the enfranchisement of eight million electors as 'a very alarming prospect' which without proportional representation might lead to something like anarchy or revolution. He also listed the measures which in his view were disastrous and would not have been passed in recent years with a proper system of representation; these included the 1909 budget, the Parliament Act of 1911, Home Rule for Ireland, and Welsh Church Disestablishment.[26] Some Liberal advocates of proportional representation (such as J. M. Robertson and Aneurin Williams) were naturally disturbed by these arguments for the proposal, as they based their case on the more principled grounds of justice, and they regretted that, by making points such as these, Cecil weakened the force of his efforts to raise the discussion from comparatively unimportant issues on to the theory of representation and tests of political legitimacy.

The trouble with what can be called 'the Conservative case' for proportional representation was that it failed to win over enough Unionists to secure a majority for it in the Commons, and that it also alienated some Liberals and many Labour MPs. Moreover the Conservative case seemed to conflict with the very different argument put forward by some speakers that proportional representation was needed in order that the true strength of Labour should be represented. The idea behind this position seems to have been that there was a danger of disorder or even revolution if the majority of the people were not represented, especially at a time when the work of reconstruction after the war was to be undertaken.

Much was also said about how proportional representation with the single transferable vote would reduce the power of party machines and caucuses, and thus enable differing views in a party to be represented and even independent MPs to be elected. This argument naturally reinforced the already strong opposition of party agents, who saw proportional representation or at least this form of it as a threat to their professional position; and members of the government did not relish the

---

[26] *HC Deb.* 94 (12 June 1917), 836–43. Lord Hugh Cecil, 1869–1952. MP, Conservative, 1895–1906 and Jan. 1910–37. Brother of Lord Robert Cecil. Both were members of the PRS.

idea that the power of the Executive over parliament would be curtailed. Moreover MPs did not like being told that some of them were inadequate and that the prestige of their House was deteriorating, whereas under proportional representation 'the strong man, the honest man, the man who has breadth of vision, and political foresight' would be elected.[27] It was not difficult to ridicule this kind of picture of the salvation of the House of Commons. Ramsay MacDonald put it well when he said, 'A small group of special, superior, selected men, from twelve to twenty of them, sitting below the gangway . . . are going to save this Sodom and Gomorrah from complete destruction.'[28]

Some other inflated claims were made, for example that the country would not be then engaged in a European war if proportional representation had existed in 1910, and the older one that a proportional electoral system would have prevented the Civil War in the USA in the 1860s. It was also claimed that bribery at elections would be reduced or eliminated.

Whilst these parliamentary debates were taking place, a lively correspondence was being conducted in *The Times* by protagonists and opponents of proportional representation; here too most of its advocates did not argue their case by emphasizing that it frequently misrepresented voters' opinions and party sympathies. Thus H. G. Wells recommended proportional representation because it was 'organiser-proof'; he thought great masses of people were 'utterly disgusted with party'; he wanted to help independent men of repute to defeat official candidates put up by caucuses and agents.[29] Earl Grey too claimed that proportional representation would enable men of high character with national ideals to enter the House of Commons; he also criticized the existing electoral system because it had allowed a powerful minister to overthrow the constitution by depriving the House of Lords of its power of veto.[30] Others referred to the unsatisfactory working of the first-past-the-post system in South Africa, Canada, Australia, and the USA. This point probably had little effect; in particular it seems unlikely that the

[27] *HC Deb.* 93 (23 May 1917), Leslie Scott, Unionist, at 2363.
[28] *HC Deb.* 93 (22 May 1917), 2224.
[29] *The Times*, 30 Mar. 1917, 7e.
[30] Ibid. 2 Apr. 1917, 3b.

oft-quoted views of the American President, Garfield, carried much weight, although he had long experience in Congress.

The opponents of changing the electoral system marshalled a vast array of arguments to support their case. The most fundamental one was that it was not necessary or even desirable that the House of Commons should be a mirror of the nation, a sentiment which was put quaintly by Ramsay MacDonald who praised the 'Gothic roughness and peculiarities' of the existing system of representation. 'Democracy', he said, 'does not consist of counting noses.'[31] This was really an attack on the generally accepted theory of representative government, revealing scepticism about its basic premiss, though its proponents did not indicate whether there was any degree of 'unrepresentativeness' or distortion at which they would baulk.

It was however more frequently argued, though without any supporting figures, that the existing system did enable the opinions of the electorate to be reflected fairly accurately in parliament, so that no change was necessary, and that in so far as it did not, the redistribution of seats which was to take place would assist the representation of minorities. It was even said that 'the liberal party were entitled to their majority' in 1906.[32] Other speakers emphasized not the accuracy of the results, but the notion that exaggerated parliamentary majorities were usually returned, and that these were good, as they produced strong government. Wisely they did not discuss the theoretical possibility that the party getting most votes might not get most seats, a situation which some people considered had actually happened in 1874 and 1886 and could happen again.

When the opposition turned from defending the *status quo* to attacking the changes proposed, they put forward a great many objections to proportional representation. Some of them were not deterred by the fact that on their own admission they did not understand the subject. Others made objections which revealed distrust of the efficacy of the change proposed. They claimed that proportional representation would not produce a more proportional parliament; to suggest that it would was

---

[31] *HC Deb.* 93 (22 May 1917), 2230, 2227.
[32] *HC Deb.* 95 (4 July 1917), Walter Long at 1244.

mere conjecture; the majority should govern, but (they alleged) at the bottom of the minds of the advocates was the notion that nothing but a minority ought to be represented; proportional representation would not represent majorities; a minority could elect a majority; it was an unfair system; in particular socialists would be over-represented; the people had a right to say who should govern them and this they would lose with proportional representation.

In contrast to this view, some, indeed many, opponents were afraid that the representation of parties in parliament would be only too exact, with the result that governments would have small majorities; this would make them weak, ineffective, timorous, and vacillating. The legislature would be almost unworkable.

The opposition also stressed that MPs elected under a proportional system would represent particular interests and not principles, or the will of the nation, or great national forces. They would be 'single-issue MPs', and, as had been so much stressed by earlier opponents, cranks, and eccentrics. Parliament would be 'a patchwork quilt', 'a bear garden', as Lord Harcourt so graphically put it.[33]

A great many speakers were certain that, contrary to the views of the advocates of proportional representation, it would not diminish but would increase the power of caucuses and of party machines outside parliament, though they did not explain why, if this was so, it would also, as they feared, introduce cranks and faddists into the House, or why all party agents were strongly opposed to the change. The experiment with the limited vote during the years 1867 to 1885 was cited in support of their contention, as was the use of the cumulative vote for school board elections, though under pressure it was usually admitted that these systems were different from the single transferable vote which was being proposed in 1917. Some objectors also urged that inside parliament, on the other hand, the party system, meaning apparently party discipline, would be weakened; parties would be replaced by groups whose support would shift and be unreliable.

[33] *HL Deb.* 27 (21 Jan. 1918), 845. This was Lewis, 1863–1922. MP, Liberal, 1904–16. Son of Sir William Harcourt, he held various government posts from 1905 to 1916. Created Viscount Harcourt in 1917.

Other objections included the difficulties with which the system would face electors, especially new electors. How could one expect them to understand it if the Prime Minister found it baffling? As late in the debates as May 1918, Austen Chamberlain alleged (wrongly) that voters would have to mark all the names on the ballot paper, which might amount to as many as twenty-five. Several speakers saw serious drawbacks to the increase in the size of constituencies which the system would entail; it would result in great costs and would weaken links between the MP and his constituents. But others considered that if minorities were to be adequately represented one needed larger constituencies than those contemplated, which mainly ranged from three to five MPs; and they were particularly critical of constituencies of four members on the (curious) ground that a place would in effect be unrepresented if two of its MPs belonged to one party and two to another. The problem of by-elections was also mentioned occasionally.

Apart from these specific objections which focused on how the proposed system would allegedly work, more general ones were made. The most important of these was the argument that if the change was desirable, it should be applied to the whole country and even to local authority elections, and not limited to some constituencies, i.e. the larger towns. In particular it was pointed out that it left untouched the areas which were so often mentioned as examples of the deficiencies in the working of the existing system, namely Wales, Scotland, and many of the Home Counties in the south of England. Moreover whilst the bill was being debated certain agricultural organizations argued that their interests would be better protected if proportional representation were introduced in the areas where agriculture predominated.

Other opponents made a very different objection, namely that the scheme should not be forced on to places which were against it, though they did not specify what groups or persons were entitled to give or withhold consent for an area. This objection was particularly effective in the case of London, for whose existing fifty-nine seats proportional representation had been recommended by the Speaker's conference. Early on the majority of both Conservative and Liberal London MPs declared themselves hostile to the proposal. Some of them were probably influenced by the case so passionately put by Lord Eversley, who argued that the quality of London MPs had improved markedly since single-member constituencies were introduced in 1885.[34] In claiming that before 1885 London MPs were not 'distinguished', Eversley seems to have overlooked the fact that they included at various times such figures as Gladstone, Charles Dilke, Goschen, Bryce, Ritchie, W. H. Smith, and J. S. Mill. But the pressure from London MPs was so great that even the parliamentary committee of the PRS decided in June 1917 to accept the exclusion of London from the scheme. This was an unfortunate decision for it did nothing to mollify the London members whilst encouraging MPs for other large cities to discuss proportional representation primarily in terms of their own convenience and to ask for exemption from the scheme. The result was that the debate often deteriorated into pleas not to be experimented on and into offers of sympathy for the places affected—'the victims'. This attitude was commented on adversely by Lord Burnham who said that MPs spoke of their constituencies 'as if they had some private and proprietorial right in them, as if they were to be expropriated from their favourite rabbit-warren'.[35]

The idea that local agreement was necessary became increasingly accepted and was at the root of the final compromise of a Commission which could hold local inquiries and recommend the application of proportional representation in 100 seats. The arguments which ensued subsequently about how much support for a proportional system was revealed by the Commissioners and whose support was relevant illustrate the drawbacks of this method of procedure.

The opposition was able to cite the names of several prominent and diverse politicians of the past in support of their case:

---

[34] See Eversley's letters to *The Times*, 1 June 1917, 9d, and 28 Jan. 1918, 7d. He also sent all MPs a pamphlet emphasizing his long experience of the question. Certainly great changes in the electoral arrangements in London boroughs were made in 1885: instead of 9 constituencies returning two members each under the block vote system, 57 constituencies returned one member each under the first-past-the-post system. This resulted in substantial reductions in the size of constituencies and electorates, which no doubt made them easier to manage. But it is not apparent why this should have improved the calibre of London MPs.

[35] *HL Deb.* 28 (4 Feb. 1918), 415.

Gladstone, Bright, Joseph Chamberlain, and Disraeli were all mentioned. Advocates of proportional representation could not produce a rival list of heavyweights, and they were no doubt wise to refer only occasionally to philosophers. They tried to dispel the host of misconceptions which still existed, despite all the pre-war propaganda, about the reform they proposed; but although some of these misconceptions were genuine and not contrived, the advocates' task was difficult given the vehemence which the subject aroused amongst many opponents, including members of the front bench such as Long, Austen Chamberlain, and Hayes Fisher.

The type of rhetoric which had been evident in earlier debates was still used. 'I am sufficiently of an Englishman to prefer a straightforward stand-up fight, win or lose, a fight fair and square, in which the best man . . . will win, and let the devil take the hindmost', declared Sir Francis Lowe, a Conservative MP for Birmingham, a town where proportional representation would have enabled the substantial number of electors who voted Liberal to procure some representation instead of none since 1886. Birmingham was divided into seven single-member constituencies. In many contests since 1886 the Liberals had secured 30 to 40 per cent of the vote. The power of the opposition's rhetoric is well demonstrated by the fact that in spite of this imbalance Chamberlain and Lowe persuaded the Commons to delete Birmingham from the list of towns to which proportional representation would apply if it were introduced.[36]

The difficulties and horrors which the proposed change would create were painted in lurid colours: it was compared to vivisection, and inspired alarming references to surgeons and quack doctors. It was also said that it would strike a blow at the freedom and liberty enjoyed for so long by the people of this country, which had the most democratic constitution in the world.

Several other factors contributed to the defeat of proportional representation besides the rather poor case put up for it by

---

[36] *HC Deb.* 101 (5 Feb. 1918), 2173–8. Sir Francis Lowe, 1852–1929. MP for Birmingham (Edgbaston), 1898–1929. President of the Birmingham Conservative Association, 1892–1918.

many of its supporters and the barrage of objections expounded with such passion by opponents. The absence of support from the government, especially from the Prime Minister (Lloyd George), was obviously crucial. Indeed towards the end of the controversy, government neutrality turned into opposition.[37] In the final vote on the Commissioners' scheme affecting 100 seats, twenty members of the government voted against it and only nine in favour.

Another material factor was that the PRS was hampered in its activities by a severe decline in membership and funds.[38] The cause also suffered from the deaths of leading members: in 1913 of Lord Avebury, one of its best and most sober advocates, in 1914 of Sir William Anson, the able chairman of the society's parliamentary committee, and in 1917 of the fourth Earl Grey, the society's president. The world tour of the PRS's secretary, Humphreys, did little, if anything, to help the campaign in the United Kingdom, as had been hoped. References to the Tasmanian experiment with the single transferable vote carried little weight in parliament. Moreover, foreign demands on the society which were encouraged by Humphreys' travels overtaxed its strength and resources. Nevertheless some propaganda and pamphlets were sent out in particular to MPs, and the arguments were disseminated through the press, the *Manchester Guardian*, *The Times*, and the *Daily Telegraph* being the main supporters. But the impact of these efforts was probably neutralized by the literature of the Anti-Proportional Representation Committee, an organization formed in 1917 by Conservative and Liberal MPs, especially from London. It concentrated on the disadvantages for both candidates and MPs of having multi-membered constituencies, and the disruption this would cause to existing arrangements and contacts, a much more telling consideration for many MPs than the case for a fair and fully democratic electoral system.

In spite of the ultimate failure to get proportional representation adopted in 1918 even as an experiment for a limited number of seats, its advocates, with their usual resilience, comforted

[37] See speech by the Home Secretary, Sir George Cave, on 30 Jan. 1918, *HC Deb*. 101, 1691–9, and that of Lord Peel, the government spokesman in the Lords, on 21 Jan. 1918, *HL Deb*. 27. 858–66.

[38] See Appendix E.

themselves with the thought that they had come nearer to success than at any time previously, and that the subject had had considerable publicity. They had not expected at the beginning of 1917 that there would be sixteen debates on it in the Commons and more controversy over the electoral system than over the rest of the bill put together. They were naturally pleased that interest in the subject among the public generally or at least among the political nation had been stimulated, though they regretted that the debate had focused so much on detailed difficulties rather than on general principles, such as the essential attributes of representative government and democracy, and on questions about fairness and justice in an electoral system. So, undeterred by the defeat of 1918, the PRS began at once planning its next campaign, buoying itself up with the belief that the advance which the cause had made in public opinion here and in other countries foreshadowed its ultimate triumph.

# IX

# Success and Failure, 1919–1929

DESPITE the setback of 1918, the cause of proportional representation made some progress during the three following years. For the British parliament passed Acts applying it in Ireland to the election of all local authorities and of the parliaments to be set up in both the south and north of that country; in Scotland for all local education authorities; and outside the United Kingdom in Malta and for some constituencies in India.

The impetus to at least some of these developments can curiously enough be traced to the events in a small town in the north-west of Ireland—Sligo. There, as indeed in many other places in Ireland, the more heavily rated citizens found themselves outvoted at local elections, as the Local Government (Ireland) Act of 1898 had broadened the franchise but made no provision for the representation of minorities, a feature of the Act which was criticized by Courtney and Lubbock when the legislation was being passed. So after a time many ratepayers in Sligo ceased trying to obtain representation on the council and merely criticized it from the outside. The local authority laboured under great difficulties: it was heavily in debt and became bankrupt. Its furniture was auctioned, but even so local services could not be maintained: the streets were not swept and the lamps were not lit. The result was the formation of a vigorous Ratepayers Association in which members of the unrepresented minority played a prominent part. They opened negotiations with the council, and it was agreed that a private bill should be promoted increasing the rating powers of the borough and providing for the election of councillors according to the principle of proportional representation, in order to encourage the minority to play a more active part in public affairs. The bill, sponsored by Thomas Scanlan, the Nationalist

MP for Sligo county, was passed without opposition or debate in July 1918.[1] An election was held in January 1919. Over 2,000 electors (73 per cent of the electorate) voted. Only 1 per cent of the voting papers were spoiled as a result of the new voting system (the single transferable vote) although 10 per cent of the electorate was illiterate. Most voters marked second or later preferences, many of them as many as eight, which was the number of candidates to be elected in each of the three wards of the borough. The election resulted in the representation of certain sections of the population who had had little or no representation since 1898.

Within a few weeks of the election in Sligo, several Irish local authorities passed resolutions in favour of proportional representation, and in February 1919 the Chief Secretary for Ireland, Ian Macpherson, announced that the government would introduce a bill applying the system to all Irish local elections. The result was the Local Government (Ireland) Act, passed in June 1919. The supporters of proportional representation were as amazed as they were delighted to see this considerable extension of the system following so quickly on a single experiment, but in fact it did not signify a conversion of the government to the general principle of proportional representation: ministers were simply trying to deal with the particular problems evident in Ireland. The government spokesman (A. W. Samuels) alleged that Sinn Fein intended to break down British rule by capturing local bodies and making local government virtually impossible. Under the existing electoral system, he said, they were able to do this; ratepayers were hardly represented on local authorities which were consequently very extravagant; it was necessary to enable responsible persons with business and commercial interests to serve on them.

The government's scheme was welcomed by southern Unionists and northern Nationalists, and by others on general principles, but was strongly criticized by Ulster Unionists, in particular Charles Craig and Edward Carson who made the astonishing statement that he did not know anybody from Ireland who understood the subject. He too had not got the faintest idea of what proportional representation meant

---

[1] Local and Private Acts, 1918, ch. XXIII.

although he had listened to discussions about it for twenty years or more. The bill was passed in the Commons by 170 votes to 27.[2] In the Lords the government spokesman introducing the bill (Viscount Peel) referred to the peculiar circumstances of Ireland which made it desirable to extend the Sligo experiment to all local authorities, and the Earl of Mayo emphasized the need for respectable and loyal citizens to be represented on these bodies to counteract the influence of republicans.

After the Local Government (Ireland) Act was passed, the Irish PRS took on the task of educating the one-and-a-half million persons who were to vote in municipal elections in January 1920. Funds were raised locally, and donations were received from the British PRS, from its Manchester branch, and from the American Proportional Representation League. Although the country was in a disturbed state and the political situation difficult, lectures were given with illustrative elections in almost all the 126 districts affected, and tens of thousands of explanatory leaflets were distributed. These remarkable efforts bore fruit, for at the municipal elections the turnout averaged 70 per cent with very few spoiled papers. It proved more difficult to conduct a similar campaign in the rural areas where elections were held in June 1920. At these many seats were not contested due to Sinn Fein terrorism, but where constitutional methods prevailed the electoral system secured fair representation.

The government had at the same time to decide what to do about Ireland more generally as the provisions of the Home Rule Act of 1914, suspended on the outbreak of war, were no longer appropriate. Their 'solution' was the Government of Ireland Act, 1920. This measure divided the country into two parts, northern Ireland consisting of six Ulster counties, and southern Ireland consisting of the remaining twenty-six counties. Each was to have its own parliament, made up of a Senate, and a House of Commons the members of which were to be elected according to the principle of proportional representation

---

[2] *HC Deb.* 114 (24 Mar. 1919), 99–183; (31 Mar. 1919), 861–2; (27 May 1919), 1098. Charles Craig was the brother of James Craig, the later Viscount Craigavon. James Craig could not oppose the bill in parliament as he then held a government post.

with the single transferable vote. Most members of the Senate were to be elected on the same principle. This provision followed naturally from the fact that there had been an element of proportional representation in the 1914 Act; and a proportional electoral method was recognized as having a special value for Ireland because of the existence of irreconcilable minorities. The 1920 Act thus followed in this respect the provisions of the Local Government (Ireland) Act, 1919.

The inclusion of proportional representation in the bill of 1920 was opposed in the Commons by the Ulster Unionists who tried without success to get it deleted. Thomas Moles, a Belfast MP, cited many drawbacks to proportional representation and said that it would do little to represent the Unionist minority in the south as they numbered so few. He showed no similar concern for the much larger number of Nationalists in the north.[3] Charles Craig and Carson tried to undermine the government's proposal by challenging them to impose it on themselves and not just on Ireland if they thought so highly of it. Others clothed their opposition with flippancy, sarcasm, and rhetoric. Thus Lt.-Com. Charles Williams, who admitted he could not understand proportional representation, saw it as 'a mild form of amusement which people with nothing better to do indulge in from time to time if they are not particularly strong in their minds'. Beyond that he thought it was 'a very harmless form of pleasure'. Sir J. D. Rees described proportional representation in apocalyptic language as an endeavour of cranks, pressed on the House 'with the most persistent malevolence' by those who are 'determined to reform everything out of its original shape, and to turn everything inside out and upside down . . . It was contrary to the spirit of our elections and constitution.'[4]

In the Lords a further attempt was made to delete proportional representation from the bill. Lord Killanin saw great drawbacks to large constituencies: the local man would have no

[3] The cause of the southern Unionists was also pressed by others, supporters of proportional representation from English constituencies (Lord Hugh Cecil, J. W. Hills, J. Pennefather, and W. E. Guinness) who wanted larger constituencies in Southern Ireland.

[4] *HC Deb.* 130 (15 June 1920), 1164–93, and 134 (10 Nov. 1920), 1240–44, Williams's remarks are at 1202–4 on 15 June, and 1243 on 10 Nov.; Rees's are at 1243 on 10 Nov. Both were Conservatives from English constituencies.

chance of election; only sheer party men, extreme politicians, would get elected. Lord Clifford of Chudleigh, speaking from Australian experience, made the curious statement that proportional representation represented neither minorities nor majorities. The Marquess of Dufferin and Ava was very frank, saying that 'We in the north who are a majority do not like proportional representation'. This was undoubtedly true, but he was less accurate when he said that 'No Irishman has ever asked for it, and there is absolutely no demand for it'. The case for leaving proportional representation in the bill was put with force by Lords Parmoor and Selborne, who both stressed that experience in Ireland and elsewhere belied the opposition's view that the system could not work satisfactorily because it was complicated. The government spokesman, the Earl of Crawford, spoke with less conviction, but succeeded in preventing the deletion of proportional representation from the bill.[5]

The opposition tried also to secure that the Irish parliaments could alter the electoral system after one year had elapsed, instead of the three years prescribed in the bill. Others recommended a much longer period, even ten years. The government relented to the extent of proposing six years so that two elections would be held before the system was altered. This was turned down on a free vote. Six was reinstated by the Lords, but they ultimately gave way to an adamant Lower House; so three years remained.[6]

In southern Ireland, the Government of Ireland Act, 1920, was a dead letter. At the election of May 1921 which was to create a parliament in Dublin, Sinn Fein prevented contests in all constituencies except Dublin University, and returned 124 Sinn Feiners unopposed. Proportional representation therefore only operated in the election of the University members. They alone turned up for the meeting of parliament which was adjourned indefinitely. Throughout this time, the period of the 'troubles', the Irish Republican Army and the British were at war with each other. During the negotiations which culminated in

---

[5] *HL Deb.* 42 (2 Dec. 1920), 928–38. Dufferin and Ava's remarks are at 934.
[6] *HC Deb.* 134 (10 Nov. 1920), 1240–4; 136 (16 Dec. 1920), 808–26. *HL Deb.* 42 (2 Dec. 1920), 928–41; 43 (13 Dec. 1920), 54–8; (17 Dec. 1920), 400–22.

December 1921 in the Anglo-Irish Treaty, leaders of both the independence movement in Ireland and the British government were committed to proportional representation. Arthur Griffith, the leader of the Irish plenipotentiaries, had been a founder member of the Irish PRS, so he was willing to promise that the single transferable vote system would be used in the future independent state to secure, as the British government wished, full representation for the Protestant and Unionist minority in the Irish parliament. The result was that proportional representation for both Houses of the legislature was included in the constitution of the Irish Free State which was produced by a Constituent Assembly in Ireland and ratified by the British parliament in the Irish Free State Constitution Act, 1922. There was, it seems, no discussion in Ireland about the inclusion of proportional representation in the settlement: it was just accepted both as correct in principle and as a means of conciliating the southern Unionists. Already in June 1922 elections to the third Dail Eireann, the self-constituted Irish parliament, had been held under a proportional system which has continued to operate ever since. A proposal to substitute the simple majority system for proportional representation has twice been put to the people of Eire in a referendum and twice rejected—in 1959 and 1968. It is not altogether fanciful to see the history of proportional representation in southern Ireland as the outcome in some small part of the visit paid by Courtney to Dublin in 1911.

In Northern Ireland the history of the issue has been very different. At the first elections of the fifty-two members of their House of Commons held in May 1921, proportional representation was in operation. There were ten constituencies of four to eight members each. The method of selecting candidates was fairly democratic, and they were chosen by the party associations to represent as far as possible the different forces within the party. This had always been one of the subsidiary goals of the advocates of proportional representation. All seats were contested and the poll was high, averaging 89 per cent. Only 1 per cent of the voting papers were invalid. The supporters of proportional representation regarded the election as a success for the system, although on a strict mathematical criterion the

Unionists with 40 seats were slightly over-represented and the Nationalists, including Sinn Fein, with 12 seats were slightly under-represented. This was due to the small number of members to be elected in some constituencies.

Another general election with proportional representation was held for the parliament of Northern Ireland in 1925. Electors were able to choose between candidates within a party and did so. Seventy-seven per cent of the electorate went to the poll and less than 2 per cent of the votes were invalid. Supporters of the electoral system were pleased with the results which showed almost exact proportionality between votes and seats: thirty-two Official Unionists were returned, ten Nationalists, four Independent Unionists, three Labour representatives, and one independent.

But the experiment with proportional representation in Northern Ireland was not to last. The Prime Minister, Sir James Craig, had always been hostile to it. His government therefore soon abolished the use of proportional representation in local elections. In introducing into the Northern Ireland House of Commons in 1922 a bill to effect this, the government spokesman, Robert Megaw, argued that the great changes in the membership of local councils which had been prophesied by the doctrinaires who were responsible for the Local Government (Ireland) Act, 1919, had not materialized: the local bodies elected under proportional representation were no better than their predecessors. He laid considerable stress on the disadvantages of large constituencies and alleged that the system was not generally understood. It was only suitable for academic constituencies because university people were trained in allotting percentages and marks at competitive exams. 'So', he added mockingly, 'the study of the various points of the candidates would give them pleasurable excitement.' There was some opposition to the bill on the ground that it had been rushed and that the block vote system which was to replace proportional representation could prevent a minority as large as 42 per cent of the electorate having any say in the management of anything. But the only two MPs who spoke against the bill (W. T. Miller and T. Donald) admitted that there were defects in the existing arrangements.

In the Northern Irish Senate, the government spokesman,

Lord Londonderry, denied that minorities received the protection which they believed they would get under 'the specious arguments of advocates of proportional representation'. The people of Northern Ireland had not wanted the Act of 1919 which was forced on them to meet circumstances which existed elsewhere. (He clearly had Southern Ireland in mind.) What was considered good enough for Ireland was not considered good enough for Great Britain. The system was excessively costly and difficult for electors and officials, criticisms agreed to by members of the Senate who were in principle in favour of proportional representation. The Local Government (Northern Ireland) Bill, 1922, therefore went through quickly and easily.[7]

The lack in 1922 of any considerable opposition to the abolition of a proportional system for local government elections in Northern Ireland was due to the fact that most members of the opposition parties had refused to take their seats in parliament as a protest against partition. Later, after they had relented, and seen the results of abolition, they tried to get proportional representation restored for local government, bringing in a bill to effect this in 1928. They argued that since the electoral system had been changed, the representation of labour, Nationalists, and independents on local councils had declined; the party in power in the government was so strong, it could afford to be fair to minorities who were treated in Northern Ireland with less consideration than minorities in India; it was dangerous for the government thus to perpetuate old passions instead of trying to gain the confidence and co-operation of all sections of the community. Government supporters, in opposing the bill, said that proportional representation worked badly where it had been tried, in New South Wales, Europe, and the Irish Free State, and they made much of the fact that it had been turned down by the Labour party in Great Britain in 1924. The vote went inevitably against the bill.[8]

The government of Northern Ireland had been determined from the start also to abolish proportional representation for elections to their parliament, but they delayed doing this until

[7] Northern Ireland Parliamentary Debates. *HC Deb.* 2 (26 June 1922), 829–52. *Sen. Deb.* 2 (3 July 1922), 198–212. The quotation from Megaw is at 831, and from Londonderry at 210.

[8] *NI HC Deb.* 9 (24 Apr. 1928), 958–1014.

1929. The question had been debated in their House of Commons in 1925 and at great length in 1927, when those against abolition tried without success to get a select committee appointed to determine whether the government had the legal authority to set aside the provisions of the Government of Ireland Act, 1920, which they clearly had.[9]

When introducing into the Northern Irish parliament in 1929 the bill to substitute the first-past-the-post system for the single transferable vote, except for Belfast University, the government hardly bothered to argue the case for abolition of proportional representation. The Prime Minister, Viscount Craigavon, simply asserted that 'There has been for a long time a general desire throughout the whole of Ulster to get rid of that horrible system of proportional representation', and he professed not to understand why the British government had adopted it for Ireland in 1920. The Attorney-General, A. B. Babington, said that the system besides being cumbersome and complicated was unfair to the electorate because often MPs represented the people on one point only. He also made the trivial objection that with multi-membered constituencies it was difficult to know how to refer to MPs in parliament, as the convention was to speak of them as the Hon. Member for a certain place.

In the long Commons debates on the bill, which occupy 280 columns in Hansard, only four MPs spoke on the government's side, for it was clear the measure would be passed however much it was criticized. This it certainly was and with tremendous passion and bitterness by no less than seventeen different MPs. They demonstrated that it was misleading to say, as the government did, that 'the country' had asked for the abolition of proportional representation, since it was liked by Nationalists, Labour, and Independent Unionists. They alleged that the Prime Minister wanted only two parties, the Unionists and the Nationalists, denying representation to Labour and independents. This was true, as speaking on the 238th anniversary of the Battle of the Boyne in 1928, Craigavon said: 'I say most solemnly, there is no room for a third party in Ulster politics. We live on too narrow a majority.'[10] At the back

[9] *NI HC Deb.* 6 (21 Apr. 1925), 143–50; 8 (12 Oct. 1927), 1938–40; (25 Oct. 1927), 2253–2306; (26 Oct. 1927), 2307–68.

[10] Quoted by S. R. Daniels in *The Case for Electoral Reform* (1928), 96.

of Craigavon's mind was probably the fear that proportional representation might, through its complications, trick electors into making a mistake, resulting in the end of the partition of Ireland.[11] The opposition foretold, with some justification as it turned out, that the abolition of proportional representation would encourage sectarianism by dividing the country along religious lines. They considered that the government should be satisfied with the large, unbeatable majority which the existing electoral system provided for it. The only motive for changing it, they said, must therefore be a desire to stamp out independent thought in parliament; the government had initially asked for their co-operation in solving the province's serious economic and industrial problems, but this was not the way to obtain informed advice or to diminish animosity; on the contrary denying them the representation they were entitled to would encourage unconstitutional, even revolutionary, behaviour.

The Prime Minister and Attorney-General had supported their case by quoting Ramsay MacDonald, who may thus paradoxically have contributed to the under-representation of Labour in Northern Ireland. The opposition countered by quoting Lord Birkenhead, L. S. Amery, and others, and by pointing out that several prominent British Labour politicians were in favour of proportional representation.[12]

In a brief debate in the Senate, which did not contain one Roman Catholic amongst its twenty-six members, the bill was justified on the ground that 'the country' had asked for the change; the system in operation was complicated and not easily understood by many electors; constituencies were too large, a complaint which was justified in the case of the counties of Fermanagh and Tyrone which together formed one constituency returning eight members. Only one senator, Robert Dorman, opposed the bill, stressing that the majority system would encourage inherited prejudices and passions, and religious animosities; Labour in particular would suffer, as it had

---

[11] This is suggested by St John Ervine in his book *Craigavon: Ulsterman* (1949), 516–17.

[12] *NI HC Deb.* 10 (5 Mar. 1929), 427–53; Craigavon's remark is at 433; (6 Mar. 1929), 505–59; (7 Mar. 1929), 577–650; (21 Mar. 1929), 1143–1200; (27 Mar. 1929), 1505–76.

in Belfast after the abolition of proportional representation for local elections.[13]

The government's aims in abolishing proportional representation were fulfilled at the general election of 1929 which substantially reduced the representation of the smaller parties—Independent Unionist, Labour, and Liberal—giving them seven too few seats in relation to their votes in contested constituencies. The Official Unionists secured 37 seats (five too many), and the Nationalists eleven (two too many). Barely half the constituencies were contested.[14]

Meanwhile the single transferable vote had made progress in another quarter, namely Scottish Education Authorities. Elections to Scottish school boards were still conducted under the cumulative vote (introduced in 1872) although it had not operated for English education authorities since 1902. Advocates of proportional representation, whilst preferring the cumulative vote to the simple majority system, had for many years tried to get the cumulative vote replaced by the single transferable vote. The PRS had had a strong branch in Scotland since 1907 with Lord Balfour of Burleigh as president, and some of the larger school boards had passed resolutions in favour of the single transferable vote. Little surprise therefore was expressed when in June 1918 the government inserted this electoral system into its bill reorganizing the administration of education in Scotland on a wider basis than the parish. The Secretary of State, Robert Munro, pointed out that the cumulative vote sometimes over-represented minorities, but considered that their interests would not be adequately protected by the simple majority system, whereas they would be by the single transferable vote. There was no opposition in parliament to the change.[15] Elections were held under the new electoral system four times, at three-yearly intervals between 1919 and 1928. It achieved its main purpose of fair representation of religious opinions, and ensured that few votes were wasted. But criticisms arose: in

[13] *NI Sen. Deb.* 10 (4 Apr. 1929), 109–38; (10 Apr. 1929), 153–6.
[14] Figures taken from James Knight and Nicholas Baxter-Moore, *Northern Ireland: The Elections of the Twenties* (1972).
[15] *HC Deb.* 107 (26 June 1918), 1078–9. Balfour of Burleigh (A. H. Bruce), 1849–1921. Secretary of State for Scotland, 1895–1903.

particular it was said to be confusing for electors to have to work two different systems, marking their ballot papers with a cross when voting for local authorities generally, and putting names in order of preference when voting for education authorities. The experiment ended in 1928 when local education authorities in Scotland ceased to be elected separately, their powers being transferred to County Councils.

At the UK general election of December 1918, the parties supporting a continuation of the wartime coalition government of Lloyd George won vastly more seats than their voting strength warranted, and the other parties, particularly Labour and Asquithian Liberals, were correspondingly under-represented.[16] This naturally stimulated highly critical comments from supporters of proportional representation. The PRS annual report for 1918–19 considered that the election showed the 'utter failure of the present system'. Different people produced different figures to illustrate what they saw as distortion in the results. Thus the journal *Representation* considered that the coalition got a majority of 414 instead of about 114, and Sir Donald Maclean, the chairman of the parliamentary Liberal party, calculated that in Great Britain the coalition parties got one seat for every 13,000 votes, Labour one seat for every 48,000 votes, and the Independent Liberals one seat for every 51,000 votes. However it was encouraging to the proportionalists that the press devoted far greater attention than ever before to a comparison of the votes recorded with the number of seats gained by the various parties.

During the next five years (1919–24) the PRS, at any rate in its annual reports, remained optimistic about ultimate victory. They were encouraged by developments in Ireland and in the world generally, especially in Europe where proportional representation had been included in many of the constitutions

[16] There are many complications involved in presenting the statistics for this election in particular, but there can be no doubt that the general picture is as stated. F. W. S. Craig in his *British Election Statistics 1918–1970* (1971) gives the coalition parties 47 per cent of the votes and 67 per cent of the seats; and the Independent Liberals 13 per cent of the votes and 5 per cent of the seats. These figures tally substantially with D. and G. Butler's *British Political Facts 1900–1985* (1986).

introduced after the war, though they regretted that these adopted party list systems rather than the single transferable vote. They noted with pleasure that various non-governmental bodies such as the Church of England and some trade unions were using the single transferable vote for their own elections. The society maintained a high level of activity, issuing many pamphlets and leaflets and organizing hundreds of public meetings every year all over the country, assisted by their local branches which existed in several important towns.

Support for proportional representation at this time also came from women's organizations. Before 1918 several advocates of women's rights and particularly of votes for women were also advocates of proportional representation, such as Mill, Courtney, Henry and Millicent Fawcett, but the two movements were not interconnected, and it was quite common to believe in one of these causes but not in the other. In any case the women's suffrage organizations were not concerned with the electoral system, as they were not pressing the case for women MPs. On the contrary they attempted to calm the fears of opponents by forecasting a long interval after the franchise was granted before women stood for parliament. (The Law Officers regarded it as part of the Common Law that women were not eligible to become MPs.) However soon after women aged 30 and over got the vote, a statute was passed in November 1918 enabling them to sit in parliament. Mrs Fawcett immediately and successfully urged the appropriate women's organization, the National Union of Societies for Equal Citizenship, to include proportional representation as one of its objects in order to help women to get into parliament, and since then other societies such as the National Council of Women and the Women's Freedom League, disappointed by the small number of women candidates and the even smaller number of women MPs, have backed proportional representation. They thought that when a local party had to find candidates for a constituency returning several members instead of just one, it would probably include a woman amongst them so as to appeal to as many kinds of electors as possible, and the subsequent experience of countries with proportional electoral systems does suggest that these give women a better chance of political success than the single-member constituency system. Thus even in the late 1970s, only 3 per cent of UK MPs were women, and 4 per cent in the USA Congress, whereas in all countries with proportional systems the percentage was higher, amounting in some cases to nearly a quarter.

The women's lobby was not powerful, but the advocates of proportional representation were encouraged by the feeling that the cause was gaining support among the general public and that it had some sympathizers in the coalition government; so they renewed their attack on parliament with the aim of changing the electoral system used in parliamentary and local elections. Soon after the general election of 1918, the government was regularly asked about its intentions on electoral reform; the answer was invariably that it had none, and no bill providing for the single transferable vote in parliamentary elections secured a second reading until April 1921 when a debate was held on one introduced by the Independent Liberal Sir Thomas Bramsdon.[17] For several months beforehand the PRS set about preparing the ground carefully. Two thousand circular letters were sent to every sort of influential person and institution. A deputation to the Prime Minister (Lloyd George) was elaborately organized, though it did not take place. The help of the national press was secured with a model election in which 35,000 ballot papers were returned. Another model election was held in the Commons, 350 MPs taking part. All this activity led the Anti-PR committee which had existed in 1917–18 to revive itself and to organize determined opposition.

In parliament supporters of Bramsdon's bill (from all parties) put the traditional arguments for proportional representation, but they also introduced a new note of urgency into the debate by emphasizing the danger of 'direct action', i.e. various forms of allegedly unconstitutional behaviour by the labour and trade union movements. There had been acute industrial unrest since the war ended and recurrent threats of a general strike. An alarming coal strike had started a week before the debate. Some MPs (and not only Conservatives) therefore argued that proportional representation, by producing a properly representative parliament, would restore respect for constitutional government

---

[17] Sir Thomas Bramsdon, 1857–1935. MP, Portsmouth, Liberal, May–Oct. 1900, 1906–Jan. 1910, 1918–22, and 1923–4. He was a solicitor with many public interests and appointments, local and national.

and discourage irregular extra-parliamentary activities. It was also pointed out that just as the existing electoral system had given the coalition government an unwarranted majority, it might do the same for the Labour party, a 'false' situation not welcomed even by some Labour supporters.

The opposition spokesmen, who were all Conservative except for one coalition Liberal, mounted wide-ranging arguments against the bill. They said the electorate had not been consulted and that there was no public demand for the change; large constituencies would pose problems and be expensive for candidates, particularly young ones; governments would not have adequate majorities in parliament; there would be frequent general elections, even every three weeks; the power of cau-cuses would be strengthened; the nineteenth-century experi-ment with the limited vote had not been a success; the proposed system would not produce a representative House of Commons; this could only be obtained by making the whole country one constituency, as advocated by Thomas Hare, and that was a ridiculous idea, favoured only by cranks, doctrinaires, and pedants. Some of the opponents drew on the political philo-sophy of Edmund Burke to support their case: the test of any political institution, they said, was not logic but expediency and the way it worked in actual practice; one should not apply philosophic or abstract notions, such as proportionality, to political machinery.

The government, admitting that it was divided on the ques-tion, did not put on the whips, but made no promise to facilitate the passage of the bill, should it be accepted. It was however defeated by 186 votes to 87.[18] If pairs are included, the parties divided as follows:[19]

|                       | For | Against |
| --------------------- | --- | ------- |
| Conservative          | 34  | 176     |
| Coalition Liberal     | 31  | 24      |
| Independent Liberal   | 20  | 4       |
| Labour                | 25  | 5       |
|                       | 110 | 209     |

[18] *HC Deb.* 140 (8 Apr. 1921), 613–92.
[19] Source: *Representation*, July 1921.

The PRS considered these figures showed that proportional representation was not a party issue, because although the opposition consisted almost entirely of members of the coalition, coalitionalists also constituted the major part of those who voted for the bill. But in fact the voting suggests that opinion amongst Conservatives was swinging against proportional representation and amongst Liberals in favour of it, thus foreshadowing future party alignments on the issue.

At the general election of November 1922, held on the break up of the coalition, proportional representation was included in the Independent Liberal manifesto, thus appearing for the first time in a party programme. The results of the election were thought by some to strengthen the case for electoral reform, as one party (the Conservatives) was over-represented, and others, particularly Labour and Independent Liberal, were under-represented, and a single-party (Conservative) government was formed with only 38 per cent of the vote.[20] But there was no wide public concern about the results; and the Labour party was more impressed by the fact that it had greatly increased its representation in parliament (from about 60 to 142) than by the overall lack of proportionality between votes and seats. Moreover opinion in the Labour party was hardening towards a desire to weaken or even destroy the Liberals, and was seeing more and more clearly that proportional representation would impede this objective.

Pressure to change the system by which local government councils were elected ran concurrently with activity about parliamentary elections. In the sessions of 1919, 1920, and 1921, bills giving local authorities (counties, boroughs, and urban districts) the option of being elected by proportional representation passed in the House of Lords with no opposition. Parmoor pointed out that many very important local authorities

[20] The PRS calculated that in contested seats, except universities, the Conservatives got 88 too many, the Independent Liberals 47 too few, and Labour 26 too few (PRS Annual Report 1922–3). The secretary of the society, Humphreys, in his book on the election, pointed out that a minority of votes (5½ million out of 14 million) obtained a majority of seats (J. H. Humphreys, *Practical Aspects of Electoral Reform: A Study of the General Election, 1922* (1923)).

in all parts of the country supported the proposal, and both he and Monteagle drew attention to the successful conduct of municipal elections in Ireland with the single transferable vote in 1920. The Minister of Health (Addison) and his parliamentary secretary (Viscount Astor) were in favour of the bill partly because they thought proportional representation would improve the calibre of local councillors, on whom a great deal of extra work had been placed; but the government withdrew its offer of support when it discovered that the bill would be opposed in the Commons.[21]

A further attempt was made in 1923 to get a similar bill through the Commons. The mover was a new National Liberal MP, Harold Morris, KC.[22] The parliamentary debate illustrates some of the problems confronting advocates of proportional representation. They gave many examples of the anomalies which resulted from the system under which local authorities were elected (often the block vote), pointing out that it was exceedingly capricious: a small swing in votes could result in a large and misleading change in seats; at times it gave power to a minority; at other times it failed altogether to represent, or grossly under-represented, substantial minorities. Referring to John Stuart Mill they pressed that arguments and views, even if unpopular, extreme, revolutionary, or reactionary, should be exposed to the test of contact with other points of view through representation on elected bodies where they could be dealt with. They pointed out that experience in Ireland and Malta showed that electors were able to cope with the single transferable vote system: the 'Chinese puzzle' objection, they averred, had been killed.

But these arguments carried little weight against the emotive rhetoric of those who objected to the bill. One MP, Gerald Hurst, (of German origin) declared that it 'subverted one of the historic and traditional aspects of our constitutional system', in existence since the time of Edward I. Another, Sir Henry Craik, considered that a man should be wedded to one constituency, which he thought impossible under a proportional system. 'The

---

[21] *HL Deb.* 35 (3 July 1919), 188–94; 39 (2 Mar. 1920), 160–4; 40 (9 June 1920), 569–72; 44 (24 Feb. 1921), 161. *HC Deb.* 131 (8 July 1920), 1653.

[22] Harold Spencer Morris, 1876–1967. MP, National Liberal, 1922–3.

bond is a more sacred one', he said, 'a more satisfactory one in every way, just as in the conjugal relationship.' Yet another, R. W. Barnett, said the bill 'upset a very good, old sound British principle which you have got on the turf and in many other things in life—"the first past the post the winner".' The historian Sir Charles Oman, obviously thinking more about national than local government, quoted the Duke of Wellington and feared it would be impossible to carry on His Majesty's Government if the change were made. Coalitions, he added, were undesirable because their members would have to sacrifice some of their views of what was right and wrong. Other MPs raised once again the bogy of cranks: flat-earth men would decide elections; proportional representation aimed to disfranchise majorities; it was an artificial scheme. Reference was also made to the 'disastrous failure' of the 1867–85 experiment (with the limited vote). The most valid criticism of the bill was that complications might result if one electoral system was used for some local elections and not for others in the same area. The Home Secretary (Bridgeman) for some strange reason thought that it would be very difficult for the government to prescribe the method of voting and to ensure that it was understood by electors even after affirmation, which was not in fact proposed.[23] The bill was defeated, though only narrowly (169 votes to 157) on a free vote. The Conservatives who voted were divided 155 to 25 against it; Labour members favoured it by 69 to 11.

No further bills concerning the election of local authorities were introduced in parliament in the 1920s, but the PRS submitted memoranda to the Royal Commission on London Government in 1923 and to the Royal Commission on Local Government in 1927 and 1929 urging the reform. They gave many examples of what they considered extraordinary results, which often showed little correspondence between the composition of the electorate and that of the elected council, whereas, they argued, the idea of proportionality was implicit in the word 'representation' itself. They also stressed that proportional

[23] *HC Deb.* 160 (23 Feb. 1923), 1429–1520. Second reading of the Local Elections (Proportional Representation) Bill. Hurst's remark is at 1441, Craik's at 1468, and Barnett's at 1479.

representation would result in an improved quality of councillors. Neither commission recommended the change, but in 1923
two commission members (Robert Donald and Stephen Walsh)
submitted a minority report in favour of the election of all local
authorities in London including the London County Council by
proportional representation.[24]

Opponents of proportional representation had another opportunity in 1923 to put their case during debates on a bill providing
for the use of the alternative vote in single-member constituencies. The bill was introduced in both the Commons and the
Lords. It was defeated in the Commons on first reading by 208
votes to 178. There was some cross-voting, but it was in the
main a straight fight between a Conservative majority against
and a Labour and Liberal minority for the bill. In the Lords
there was no vote as the bill was withdrawn after debate. In the
Commons Gerald Hurst said that no elector wanted to express
a second choice and he denounced 'the alternative vote and
other methods of gerrymandering'. In the Lords Viscount Long
revealed the wide and unbridgeable gap between the advocates
of a change and defenders of the *status quo* when reflecting on
the working and essence of representative government. Thus
he admitted that the government, like others before, had not
obtained at the last election (1922) 'what is called a majority of
the electorate' which was, he said, anyway unattainable in
existing conditions; indeed he did not want 'a majority of
electors as a whole' to be represented, or for a party 'in an
absolute minority' to obtain representation; it was sufficient if a
government represented, as it necessarily did, the particular
group which was in the majority; the existing system usually
produced a government with a strong majority behind it.
Viscount Peel, speaking for the government, saw nothing
wrong in a candidate being returned without an absolute
majority: it was the verdict of the constituency.

The debate also revealed a weakening in the ranks of members of the PRS. For the bill was introduced in the Lords by
Lord Beauchamp, a vice-president of the society which believed

[24] PP 1923 XII. Part I. Report of Royal Commission on London Government,
771.

in the single transferable and not in the alternative vote. Moreover Beauchamp said that the existing system was excellent when there were only two parties. The bill was also supported by Earl Grey, the president of the PRS, who apparently thought that the alternative vote would produce fair and adequate representation of the real opinions of the country.[25] Discussion about the aims and results of the two systems—the alternative vote and proportional representation—was later carried on in *The Times*, Lady Courtney being critical of those who thought the alternative vote would produce greater proportionality in the representation of parties over the whole country.[26]

At the general election of December 1923, the state of opinion amongst the electorate was reflected in parliament much more closely than at the 1922 election, though on strict mathematical calculations the Conservative and Labour parties were slightly over-represented and the Liberals rather under-represented in the light of the votes received. But the striking thing about the election was that it appeared to illustrate the haphazard nature of the electoral system: for whilst the three main parties each retained about the same percentage of the total votes as they had secured in 1922, their representation in parliament changed substantially. Thus the Conservatives lost 88 seats, Labour gained 49, and the reunited Liberals gained 44. It has been argued forty years later by a leading psephologist that these figures are very deceptive and that they do not warrant the view that our electoral system is a complete gamble;[27] but at the time a simpler interpretation was put on them by advocates of proportional representation. Whatever the truth of this matter, the election undoubtedly showed something else, viz. that the existing electoral system did not always produce a clear majority for one party and 'strong' government, as many of its supporters from Bagehot onwards had frequently contended. For although

[25] *HC Deb.* 161 (7 Mar. 1923), 501–4; *HL Deb.* 53 (20 Mar. 1923), 413–39. Long's speech is at 417–22.
[26] *The Times*, 7 Dec. 1923, 17d, and 13 Dec. 1923, 17d. Lady Courtney was the widow of Leonard Courtney.
[27] D. E. Butler, *The Electoral System in Britain since 1918* (2nd edn., 1963), 175–8.

the Conservatives with 258 MPs were still the largest party in the Commons, they had not got a majority over the other parties, and a Labour government was formed with only 191 MPs in a House of 625. It survived with Liberal support for ten months.

Proportional representation had not been included in the Liberal manifesto of 1923, published over the signatures of Asquith and Lloyd George. It seems clear that Lloyd George would not have agreed to its inclusion. He was by this time not quite as ignorant about it, and hostile to it, as he had been earlier, but his support was still only lukewarm. Thus he refused in April 1923 an invitation to speak at the annual meeting of the PRS; in 1924 he said he believed in the second ballot; and as late as 1926 he was still making rather hostile remarks about proportional representation.[28] Nevertheless some Liberals thought that their support of the Labour government should be conditional on the introduction of proportional representation; but there was never any possibility of such a bargain being struck when the government was being formed. If the Liberal party had tried to make conditions for their support, it seems certain that this would have been refused by Labour. For feeling in the Labour party was overwhelmingly against not only coalition or alliance, but any compromise with the Liberals. In addition they were irritated by Asquith's patronizing attitude as exemplified by his remark (as early as December 1923) that whatever party was in office, it was the Liberal party who really controlled the situation. Indeed not only was Labour determined to avoid the Liberal embrace; some of them hoped to destroy the Liberals and to return to a two-party system; so they constantly stressed the unbridgeable gap between the party of socialism and any capitalist party. On the Liberal side, the party accepted Asquith's advice, given soon after the election, not to compromise or fetter itself by making any agreement with the Labour government, and it repeatedly declared its independence. Moreover, the Liberal party was divided about the urgency of electoral reform, the tactics by which it should be secured, and the form it should take, viz. proportional representation or the alternative vote.

---

[28] Lady Courtney to John Fischer Williams, 14 Apr. 1923; *Manchester Guardian*, 12 Sept. 1924; and JFW to Lady C., 16 Jan. 1926.

There was however a breach in the Liberals' uncompromising policy of independence when a bill providing for proportional representation was introduced by one of their back-benchers, Athelstan Rendall.[29] Two days before its second reading on 2 May 1924, the parliamentary Liberal party indicated their hope that in return for Liberal support of the budget, the government would assist the passage of the bill. But Labour members were incensed by what they saw as an ultimatum and refused to bargain. They decided by a large majority at a special meeting of the parliamentary party that the bill should be left to a free vote (in spite of the fact that the cabinet had recommended them to support it), and that no facilities for the bill should be afforded by the government if it passed a second reading (which it did not).[30]

It is difficult to know whether many Liberals were seriously intending to threaten withdrawal of support for the government unless they obtained proportional representation. This seems unlikely, as they did not at that time want to bring the government down; they wished to continue criticizing it severely, whilst exercising great care not to vote it out of office. What is certain is that the incident worsened the already strained relations between the two parties.

In the parliamentary debate on Rendall's bill, speakers for it argued that the existing system was not based on democratic principles and was 'a chapter of accidents'; it was absurd to go to the great trouble and expense of a general election only to produce chancy and inaccurate results; it was even possible for a minority in the country to obtain a majority of the seats; strong government with a good working majority was admittedly desirable, but only if it had a majority of electors behind it. Asquith confessed that he had changed his views. 'I started with every conceivable prepossession and prejudice against it [proportional representation]', he said. 'I have repeated, in my own unregenerate days, the Philistine formula of Sir William Harcourt, that the only right of a minority is to turn itself into a

[29] Representation of the People Act (1918) Amendment (No. 2) Bill, 1924. Athelstan Rendall, 1871–1948. A country solicitor. MP, Liberal, 1906–22, and 1923–4. He described himself as 'an advanced radical'. He was a member of the Fabian Society and in 1925 joined the Labour party.

[30] *The Times*, 1 and 2 May 1924. Parliamentary correspondent's reports.

majority.' But he had learnt from observation and experience, and now thought that no substantial minority should be left without representation. The fate of his group of Independent Liberals since the general election of 1918 was clearly uppermost in his mind, but in fact his attitude had already been changing in 1917–18. The case for proportional representation was on the whole put in more sober terms than sometimes in the past, though some speakers were still throwing in points in its favour other than the need for proportionality. Thus they argued that it would assist leaders, and men of value to their parties and the state, to remain in political life instead of being thrown out as a result of 'wobblers' in their constituencies. The Conservative supporters of the bill (Amery and Samuel Roberts) made it clear, rather tactlessly, that they were concerned to ward off the danger of a Labour government obtaining power, particularly if it was supported by only a minority of voters.

The opposition to the bill was led by the curious combination of the Duchess of Atholl (not yet in her 'red' phase) and Herbert Morrison who was then a new back-bench Labour MP.[31] One of the Duchess's objections to proportional representation was that, contrary to what was often said by its advocates, it would not assist women candidates, because of the fatigue caused by electioneering in large constituencies. Morrison considered that on the whole the present position did secure representative government; public opinion could always bring effective pressure on the government; though at the same time he wanted government to be strong; indeed he preferred a bad government if strong and logical to one that 'wobbled'; proportional representation would result in coalition government which, involving as it did the coming together of opinions which were really antagonistic, was contrary to democracy. Other speakers too hoped that the country would return to the two-party system or at least to exaggerated majorities; proportional representation

[31] Duchess of Atholl, Kathleen Stewart-Murray, 1874–1960. MP, Conservative, 1923–38. Held government office, 1924–9. She was known in the 1930s as 'the Red Duchess' because of her passionate opposition to the government's foreign policy. Herbert Morrison, 1888–1965. MP, Labour, 1923–4, 1929–31, and 1935–59. Morrison's hostility to proportional representation may have been due to the fact that he was a protégé and admirer of MacDonald's; it was not weakened by some odd results in local and parliamentary London elections.

besides all its other disadvantages would perpetuate three parties.

Arthur Henderson speaking for the government said that a free vote would be allowed, but that the government would not give the bill further facilities or bring in one of its own; for the question had not been put to the electorate; the parties were divided on the issue; and it had been turned down by the Commons previously on several occasions. He admitted that the government was not satisfied with the present situation, but he thought it was difficult to ensure that any new system would not perpetuate some of the worst anomalies of the existing one. Obviously worried that the Liberals would make proportional representation a condition of their support, he promised that the government would not lose sight of the question.[32]

The bill was then defeated by 238 votes to 144. There was a more clear-cut party division than ever before. The figures were:

|  | For | Against |
|---|---|---|
| Conservative | 7 | 148 |
| Labour | 28 | 89 |
| Liberal | 105 | 1 |
| Others | 4 | – |
|  | 144 | 238 |

The government was more equally divided than the rank and file of the Labour party: ten of its members voted for the bill and six against. Those in favour included Snowden, Thomas, Trevelyan, and Jowett, those against Webb, Wheatley, and Adamson. The Prime Minister (MacDonald) did not vote. He was less hostile to proportional representation on general grounds than he had been, admitting that it was 'good up to a point'. But when contemplating the subject with his party's fortunes in mind, he was worried that they might find themselves in an even worse position than they were then.[33] Earlier,

---

[32] *HC Deb.* 172 (2 May 1924), 1937–2072. Asquith's remark is at 2024. Arthur Henderson, 1863–1935. MP, Labour, 1903–18, 1919–22, 1923–31, and 1933–5. Held office in wartime coalition government and in Labour governments of 1924 and 1929–31.

[33] *The Times*, 17 May 1924, 9d, reporting MacDonald's speech at the opening of the Parliamentary Labour Club.

in 1921, MacDonald, shocked by the results of the general election of 1918, considered that 'Proportional representation, with all its deficiencies, alone seems to afford a practical working scheme', but at the same time he said it would 'tend to diminish rather than increase the representative character of parliament, and to produce governments also less representative than those we now have'.[34] As so often with him, it is difficult to see where he stood on a question or to unravel his Delphic processes of thought.

Although the PRS had not sponsored Rendall's bill, they were naturally disappointed by its defeat, and particularly that the voting was to a greater degree than usual on party lines. They tried to take some comfort from the fact that it was supported in their view by important and representative members of all parties;[35] but the more realistic members of the PRS could not help admitting that the cause was increasingly losing the kind of high principled support it had once received: there was much less talk about what was a fair electoral system, and much greater consideration of whether it would help or hinder this or that party. To counter this tendency the society tried to extend its work amongst the general public, but it was severely handicapped by shortage of funds. Income from subscriptions and donations declined dramatically in the 1920s, and in 1929 was, at just over £2,000, only half of what it had been in 1920.[36] It was also worrying that the society depended largely, as before, on a few generous donors.

The PRS hoped to stimulate Tory support by persuading a prominent Conservative, such as Amery or Birkenhead, to act as their leader. Lord Robert Cecil was proving more and more disappointing, and the society's President, Earl Grey, was considered by some members to be useless as a leader. He attended very few meetings of the Executive Committee, and relations between him and the society's secretary (Humphreys) were strained: Lady Courtney reported in 1922 that Grey was

[34] J. Ramsay MacDonald, *Socialism: Critical and Constructive* (1921), 244–5 of 1924 rev. edn.
[35] The most important of the seven Conservatives who voted for the bill were Amery, Moore-Brabazon, and Ormsby-Gore.
[36] See Appendix E.

'very critical with Humphreys for all he writes and says lest it should be anti-conservative'. It was even thought that Grey actually did harm.[37] He had become president of the PRS in 1917 on the death of his father, the fourth earl. This may have been an unwise appointment by the society, for he seems to have played little part in public life after the war, in which he served.

An increase in Tory support became less and less of a realistic aim for the PRS after the general election of October 1924. It had resulted in the Conservatives being heavily over-repre-sented, getting 68 per cent of the seats with only 48 per cent of the votes; they had therefore little incentive to change the system. The Liberals were badly under-represented (71 seats too few in Great Britain, they estimated) and were shocked that they won only 40 seats in lieu of the 159 they had had previously; so some of them were keener than ever on electoral reform, the need for which had been included in the Liberal election manifesto of 1924. Labour returned 40 fewer MPs than in 1923 although they received one million more votes, and were under-represented (50 seats too few in Great Britain), but many of them took heart from the feeling that the Liberals were indubitably in decline. Proportional representation still had supporters among Labour leaders and in some trade unions, but in 1926 the Labour party annual conference passed a resolution against it. This condemned proportional representa-tion on the ground that it was 'not in the interests of democratic government', as it involved large constituencies and numerous representatives for each constituency. What supporters of the resolution clearly had uppermost in their minds was that proportional representation would not help the Labour party. They were suspicious of it because, they said, it had long been supported by reactionaries afraid of democratic majorities, such as Hare, Robert Lowe, Lord Robert Cecil, and the House of Lords; Labour, if wise and determined, could make the existing system work for them; they did not want to load it against the advancing forces of Labour. (It did work for them at the general election of 1929, but not in 1931 or 1935.)

[37] Lady C. to JFW, 21 Nov. 1922; JFW to Lady C., 25 Nov. 1923 and 2 Dec. 1923. Grey was Charles Robert, the fifth Earl, 1879–1963. He stood for parlia-ment once unsuccessfully in Jan. 1910 as a Liberal Unionist. By 1917 he was a Conservative.

Labour hostility to proportional representation received some stiffening from the Fabian Society, which had not abandoned its previous opposition though some individual members of the society favoured it. A Fabian tract issued in May 1924 showed considerable and remarkable confidence in the working of the existing electoral system and in the conventions operating in British politics. Thus it admitted that there was a theoretical possibility that a minority in the country could get a majority of seats, but if that ever happened the majority would behave decently and not take advantage of the accident. Similarly even if a ministry had a huge majority, its views would inevitably be tempered by the arguments of the opposition and by the views of MPs who knew the opinions of their constituents. An electoral system should provide a clear and unambiguous answer to the question which government we were to have, and a cabinet should rest upon the support of a single party. The fact that it had not done so recently was due to a temporary dislocation, not to permanent error: the problem would disappear as the Liberal party petered out. There was no need therefore for a change, and the one proposed by various minorities, proportional representation, was open to many objections. The tract assumed that its advocates wanted representation to be mathematically exact so that every small group would return a representative; this would result in an unworkable assembly and in surreptitious political bargaining, leading to contracts on policy not submitted for popular ratification.[38]

With this falling off in Conservative and Labour support, the PRS came to be more and more identified with the Liberals who were the main attenders at committee meetings. This obviously restricted the society's influence as the Liberals in the years 1924–9 were not only still divided on many issues but politically impotent, the Conservatives having a large parliamentary majority over all the other parties. In any case several leading Liberals did not give full support to the cause. Lloyd George was ambivalent; Herbert Samuel was still playing with the idea of the alternative vote or the second ballot as the means of

---

[38] Fabian Tract No. 211, 'The Case Against Proportional Representation', by Herman Finer (May 1924). Finer was then a lecturer in Public Administration at the London School of Economics. For criticism of Finer's arguments see J. M. Robertson, *Electoral Justice* (1931), 71–8.

preventing minority government, and some rich Liberals, even vice-presidents of the PRS such as Sir John Simon, did not contribute to the society's funds, a fact much resented by the treasurer.

Nor did proportional representation receive much help from the liberal press, apart from the *Manchester Guardian*. The main Liberal weekly, the *Nation*, hardly ever referred to the subject after 1923 when it was taken over by Maynard Keynes as chairman of the board and the economist Hubert Henderson as editor, in order to make it an organ of 'new Liberalism' and the views of the Liberal Summer School. Liberal Summer Schools, attended by large numbers, were the linchpin of Liberal and progressive thought in the 1920s. They revived Liberalism as an intellectual force, but Keynes was bored by questions of government. He thought them dull; so he was not interested in electoral systems. He wanted to see the Liberal party preserved, and he was right in thinking that more people would vote Liberal if the party had a more positive philosophy and constructive economic policies; but he and others in his group do not seem to have realized that a change in the electoral system was necessary if these votes were to be adequately reflected in parliamentary seats.[39] What was in effect the Liberal party manifesto of 1929, *We Can Conquer Unemployment*, made no reference to electoral reform; nor did Lloyd George in his address to his constituents, though about 40 per cent of Liberal candidates included it in their election addresses. According to the *Nation* there was even an 'anti-P.R. trend' in the Liberal party; this was revealed by the narrowness of the majority in favour of proportional representation at the Summer School of 1928. The next year, depressed by the result of the general election, members of the Summer School had changed their views; no vote was taken, but it seemed clear that the overwhelming majority were in favour of proportional representation.[40]

In spite of these many difficulties in the second half of the 1920s, the critics of the electoral system were not altogether

---

[39] 'Am I a Liberal?' (1925), and 'Liberalism and Labour' (1926), reprinted in J. M. Keynes, *Essays in Persuasion* (1951).

[40] *Nation*, 11 Aug. 1928, and 17 Aug. 1929.

inert. They pressed that the system of voting should be included within the terms of reference of the Speaker's conference which the government had in 1925 promised to appoint to consider lowering the voting age for women from 30 to 21. Nothing came of this request, as the franchise was equalized in 1928 without consideration by a conference; but advocates of proportional representation took the opportunity to point out during debates about women's suffrage that people should have a right to representation as well as a right to vote.

The subject was brought up in parliament on five other occasions in the late 1920s. In 1926 during a debate in the Lords on compulsory voting, Burnham and Beauchamp asked for an inquiry into electoral reform generally. They were supported by the Earl of Mayo who countered Haldane's objections to proportional representation (wire-pulling by well-organized minorities) by drawing on Irish experience of the system.[41]

In 1927 the Lords held a debate on the second ballot. Its most marked feature was the falling off in support for the single transferable vote which occurred at this time. Two vice-presidents of the PRS (Burnham and Beauchamp) spoke as if the existing electoral system worked satisfactorily in a two-party system and that problems had occurred only because there were then three parties. Burnham saw the second ballot as the solution: it would prevent the return of a socialist government.[42] Beauchamp admittedly preferred proportional representation to the second ballot or the alternative vote, but only 'on the whole'. Birkenhead, who had been an enthusiastic advocate of proportional representation for fifteen years, now only 'inclined' to it.[43]

In 1928 electoral reform was debated twice in the Lords and once in the Commons. On the first occasion in the Lords, Grey asked that the government should collect and publish accurate

[41] *HL Deb.* 63 (17 Mar. 1926), 601–21. Haldane curiously thought that if the electorate was educated and interested 'you will get electoral majorities which will ensure that the opinions carried into effect are the opinions of the nation, and not the opinions of mere groups' (608).

[42] Burnham was previously Sir Harry Levy-Lawson, 1862–1933. He had sat in the Commons intermittently as a Liberal and then Liberal Unionist from 1885 to 1916, when he went to the Lords. Managing proprietor of the *Daily Telegraph*, 1903–28.

[43] *HL Deb.* 66 (20 Mar. 1927), 812–34.

information about the working of other electoral systems in foreign countries. Grey spoke at times as if he thought the British electoral system would be satisfactory if it were not for three-cornered contests, but as the two-party system was, he thought, unlikely to return, he wanted alternatives to be considered. Parmoor, whilst supporting the request for more information, made it clear that he was not in favour of the second ballot or the alternative vote and put the subject in a wider context: the existing system did not comply with the principles of representation; the House of Commons should be a microcosm of general public opinion; this would not result in weak governments as a government under a proportional system would have the largest amount of support in the country. No other peer spoke in favour of proportional representation though Desborough acknowledged that it looked attractive on paper and that he had supported it in the past. Southwark wanted to do away with three-cornered contests and spoke in favour of the alternative vote, but Banbury saw no need for a change as the Liberals would disappear in a few years. He added that he had never met anyone who understood proportional representation. Viscount Younger did not consider the present system satisfactory, but thought it was not possible to find a better one. Salisbury, speaking for the government, said he would see if more information could be produced, but he considered it was difficult to understand the working of electoral systems, including the English one. He admitted he had been a 'great supporter of proportional representation', but he was no longer, as it involved large constituencies, machine-made politics, and disciplined voting. (He presumably had party list systems in mind.)[44]

Soon after this debate Southwark pressed the government to introduce the second ballot before a general election was held under the extended franchise. He said he had no party object; but he must have feared that the new young women voters would support the Labour party, for he thought it was dangerous to leave things as they were. Lord Jessel agreed that the

---

[44] *HL Deb.* 70 (7 Mar. 1928), 382–403. Salisbury, 1861–1947, was the fourth Marquess, son of the third Marquess whose views on electoral systems are discussed in Ch. V. He was the elder brother of Lords Hugh and Robert Cecil.

present system had grave defects, but he thought it led to 'a clear majority on one side or the other'. Desborough announced that the government had no intention of making any great change in the electoral system.[45]

At the same time, in March 1928, the Commons debated a Liberal member's motion deploring the unrepresentative nature of the electoral system. Its sponsor, W. M. Wiggins, had been for some time a strong supporter of proportional representation, but now saw difficulties in its working; so he was in favour of the alternative vote. Two of those who spoke for the motion (a Liberal and a Conservative) based their case partly on fear of socialism. The Conservative, Sir Samuel Roberts, who was chairman of the Executive Committee of the PRS, put the danger he foresaw graphically by saying that Labour 'could skin us all alive and ruin us' even without a majority of support in the country. Opponents of the motion tabled a comprehensive criticism of any departure from the 'proved wisdom of the present system of voting'. New devices, it said, would inevitably add to the dangers of political corruption, to the instability of the state, to the powerlessness of the governments in office, and to the burdens of individual MPs. They contended that the existing system expressed the will of the people and that it had worked with tremendous success since 1800. They saw no reason to save the Liberal party from decline, as they believed in the two-party system of government. The government spokesman (Sir Vivian Henderson of the Home Office) contrasted the position in Britain with that abroad. We had strong governments which could and did govern; in countries with a proportional system, which he admitted were numerous, there was less stability: Italy had had a revolution and Bulgaria a *coup d'état* with political murder. Our status and prestige in Europe would decline if we had proportional representation, and he listed many other objections to any change in the electoral system. One Liberal, H. E. Crawfurd, answering Henderson, pointed out that a stable government, i.e. a government with a working majority, could be tyrannous and not act according to the wishes of the people. What was desirable was continuity of policy; this was not produced by the existing system, as evi-

[45] *HL Deb.* 70 (22 Mar. 1928), 595–604.

denced by our policies towards Russia and on fiscal issues. The motion opposing change in the electoral system was carried by 204 votes to 41. The minority was composed of 30 Liberals, 10 Labour, and one Conservative.[46]

The decade (1919–29) had started with some successes, but these were either reversed (as in Northern Ireland) or not followed up. Some previous supporters of proportional representation, even Mrs Fawcett, had changed their minds or had switched their allegiance from the single transferable to the alternative vote. Advocates and opponents divided much more on party lines than they had previously when support had cut across other political allegiances. The cause lacked the leadership of a front-rank politician or even of a maverick such as Courtney who, in spite of all his shortcomings, had analysed so incisively and persistently the basic features of non-proportional electoral systems. Some prominent politicians (for example, MacDonald, Lloyd George, Churchill) were losing confidence in the British electoral system, but it did not always follow from this that they saw proportional representation as the remedy for its defects. There was considerable disagreement about the working of the proportional systems which were operating at this time in Scotland, Ireland, Europe, and elsewhere, and no authoritative and impartial inquiry which would have enabled factual errors to be corrected. Misstatements about France in particular abounded.[47]

In spite of all these difficulties, the secretary of the PRS even in the late 1920s expressed confidence in the final success of the cause: proportional representation in his view was irresistible.

[46] *HC Deb.* 215 (28 Mar. 1928), 1248–1304. Roberts's remark is at 1278. Vivian Henderson, 1884–1965, had been Parliamentary Private Secretary to James Craig in 1919–20.

[47] The French electoral system at this time was not a proportional one, but a rather complicated majority system with multi-membered constituencies and the second ballot. It was therefore wrong, though common, to attribute the short life of French cabinets to proportional representation. See Peter Campbell, *French Electoral Systems and Elections since 1789* (1965), 91.

# X

# The Labour Government and the Alternative Vote, 1929–1931

AT the general election of May 1929, the Conservatives won more votes than Labour—8.6 million as against 8.3 million, but fewer seats—260 as against Labour's 289. The Liberals obtained 5.3 million votes—nearly a quarter of the total vote—but only 59 seats, less than a tenth of all seats. Thus Labour was the largest party in the House of Commons, but had not got a majority of the 615 seats. The electoral system had failed to fulfil the role attributed to it by many of its suporters, namely to give a clear indication of the nation's choice of government.

There were few contemporary comments on the fact that the Conservatives had received more votes but fewer seats than Labour, a result which reformers had for many years been showing was a possibility. Labour people naturally did not wish to draw attention to this aspect of the result; and the Conservatives, speculating on the causes of their defeat in terms of seats, blamed not the electoral system but the Liberals for fielding so many candidates, 573, which was not far off the Conservatives' 590. At the previous general election in 1924, the Liberals had put up only 340 candidates, so it was assumed that because of this and for other reasons, many erstwhile Liberals had then voted Conservative, whereas in 1929 they were given the chance to vote Liberal. A leading article in *The Times* considered the Liberal poll was 'swollen by the numerous driblets contributed by a large number of hopeless fights' and criticized the Liberal party for causing the indeterminate verdict and great constitutional difficulties.[1] Some Conservative commentators went fur-

---

[1] *The Times*, 1 June 1929, 13b.

ther and implied that the Liberal party ought not to exist; they wanted to get back to the two-party system as soon as possible, citing in support the dictum of Lord Bryce that the successful working of our government presupposed the existence of two great parties and no more.[2] By contrast other Conservatives were quite happy that the Labour government had not got a majority in parliament: it was in office but fortunately not in power.[3]

Liberals naturally complained about their under-representation, arguing that they should have won over 140 seats instead of 59. Before the general election they had had high hopes of making a sweeping advance; their campaign had not lacked money and was fought with vigour. They considered they had a distinctive contribution to make to the solution of national problems, particularly unemployment, and did not see why they should be squeezed out of the political system by the two other parties. Lloyd George denounced the electoral system as 'not democracy but the dictatorship of the croupier', and said that one should not 'trust the destinies of a great nation to a three-card trick'. He was one of the few people who drew attention to the fact that the Conservatives had a majority of votes, but were the second party in parliament.[4]

It might be thought at first glance that the political situation after the election of 1929 offered supporters of proportional representation a chance at last to get it enacted, and we must ask why they did not succeed. The answer will emerge from an account of events during the next two years.

The ambiguous result of the election produced momentary uncertainty. Tom Jones (the deputy secretary to the cabinet) thought it quite likely that Lloyd George would offer his support first to Baldwin, provided electoral reform was brought in, noting that some Liberals (Sir D. MacLean, Sir J. Simon, and others) would not want to support MacDonald.[5] But three days later Baldwin resigned, and the king sent for MacDonald, who

[2] Letters to *The Times*, 6 June 1929, 15d, and 7 June 1929, 15c.

[3] See, e.g., Winston Churchill's letter to *The Times*, 15 June 1929, 8c, and R. Boothby in *HC Deb.* 229 (4 July 1929), 315.

[4] Speech to parliamentary Liberal party, *The Times*, 14 June 1929, 9c, and *HC Deb.* 229 (2 July 1929), 155.

[5] Thomas Jones, *Whitehall Diary* (1969), ii. 187. Diary entry for 1 June 1929.

accepted the task of forming a government. MacDonald hated Lloyd George and had at this stage no contact with him or with any other Liberals to ascertain what support, if any, they would offer a Labour government. He believed the Labour party should stand on its own legs; to make an agreement with others would be humiliating. So the Liberals had no chance to negotiate terms with Labour, even if they had wanted to. However, before parliament met, Lloyd George announced that Liberals intended to use all their power in the new parliament to insist on a speedy redress of the glaring wrong of the electoral system, and the Liberal Administrative Committee expressed the hope that electoral reform would be carried in the present parliament by general agreement between the parties.[6]

It may have been pronouncements such as these which decided the government to set up an inquiry into certain electoral matters, for the Labour election manifesto had not included any reference to electoral reform. The king's speech on 2 July 1929 announced the decision in the following vague terms:

At the recent General Election an extended franchise placed in the hands of the whole of My people of adult years, the grave responsibility for guarding the well-being of this nation as a constitutional democracy, and my Government propose to institute an examination of the election so that the working of the law relating to Parliamentary elections may be brought into conformity with the new conditions.[7]

Lord Salisbury asked what precisely was intended by these words. Was it to be an inquiry into proportional representation? The reply from the government spokesman, Lord Parmoor, was discouraging, although he was himself a leading member of the PRS.[8] He pointed out, referring presumably to the events of 1917–18, that the Liberals had thrown out proportional representation not so long ago, that the party in power was always against it, that all parties were divided on the subject, and that it created grave practical difficulties.

---

[6] *The Times*, 14 June 1929, 9c, and 20 June 1929, 18e.

[7] *HL Deb.* 75 (2 July 1929), 8.

[8] Parmoor. Charles Alfred Cripps, 1852–1941. MP, Conservative, 1895–1900, and Jan. 1910–1914 when he went to the Lords. He opposed the war, became a Labour sympathizer, and took office in the Labour governments of 1924 and 1929–31. Parmoor's first wife, who died in 1893, was Lady Courtney's sister.

During the debate on the king's speech in the Commons, MacDonald said that the announcement was deliberately general and comprehensive. He added that there were different views about the purpose of an election. It seems clear, in spite of his usual cloudiness, that in his view the final purpose of an election was to elect a government rather than to produce an accurate representation of electors' opinions. This remark gave rise to the comment that the Prime Minister appeared to have changed his views, as during the last parliament the Labour party often pointed out that the Conservative government had no mandate for its actions, as it represented only a minority of voters. Did MacDonald now believe that a minority of electors should choose the government?[9] Lloyd George said that the government would get greater support from the Liberals in helping to solve the many difficulties of the time if it promised a speedy inquiry into the electoral system, and that the Liberals meant to use their parliamentary position to the full to ensure the redress of the wrong done to five million Liberal voters. He did not indicate what electoral system would achieve this, but Herbert Samuel, deputy chairman of the parliamentary Liberal party, obviously thought that the alternative vote was the solution.[10]

Indeed, many people who at that time were dissatisfied with the result of the general election for one reason or another thought the remedy was to adopt the alternative vote. This was because they focused on the fact that over half the MPs had been elected on a minority vote in their constituencies. The alternative vote would have prevented that, but its advocates were wrong in thinking that it would also secure the representation of parties according to their strength in the country, and that it was guaranteed to give one party a majority over all the others in parliament, thus preventing a stalemate like the existing one.

The government decided that the inquiry should be made by a conference on the lines of the Speaker's conference of 1916–17. The existing Speaker and his immediate predecessor declined to take the chair, but Lord Ullswater, who as Speaker Lowther

[9] Oliver Stanley. *HC Deb.* 229 (4 July 1929), 291–2.
[10] *HC Deb.* 229 (3 July 1929), 157–9, and (4 July 1929), 304–14.

had presided at the previous conference, agreed to be the chairman. Party representation at the conference was based on party strengths in the electorate rather than in the House of Commons, with the result that the Labour and Conservative parties had eight members each and the Liberals five. These were all chosen by Ullswater from the panels of names submitted to him by the parties.[11]

The conference, which had taken five months to set up, started work in December 1929 and sat until July 1930, hardly the speedy inquiry asked for by Lloyd George. During ten sittings the members examined and debated the comparative merits of proportional representation, the alternative vote, and the existing system. The secretary of the PRS presented several memoranda to the conference and gave evidence on three occasions. He was very fully examined and, according to the chairman, met with great frankness the various objections to the scheme which he advocated, the single transferable vote. The case for the alternative vote was put by a rather obscure former Liberal MP, William Clough, and by the Law Lord, Craigmyle, one of the Liberal members of the conference.[12]

As in the case of the conference of 1916–17, no official record of the proceedings is available other than the chairman's letter to the Prime Minister at the conclusion of the conference;[13] but information about what went on can be culled from the papers of some of the participants, in particular those of Sir Samuel Hoare who sent various memoranda to his colleagues in parliament asking for their advice on how Conservative members of the conference should proceed.[14]

'At the early meetings', Hoare recorded, 'we riddled with criticisms both P.R. and the Alternative Vote. I think that we may claim to have succeeded in convincing the Socialists of the dangers of P.R., and the Liberals of the futilities of A.V. Having spent much trouble upon this double task, it was agreed by our

[11] See Appendix F for membership.
[12] William Clough, 1862–1937. MP, Liberal, 1906–18. Lord Craigmyle, previously Thomas Shaw, 1850–1937. MP, Liberal, 1892–1909. Law Lord since 1909. It is not clear why he was so keen on the alternative vote.
[13] PP 1929–30 XIII. Conference on Electoral Reform, Letter from Viscount Ullswater to the Prime Minister, 17 July 1930, 341–6.
[14] Hoare's account of the conference and subsequent events tallies with the references to them in Lord Bayford's diaries.

delegation that I should bring the matter to an issue and definitely ask Samuel and Arnold [the leaders of the Liberal and Labour delegations respectively] for their concrete party proposals for reform.'[15] The Liberals proposed that any change in the electoral system should include proportional representation, with the alternative vote in a few small constituencies. Hoare himself was a strong opponent of proportional representation. This is clear from a memorandum of his written in 1929 after the general election, in which he emphasized that he disliked the conception of government involved in proportional representation—weak and unstable ministries; he also listed many other grave objections to such a change. Nevertheless he and other Conservatives on the conference decided to conciliate the Liberals, and therefore agreed in May 1930 to support the proposal that *if* any change were made it should include proportional representation, with the single transferable vote, though not for all seats. This resolution was passed by thirteen votes to eight, those against being all Labour. Every member of the conference had spoken, Hoare reported, 'Socialist after Socialist damning P.R. with bell, book and candle. The Socialists could not have been more heavy footed. Indeed they burnt their boats so completely that I do not see how they can ever get into them again.'[16]

The chairman of the conference summed up the position of the parties as follows. The Conservatives were not prepared to agree to the alternative vote in any circumstances; the Liberals would be prepared to consider its adoption generally, as being preferable to the existing system if proportional representation was not finally accepted; none of the Labour members of the conference was willing to support the alternative vote *per se*, though some of them were prepared to accept it on condition that several other reforms were adopted at the same time. Some of these such as the abolition of plural voting were considered by the chairman to be outside the scope of the conference, although it had no terms of reference. The reduction of electoral

---

[15] Memorandum of 23 May 1930. 'Further Developments of Electoral Reform', Templewood Papers, V1/2. Samuel Hoare, 1880–1959. MP, Conservative, Jan. 1910–1944, when he became Lord Templewood. He held various government offices, 1922–40.

[16] Ibid.

expenditure and the publication of party political accounts were discussed, inconclusively.

It being clear that no agreement was possible on the main issues, the conference was wound up in July 1930 without recommending any change in the system of voting. For some time before this the Conservatives had considered withdrawing from the conference on the ground that it was becoming ridiculous, as the realities of electoral reform were being discussed behind their backs in negotiations between Lloyd George and the Labour leaders. But the situation changed when it emerged that there was a possibility of an agreement between Lloyd George and the Conservative party by which a moderate scheme of proportional representation would be passed into law. Lloyd George implied in a talk with Sir Robert Horne in June 1930 that if the Liberals could get proportional representation, they would drop from their demands the alternative vote, and the abolition of plural voting and University seats.[17] Hoare was much attracted by this idea, though he shared the profound distrust generally excited by Lloyd George. He thought it was in the Conservative interest to preserve the Liberal party, because if it were destroyed, almost all of it would go to strengthen Labour. So he proposed that the government should be turned out on a favourable opportunity, not later than the beginning of the autumn session; that a Conservative government should be formed; that it should pass with Liberal support a moderate form of proportional representation and a reformed second chamber, and then dissolve parliament and hold a general election.[18]

The possibility of co-operation between the Lloyd George Liberals and the Conservatives was still being discussed in the autumn of 1930, but by December the scheme was dropped: it did not appeal to most Conservative leaders, particularly not to the anti-coalitionists of 1922 who were adamantly against making common cause with Lloyd George. Moreover they considered his terms too high, as these included not just proportional representation but inclusion of Liberals in the

---

[17] Horne was a Conservative MP who had been in Lloyd George's coalition government of 1918–22.
[18] Confidential memorandum of 2 June 1930. Templewood Papers, V1/2.

government and a veto on food taxes. They were also alienated by Lloyd George's contemptuous attitude to many of the men who would comprise a Baldwin government.

Although the conference had been a shambles and had not given a clear lead on the electoral system, the government felt that it would be wise to introduce a measure of electoral reform in the hope of securing Liberal support for its policies and preventing a Liberal–Conservative alliance. So in the autumn of 1930 consultations took place between the government, represented by Arthur Henderson, Lord Arnold, and Snowden, and some Liberals—Samuel, Sinclair, and Ramsay Muir.[19] According to Snowden the Liberals on this consultative committee realized that there was no possibility of the Labour party in parliament agreeing to proportional representation; they therefore settled for the alternative vote.[20] This decision was later endorsed by the parliamentary Liberal party, though one important member, Sir John Simon, came out against it. He admitted that he had changed his views since 1917, being persuaded by the case put by Humphreys, the secretary of the PRS.[21] Many rank and file Liberals also were unhappy about their leaders' decision to give up pressing for proportional representation. Their action was later criticized by Francis Hirst, the economist and Liberal writer, who considered that the Liberal leaders 'very foolishly kept the second labour government in office without making their support conditional on the introduction of a Proportional Representation Bill'.[22] It is impossible to say whether, if faced with such a demand at the end of 1930, the government would have complied with it in order to stay in power. It seems probable that they would not have relented, given especially MacDonald's ingrained dislike of proportional representation. If this view was correct, the

---

[19] Lord Arnold was Sidney Arnold, 1878–1945. He was at that time Paymaster-General. Sir Archibald Sinclair, 1890–1970. MP, Liberal, 1922–45. Chief Liberal whip, Nov. 1930–Aug. 1931. Ramsay Muir, 1872–1946. Prominent Liberal publicist and Director of the Liberal Summer School since 1921.

[20] Snowden, *Autobiography* (1934), ii. 288.

[21] *The Times*, 15 Dec. 1930, 14d.

[22] Francis Hirst, 'Is British Liberalism Alive or Dead?' *Contemporary Review*, 149 (Apr. 1936), 422.

Liberals' decision was the right one; for to have made proportional representation a condition of their support and thus to have precipitated a general election, held without any form of electoral reform, would probably have been disastrous for them. Moreover they would have been criticized for bringing down the government on a question which many people (rightly) considered irrelevant, and increasingly irrelevant, at a time of grave economic crisis.

The government's bill,[23] published at the end of January 1931, provided that the alternative vote should in future be used in all parliamentary elections. The bill also contained other provisions: the abolition of University seats, of the business vote, and of plural voting, limitation on the use of cars to convey voters to the poll, and reduction of permitted expenditure at elections. As foreshadowed, the bill offered no comfort to those supporters of proportional representation who thought the alternative vote was worse than the existing system, and they were hampered in the Commons by the Speaker ruling out of order all amendments which would have allowed methods other than the alternative vote to be considered.[24] Nevertheless three MPs, P. H. Oliver (Liberal), Cecil Wilson (Labour), and Eleanor Rathbone (Independent), put the arguments for proportional representation as against both the existing system and the alternative vote, and two others, Sir Hugh O'Neill (Ulster Unionist) and Joseph Devlin (Nationalist), referred favourably to the working of proportional representation in Ireland, especially in the North.

Several Conservatives emphasized the superiority of proportional representation to the alternative vote if the aim was to protect minorities and to produce a representative parliament. One of the most outspoken of them was Winston Churchill, who said that if a change had to be made proportional representation was 'incomparably the fairest, the most scientific and, on the whole, the best in the public interest', whereas the alternative vote was 'the stupidest, the least scientific and the most unreal' plan. He disliked the complications of a proportional system, but considered that with all its inconveniences it was

---

[23] The Representation of the People (No. 2) Bill.
[24] *HC Deb*. 249 (4 Mar. 1931), 455, and 251 (23 Apr. 1931), 1267.

the least objectionable way of meeting the Liberal grievance and the constitutional injustice.[25]

Other opponents of the alternative vote explained the case against it more fully. They saw as one of its defects that the second choices of those who voted for the two top candidates played no part in the outcome of the poll; if these second choices were taken into account, a candidate who came lower might have won instead of being eliminated. Thus the alternative vote did not in their view prevent large bodies of voters being (as then) entirely unrepresented. 'Unrepresented' was being used to mean 'not represented by members of the party of their first choice', or 'truly represented'; these voters were merely given a choice of masters. By contrast, with the single transferable vote, the second and later choices of *all* electors were taken into account in determining the result. Critics of the alternative vote also pointed out that it would not ensure that the parties who were successful in getting representation in the Commons were represented in proportion to their strength in the electorate. In particular it would not remedy the anomaly of a party having a majority in the Commons with no corresponding majority in the country; thus even on the most plausible of assumptions—complete mutual support between Liberals and Labour—it would not have prevented the Conservatives winning far too many seats in 1924. The claim that it would have prevented this was made by many Labour supporters of the alternative vote.[26]

When the bill was finally passed in the Commons by 278 to 228 votes on 2 June 1931, it still provided for the alternative vote, but as Hoare recorded, there had been 'complete absence of enthusiasm over the Bill in every corner of the House. With the exception of Herbert Samuel, Socialists and Liberals alike have either criticised it or damned it with faint praise. . . . As the debates went on it became clearer than ever that two out of three Socialists do not like the Alternative Vote and the Liberals regard it as a very poor substitute for P.R.' Hoare advised Conservatives in the Lords not to reject the bill, but if they

[25] *HC Deb.* 253 (2 June 1931) 102, 106.
[26] For second reading of the bill, see *HC Deb.* 247 (2 Feb. 1931), 1467–1588, and (3 Feb. 1931), 1653–1774.

thought this too risky because of the harm the alternative vote might do to the party, he recommended that they should insert in it a limited amount of proportional representation; he thought this would probably not damage the Conservative party at the next election and would create a very difficult position for the government in the Commons.[27]

Hoare's suggestion was taken up by Lord Bayford, a Conservative who had been on the Ullswater conference.[28] Debate on his amendment proposing proportional representation in 100 constituencies was allowed, in contrast to the prevention of a similar amendment in the Commons. Bayford had been a supporter of proportional representation for many years and was obviously not thinking merely of its effect on his party. The object of representative government, he said, was that representatives should represent the opinions of the represented; the alternative vote would not remedy the defects of the existing system. The Lords showed little enthusiasm for his proposal. Lord Reading, the Liberal leader in the Upper House, went no further than saying that 'it may be' that proportional representation would give all the people of the country a far better chance of just representation in the House of Commons than other systems. Ullswater complained that the government had disregarded the view of the conference that if there was to be any change it should include the single transferable vote, but at the same time he thought electoral reform should not be introduced unless all the parties agreed to it, which they did not. Earl Grey, though president of the PRS, did not speak. Parmoor said that he personally was in favour of proportional representation and always had been, but that it was not possible to introduce it at the present time. He then added a word of support for the alternative vote, saying that it would enable popular opinion to be really represented in the House of Commons. The Lords passed the bill by 50 votes to 14 on second reading. There was no vote on Bayford's amendment as he withdrew it.[29]

---

[27] Memorandum of June 1931, 'The House of Commons and the Electoral Reform Bill'. Templewood Papers, V1/2.

[28] Lord Bayford, previously Robert A. Sanders, 1867–1940. MP, Conservative, Jan. 1910–23 and 1924–9, when he went to the Lords. Held government offices, 1919–23.

[29] *HL Deb.* 81 (16 June 1931), 124–78; and (2 July 1931), 565–96.

Those who argued in both Houses of parliament against a change to proportional representation advanced a miscellaneous collection of points, some new, some old. In defence of the existing electoral system Anthony Eden asked whether anyone seriously thought that at any time the country had failed to express its will at elections; and Lord Peel spoke as if the British electoral system produced 'vigorous, consistent and authoritative government', a strange sentiment given the political situation at that time. Some speakers said that proportional representation would produce weak government as in France and Germany; others that it was not accurate unless the whole country was one constituency; that it would result in the representation of fads like anti-vaccination, anti-drink, anti-anything; that it would be dangerous to introduce such a revolutionary scheme at a time when untried and inexperienced women were being added to the voters; and that it would prevent a return to the two-party system.

The main attack on proportional representation from the government spokesmen came from Lord Passfield (Sidney Webb) who was Secretary for the Colonies. The primary object of a general election, he said, was to enable the king's government to be carried on, whereas the advocates of proportional representation wanted to give representation to as many minorities as they possibly could; it would result in the return of some Communist party members and open the door to Soviet propaganda. Arthur Greenwood, Minister of Health, considered proportional representation 'a wild and revolutionary measure', but the Home Secretary, J. R. Clynes, had to be more moderate in his objections, for he had been a vice-president of the PRS; so he confined himself to the statement that it would be more difficult for governments to reach decisions if a proportional system operated. The Prime Minister, MacDonald, too thought it would not secure a unified government; proportional representation would make the House a collection of minorities.

The bill never reached the statue book. It was returned to the Commons from the Lords on 21 July 1931 with the alternative vote still in it, though confined to one-third of the constituencies, viz. London and the larger boroughs. The Labour government resigned in August, being succeeded by MacDonald's first

National government, and nothing more was heard of this electoral reform bill.

The advocates of electoral reform had failed again. In analysing the causes of their failure it is helpful to divide them into two groups, those who opted for no change other than proportional representation with the single transferable vote, whom we may call the 'purists', and those whose first preference was proportional representation but who saw the alternative vote as the second best. Most of the latter were Liberals, whereas the purists included members of all political parties—Conservative, Labour, Liberal, and Irish Nationalist. They failed because they were not given an opportunity to vote on what system should be adopted if a change was to be made. One MP, Oliver Stanley, a Conservative member of the Ullswater conference, complained that the government had not proceeded in the customery way with regard to a bill which materially altered the electoral system, namely only to introduce it after a resolution in favour of change had been passed by the House. If such a resolution had been passed, Stanley considered that proportional representation would have received unanimous support from the Conservative benches and a very large amount of support from the other side of the House.[30] The government no doubt feared such a result and therefore proceeded without a prior resolution. They justified their position by saying that as that parliament had no mandate to make great changes in the electoral system, proportional representation was out of the question; they did not consider the alternative vote a revolutionary change.

Why did the Liberals fail to obtain any measure of electoral reform, whether proportional representation or the alternative vote, whilst the Labour party was in office and dependent on them? Their failure was due to a number of causes.

Although proportional representation had some support in the Labour party including amongst members of the government, the bulk of the party, and in particular Ramsay MacDonald, were deeply hostile to it. One Labour MP described it

---

[30] *HC Deb.* 247 (3 Feb. 1931), 1672–5.

as 'the devil' and thought it would 'destroy our constitution'.[31] It could be argued that if the Liberals *at the outset* had made proportional representation a condition of their support, the government might have been tempted to grant it in order to avoid being turned out of office, thus leaving the door open for the formation of a Conservative government supported by the existing parliament, or risking defeat at another general election. However the government did not have to face this difficult dilemma, because the Liberals, or at least their leaders, wanted to preserve the party's independence and freedom of action. They were unwilling to give the government a blank cheque; they wanted to judge each measure on its merits.

Nor did the Liberals manage to manœuvre the Conservatives into an alliance with them in order to obtain proportional representation and defeat the government. Lloyd George explored the possibility of such a plan right from the start and throughout 1930, but he could not pull it off because the Conservatives he was in touch with, particularly Winston Churchill and Robert Horne, were not the crucial ones; the more important figures of Baldwin and Neville Chamberlain were never sympathetic to the scheme.

Similarly in the case of the alternative vote, the Liberals might have obtained it if they had demanded that legislation to provide for it be introduced *at the start* of the government's term of office and had made this a condition of their support. Instead they went along with the government's decision to hold an inquiry into the electoral system. No such inquiry was in fact necessary as information about different electoral systems was readily available, and the political parties could have formulated their positions as a bill went through parliament. Five months elapsed whilst the inquiry was set up, and seven months whilst it deliberated fruitlessly. Hoare considered that Ullswater was a thoroughly bad chairman, but it seems unlikely that anyone could have persuaded the participants to reach agreement. Then another five months passed before the government finally decided to introduce a bill incorporating the alternative vote.

---

[31] Pethick-Lawrence, 2 June 1929. Quoted by J. D. Fair in 'The Second Labour Government and the Politics of Electoral Reform, 1929–31', *Albion*, 13 (Fall 1981), 278. Pethick-Lawrence was given office in the government.

During that time some Liberals were still hankering after pro-portional representation, although it should have been clear to them by then, and indeed earlier, that Labour hostility to it was entrenched. In the end the Liberals abandoned their scruples about making electoral reform a condition of support and in effect forced the government's hand. Historians dispute as to whether a 'bargain' was struck. This is immaterial. What is important in this context is that such understanding or agree-ment as there was between the Liberals and Labour came too late to secure any electoral reform.

Were the Liberals right to prefer the alternative vote to the existing electoral system? Any answer to this question is inevit-ably conjectural, as one can only make assumptions about how voters would have cast their second preferences. But even on the most cautious assumptions, it seems clear that the Liberals would have benefited from the alternative vote in the past, at the general elections of 1923, 1924, and 1929. In 1923 they might even have been the largest party in parliament and thus have formed the government. In 1929 it has been estimated that they would have received 78 more seats than they did, all wrested from Conservatives, with Labour still short of a parliamentary majority. After 1929 the alternative vote would have continued to help the Liberals, but by very much less than before, as they tended to come third or lower at the poll in an increasing number of constituencies.[32]

During this period, even the usually buoyant secretary of the PRS confessed to some despondency. He was disappointed by the attitude of the Labour party, though it is difficult to see why he should have had any hopes of it. He regretted that voting at the Ullswater conference was on strict party lines and contrasted this with the detached view taken by the parties on the contemporaneous Simon Commission on India. He was frus-trated by the fact that the Speaker ruled out of order the amendments to the government's bill which the PRS had prepared, with the result that there was little opportunity in the

[32] See the calculations made by D. E. Butler in *The Electoral System in Britain since 1918* (1963), 193–4, and Philip M. Williams in *Parliamentary Affairs*, 20 (1966–7), 13–30, 'Two Notes on the British Electoral System'.

Commons debates to put the case for proportional representation as against the alternative vote. Moreover he had to admit that parliamentary government no longer held the unchallenged position as the ideal system which it had occupied a generation or more ago.

Nevertheless the PRS continued to fight its corner. It considered that the increased number of criticisms of proportional representation at least showed its growing political importance, and the moral the society drew from the declining belief in parliamentary government was that it should be improved by proportional representation. As early as August 1929 it countered what it saw as false claims on behalf of the alternative vote and briefed MPs when the bill was going through parliament. It showed with examples from Australia and Canada what extraordinary results the alternative vote could produce, wholly excluding parties of substantial size from representation, giving a national result even less representative than would be obtained by the first-past-the-post system.[33] In spite of slender and declining resources, the PRS continued to issue propaganda literature, to organize meetings, to give talks, and to question candidates at by-elections. New members joined every year, but the impact of these activities on public opinion generally seems to have been small. Most people were understandably thinking more about the widening world depression, rising unemployment, protection versus free trade, and the financial crisis of 1931, than about electoral systems.

[33] PRS Pamphlet No. 67, *The Second Ballot, the Alternative Vote and Proportional Representation* (Aug. 1929).

# XI

# 1931–1945: Barren Years

THE general election of October 1931, held in crisis circumstances, showed how violently the electoral system could register swings of opinion, with the result that the popular vote of the minority was grossly under-represented in parliament. Opponents of the National government obtained only 10 per cent of the seats although they received a third of the total vote, whereas National candidates with two-thirds of the vote won 90 per cent of the seats. The main losers were the Labour party who put up 516 candidates and won only 52 seats. Most Liberal candidates and voters supported the National government. The Labour vote had admittedly declined substantially (by 21 per cent) since the general election of 1929, but the electoral system exaggerated enormously the influence of this loss of voting strength, and thus gave a misleading impression of public opinion.

Arthur Henderson, one of the many defeated members of the previous Labour cabinet, said that 'the new House of Commons will be a mockery of democratic parliamentary representation'.[1] Henderson had always advocated the alternative vote and been cool about proportional representation; but Labour would hardly have benefited from the alternative vote at the general election of 1931 because the second choice of almost all Liberals would have been Conservatives. It was pointed out by supporters of proportional representation that the speeches made in the last parliament to the effect that the alternative vote would yield a representative House of Commons sounded extremely foolish. On the other hand it has been estimated that if proportional representation had been in operation Labour would, assuming the same voting pattern, have won many more seats,

---

[1] Quoted by J. Humphreys in *Contemporary Review*, 140 (Dec. 1931), 'A Lesson of the General Election', 706.

189 instead of 52, and the National government parties many fewer, 413 instead of 554.[2]

At the general election of November 1935 the disproportion between votes and seats was less marked than in 1931, but it was still considerable. Thus supporters of the National government were over-represented, winning 70 per cent of the seats with 53 per cent of the vote, and Labour was under-represented, winning only 25 per cent of the seats with 38 per cent of the vote. The Liberals too were under-represented. If proportional representation had operated, the National government with 330 seats instead of 429 would still have had a comfortable majority (45) in parliament, but the opposition parties would have been more generously represented, as Labour would have secured 232 seats instead of 154, and the Liberals 41 instead of 21.[3]

In spite of Labour's electoral disaster in 1931 and their still substantial under-representation in 1935, the party showed no interest in changing the system of voting. The subject was not raised at any Labour party conference after 1931 until 1943. The figures of votes and seats obtained by all the political parties at the preceding general elections were given to the conferences of 1932 and 1936, but with no comments on disproportionate representation. Satisfaction was expressed that Labour managed to obtain as many votes as it did in 1931 in spite of the alleged calumnies and panic spread by the National government, and that the Labour vote in 1935 had almost got back to its level of 1929. No speaker at the conference drew attention to the fact that these votes had secured Labour 289 seats in 1929 and only 154 in 1935, though the party's secretary, J. S. Middleton, reflecting on the last three elections a few days after the 1935 one, described our electoral system as 'extraordinary' and said that 'There is no greater gamble on earth than a British general election'.[4] The National Executive's Reports to Conference constantly gave figures of the Labour vote since 1900 showing how it had risen steadily except in 1931, but they did not draw attention to the fact that often these votes did not

[2] D. E. Butler, *The Electoral System in Britain since 1918* (1963), 191.
[3] Ibid.
[4] Quoted by J. Humphreys in *Contemporary Review*, 149 (Jan. 1936), 'The General Election and Constitutional Reform', 39.

materialize in seats. In other words mainstream Labour thinking in the 1930s was not worried by the capricious and haphazard nature of the electoral system. This was bemoaned by Snowden who considered that the Labour party themselves were responsible for the electoral massacre of 1931 because they had refused to include proportional representation in their Electoral Reform Bill of 1931. 'There are no signs that they have realised the blunder they made', he wrote in 1934. 'They appear to be expecting that the next General Election will give them the advantage of the gamble and the chance of winning seats to which they are not entitled on the actual votes they have polled.'[5] When in 1935 the system did not work in their favour, one Labour leader, Greenwood, in the debate on the address, comforted himself by the thought that 'it was quite possible that a very small turnover of votes, not more than 250,000, might, through the accidents of our electoral system, have put us there and them here'.[6] His calculation is curious as the parties supporting the National government won nearly three-and-a-half million more votes than Labour.

After 1935 many Labour leaders thought that if they managed to increase their support in the country they could win an election. Thus Attlee, the leader of the party, was in 1937 'convinced that the achievement of power in the near future was possible if every member of the party will do his share in making converts'.[7] Dalton considered in 1936 that a clear Labour majority in parliament was possible, though he added that he did not underestimate the difficulty of the task. He also realized that the number of seats gained from a turnover in votes depended on their distribution in the constituencies, but nevertheless, when arguing against the need for an electoral pact between opposition parties as recommended by those pressing for a Popular Front, he thought a Labour victory was well within the bounds of practical politics.[8] Clearly he was not unnerved by his vastly over-optimistic forecast a year earlier

[5] Snowden, *Autobiography* (1934), ii. 889.

[6] *HC Deb.* 307 (4 Dec. 1935), 150.

[7] C. R. Attlee, *The Labour Party in Perspective* (1937), 280.

[8] Hugh Dalton, 'The "Popular Front"', *Political Quarterly*, 7 (Oct.–Dec. 1936), 481–9.

that Labour would win nearer 240 than 200 seats at the general election of 1935. (They actually won only 154.)[9]

Confidence in electoral success was also expressed by Labour's National Executive. It believed that power could be captured by disciplined loyalty, thorough organization, and widespread propaganda. When this was reported to the Labour party conference of May 1939, one speaker, J. T. Murphy, pointed out that even a 15 per cent swing to Labour would not guarantee it a majority of seats, as the distribution of the vote was the crucial factor, but this piece of realism attracted no attention. Interest at this time, and indeed during the second half of the 1930s, centred not on the electoral system, but on whether or not the National government could be persuaded to change its policies, particularly foreign policy, if all those opposed to it united together to produce a ferment of popular opinion and pressure in and out of parliament. If this strategy did not succeed before the next general election which could not be held later than the autumn of 1940, the supporters of the Popular Front wanted to prevent opponents of the government—Communists, Socialists, Liberals, and other 'progressives'—from fighting each other at the polls. This raised questions in a few people's minds about the working of the electoral system and scepticism as to its ability to transform votes into seats. Thus G. D. H. Cole as early as the autumn of 1936 warned that the Liberal electorate would refuse to disappear however weak the party was in parliament. He therefore thought that, apart from quite unforeseen circumstances, the Labour party was unlikely to win a clear majority either at the next election or at the next but one. His solution was that opponents of the National government should organize a trial run before an election so that only one candidate would emerge.[10] However he, like other supporters of a Popular or People's Front such as Stafford Cripps and Aneurin Bevan, were not recommending a proportional system of representation, but merely a way to get round the problems and uncertainties endemic in the existing one.

[9] *The Political Diary of Hugh Dalton 1918–40, 1945–60*, ed. Ben Pimlott (1986). Diary entry for 28 Oct. 1935.

[10] G. D. H. Cole, 'A British People's Front: Why, and How?', *Political Quarterly*, 7 (Oct.–Dec. 1936), 490–8.

No general election was held until 1945, by which time circumstances had changed very considerably enabling Labour to win 48 per cent of the vote and to return 61 per cent of MPs. It could be said that this result vindicated those who had stood out all along for the party to be completely independent of all other political parties, but this does not mean that if there had been no war, a Labour victory in 1939 or 1940 was more than a remote possibility. Even Dalton admitted this later when writing his memoirs.[11]

The cause of proportional representation encountered many difficulties in the 1930s, the most important of which was probably the fact that the German electoral system was thought by many people to have contributed substantially to the collapse of parliamentary government in that country. The PRS did its best to counter what it regarded as a simplistic explanation of the rise of Nazism, and pointed out *inter alia* that the system of proportional representation used during the Weimar republic was a very rigid party list system with huge constituencies and not the method favoured in England. In the society's view proportional systems, even list systems, were working satisfactorily in many countries, such as Holland, Belgium, and Scandinavia; it regretted that these passed unnoticed by the press. It made much of the success of proportional representation with the single transferable vote in Ireland, and was encouraged by its adoption in New York City in 1936.

So, undeterred as always by the generally unfavourable atmosphere, the PRS continued with its usual activities designed to keep the cause before the public and the political nation. These included many publications—pamphlets and leaflets—letters to the press, a manifesto published in *The Times* in November 1933, meetings, a talk on the BBC, weekend schools, and questioning candidates at elections. The society also sponsored a little parliamentary activity, in particular one general debate on electoral reform in 1933, and bills to alter local authority electoral systems.

The debate on electoral reform was initiated by Herbert Holdsworth, backed by Edward Mallalieu, who were both

---

[11] Hugh Dalton, *The Fateful Years 1931–1945* (1957), 221.

Liberals.[12] Perhaps for tactical reasons they hardly referred to 'proportional representation', and merely said they wanted to see greater and reasonable correspondence between the votes cast and members returned to parliament. They were supported in the debate by Isaac Foot (Liberal), Eleanor Rathbone (Independent), and two Conservatives. Besides the usual arguments, some novel points were made, reflecting the particular circumstances of the time, one of which was the disturbing policies of Stafford Cripps and Labour left-wingers. Already at the general election of 1931, Cripps had propounded a full socialist programme and recommended that parliamentary procedure should be altered if necessary to enable legislation to be passed without delay. He and the Socialist League, founded in 1932, developed these policies to include an Emergency Powers bill, the creation of peers if necessary or the abolition of the House of Lords, in order to prevent obstruction by capitalists to changes in the economic and social structure of the country. Cripps was by chance after the election of 1931 one of the three surviving Labour leaders in parliament, so although his programme of constitutional changes was not endorsed at Labour party conferences, it created considerable alarm in the country; he appeared to be a revolutionary aiming at a party dictatorship.

Supporters of electoral reform drew attention in the 1933 Commons debate to the possibility of a Labour government which had gained power on a minority vote implementing these policies, and they argued that the danger could be averted by a properly constituted House of Commons. They claimed that this would be a far more effective bulwark against loss of liberty than a reformed and strengthened House of Lords, which was being advocated once again in Conservative circles. Eleanor Rathbone made a different and so far as the cause was concerned a rather unfortunate point: she raised the bogy of 'the dictatorship of the proletariat', meaning not the taking of emergency powers by a Labour government, but the old fear that the working classes who constituted the majority of the electorate in every constituency could under the existing elec-

[12] Herbert Holdsworth, 1890–1949. MP, 1931–45, Liberal until 1938, then Liberal National. Edward Mallalieu, 1905–79. MP, Liberal, 1931–5, and Labour 1948–74.

toral system almost entirely fill the Commons with proletarian members. She warned the Conservatives to think about this, and apparently made at least one convert, Lord Scone, who said that 'PR' for him meant 'Perpetual Repression of the Socialist party'.[13]

In the debate new force was given to the old argument, used since the time of Hare and Mill, that many of the ablest men were excluded from parliament by the existing electoral system, for in 1931 all fourteen former Labour cabinet ministers who opposed the National government were defeated except George Lansbury.

The main opposition came not from government spokesmen but from the Labour deputy leader, Clement Attlee, and the Conservative ex-minister Sir Vivian Henderson. As one of the tiny band of Labour front-benchers at this time, Attlee had often to deal with subjects he had previously not much studied. Electoral systems seem to have been one of these. He was clearly unaware that stable democratic governments existed in many foreign countries with proportional systems, and thought that the British system was the only one which could produce 'effective government' and one chosen by the electors. He obstinately maintained that France had had proportional representation during the greater part of the last fifteen years, though in fact she had never had it; that the movers of the motion wanted parliament to be an exact replica of opinions in the country, which was, he said, in any case impossible; and that he did not remember voting for the alternative vote when Labour was in power, though in fact he had voted for it three times. Attlee was on surer ground when he took Labour's standard line on the Liberal party's desire for proportional representation; this was in effect that the Liberal party should not exist, and, if it did, no government, including a Conservative one, should have to pay any attention to its policies; a third group should not be allowed to tone down the policy of a government with a definite economic theory.

Sir Vivian Henderson too thought our electoral system pro-

[13] Mungo Scone, 1900–71. MP, Conservative, 1931–5, when he went to the Lords as Earl of Mansfield. Some of his anti-socialist passion may have been due to the fact that he had twice been defeated at the polls by Jennie Lee, who was soon to marry Aneurin Bevan.

duced effective government as contrasted with what happened abroad, whilst also saying that all life is a gamble and that to seek security by looking for a system without defects was a sign of defeat; politics was 'not a question of arithmetic, but very largely and primarily a question of humanity'. Another speaker (Rhys Davies, Labour) agreed that proportional representation neglected the fact that electors were human beings, and an anti-democratic MP (Michael Beaumont, Conservative) thought that proportional representation was not 'suitable for discussion'.

The motion for electoral reform was defeated by 128 votes to 32. Those voting for it included six Conservatives, one member of the ILP, and one National Labour member; the rest were all Liberals.[14]

Meanwhile before this debate a bill enabling local authorities to adopt a proportional system of election had been presented to parliament in November 1932. Its declared purpose was 'to enable any considerable section of the electorate to return one member'. A three-fifths vote of the local council would be necessary for adoption of the act, and this decision could be reversed after six years. The bill was sponsored by a Liberal, Robert Bernays, backed by members of all parties, including every section and subsection of the National government's supporters.[15] On the second reading of the bill in 1933, Bernays pointed out that the polarization of national politics in 1931 into socialists and anti-socialists was reflected in local politics, with the result that the opinions of local government electors were distorted even more than usual. For instance in Bradford in 1931, the socialists obtained more than a third of the votes but no seats on the 22-strong council, whereas in some areas the anti-socialists were grossly under-represented. There were, he said, many instances of this kind.

The bill was hotly criticized by Sir Gerald Hurst, who had been prominent in opposition to a similar bill in 1923. He

[14] *HC Deb.* 283 (6 Dec. 1933), 1725–88. Scone's remark is at 1781, Henderson's at 1752, and Beaumont's at 1785.

[15] Robert Bernays, 1902–45. Journalist on the *News Chronicle*. MP, 1931–45, Liberal until 1935, then National Liberal. He held office at the Ministry of Health and Local Government, 1937–9, but he does not seem to have used his position there to advance the cause he campaigned for earlier.

considered it 'one of the most useless bills that had ever been brought in', and he was amazed that a member of the Conservative party (Sir William Wayland) could support such a 'revolutionary and subversive measure'. Hurst may have been right in not accepting Bernays's view that the fundamental struggle between socialist and anti-socialist would be ended by introducing proportional representation, but he was on less sure ground in saying that a different electoral system would not diminish distortion of representation.[16]

This bill[17] made no further progress in parliament, and it was not until 1938 that another attempt was made to revive the question. The bill then presented by Wayland was bolder, as it made the single transferable vote compulsory for the election of some local authorities, namely the councils of county boroughs (the large towns), London boroughs, and the London County Council. Compulsion had also been a feature of a bill presented the year before requiring all London boroughs to use the single transferable vote for their elections. This failed to obtain a second reading, but Wayland's bill of 1938 did get debated. Its supporters from all parties emphasized how undesirable it was for representation to be, as it often was, wholly or largely in the hands of one party, like in a totalitarian state; apart from other objections to this state of affairs, such as unfairness and lack of interest in local elections, it could lead to suspicions of favouritism in appointments. Opponents feared that if proportional representation was used for local elections, it would be difficult not to have it for national elections, to which they advanced many objections, including the unusual one that it would tend to 'mass thinking and the destruction of individualism'. The debate showed once again a wide division of opinion about the working of electoral systems in other countries. The bill got no further at its second reading through lack of a quorum. It was reintroduced later in the year, backed again by MPs of all parties, but made no progress.[18]

[16] *HC Deb.* 274 (24 Feb. 1933), 2127–30. Sir William Wayland, 1869–1950. MP, Conservative, 1927–45. He had local government experience as Mayor of Deptford.

[17] The Local Elections (Proportional Representation) Bill.

[18] *HC Deb.* 332 (25 Feb. 1938), 685–718, and 342 (2 Dec. 1938), 829–30. The words quoted were those of the octogenarian Sir Annersley Somerville who was for many years a teacher at Eton College.

Members of the PRS also intervened in 1936 during a debate about the redistribution of seats designed to make electoral districts more equal. Sir Francis Acland (Liberal) pointed out that redistribution by itself would not produce justice between one elector and another, and that it was necessary to consider proportional representation if one wanted to produce equality of representation. Cecil Wilson (Labour) also considered the existing system unjust as large sections of the population were not represented in parliament. This would lead to disillusionment with democracy.[19]

During the Second World War, advocates of electoral reform raised the subject whenever a suitable opportunity occurred. Thus as early as October 1939, when parliament was passing a bill to postpone local authority elections and the preparation of the electoral register, Edmund Harvey said that he hoped that when a new register of electors was made up a better electoral system for both local and national elections would be introduced.[20]

In March 1940 the House of Lords held a debate on Parliament and the Electoral System at the instigation of the Liberal peer, Baron Rea, a merchant banker who had been a member of the House of Commons intermittently between 1906 and 1935.[21] Rea asked the government to set up a commission on the lines of the Speaker's conference of 1917 to examine the changes in the electoral system and the distribution of seats that might be required to ensure that the next parliament should effectively represent the opinion of all sections of the community. He wanted to avoid the mistakes of 1918 and 1919 in settling peace terms. Moreover there was, he said, a risk of revolt if government was not solidly founded on the expressed will of the people. In the debate a Scottish peer, Aberdeen and Temair, made an unusual point, reminiscent of Hare's view, that repre-

---

[19] *HC Deb.* 308 (5 Feb. 1936), 288–301. F. D. Acland, 1874–1939. MP, Liberal, 1906–Jan. 1910, Dec. 1910–22, 1923–4, 1932–9. Cecil Wilson, 1862–1945. MP, Labour, 1922–31 and 1935–44. A subscriber to the PRS since 1927.

[20] *HC Deb.* 352 (17 Oct. 1939), 748–9. T. Edmund Harvey, 1875–1955. MP, Liberal, 1910–18 and 1923–4; Independent Progressive, 1937–45, representing the Combined English Universities.

[21] Walter Russell Rea, 1873–1948. He had failed to win a seat in 1918, 1920, 1922, 1924, and 1929. Created Baron in 1935.

sentation should not be wholly based on geographical districts, as this failed to reflect the views of some interests in the community, for instance science. Two Conservative peers expressed hostility to proportional representation, but Rea when withdrawing his motion said he was pleased it had created some interest.[22]

Even in June 1940, electoral reform figured in letters to *The Times*. They were sparked off by a correspondent, Hely-Hutchinson, a Conservative MP, deploring the inefficiency in political leadership in the last ten years which he thought was due to 'equal suffrage'. He wanted heads to be weighed instead of being counted. The electoral reformers responded by attributing the poor quality of the House of Commons to the chancy nature of the electoral system which excluded some people of above average quality from public life, and they asked for a Speaker's conference to make a fresh survey of the working of the system.[23]

In October 1940 when the bill to prolong the life of parliament was being considered, the Home Secretary, Herbert Morrison, announced that the House would have an opportunity, if it so desired, to consider questions connected with changes in the electoral system, before a general election was held on a new register. Harvey and others welcomed the Home Secretary's promise, guarded though it was, and kept up pressure for some sort of inquiry, commission, or conference. They raised the issue every year when Prolongation of Parliament bills were being discussed and during the debate on the address in 1942. They also secured, in 1943, 114 signatures representing all parties to a motion for a conference on electoral reform. In the end the government relented and agreed to set up a Speaker's conference. The Prime Minister, Winston Churchill, in announcing this decision said, 'The Government are fully conscious of the importance of giving attention to all measures designed to secure that whenever there is an appeal to the country—whether at by-elections or at a general election—the result shall be fully and truly representative of the views of the people.'[24] Churchill as an ex-Liberal had always been more

[22] *HL Deb.* 115 (12 Mar. 1940), 817–30.
[23] *The Times*, 1940, 27 June, 4c; 28 June, 3d; 1 July, 5f; 9 July, 5f.
[24] *HC Deb.* 392 (14 Oct. 1943), 1047.

sympathetic to proportional representation than many Conservatives.

There was also a lively corrrespondence in *The Times* in 1943 revealing unease amongst members of all political parties about the capricious working of the existing electoral system, and the danger of a coupon election at the end of the war which, they considered, could be avoided by electoral reform.[25] A different view was expressed by the paper's editor, Barrington-Ward. Thus a *Times* leader, almost certainly written by him, advised the Speaker's conference to be guided by the sound principle that representation was not an end in itself. It also expressed the view that a House of Commons which exaggerates and distorts the broad currents of popular opinion is a more effective buttress of democratic government than one that exactly reflects every minute shade of thought at the cost of having no mind of its own; effective leadership could be exercised in this possibly cruder but always more vigorous kind of House.[26]

Before the Speaker's conference met, there was in February 1944 a two-day debate in the Commons on the electoral system on a motion welcoming the establishment of the conference. David Butler has described the Commons' discussion as 'notable for harmony rather than enlightenment'.[27] It is true that most speakers from the two main parties (Conservative and Labour) argued against proportional representation, but there was profound disagreement between them and the advocates of electoral reform, who included Liberals, Independent Labour, Commonwealth, and Communist. These disagreements were on both fundamental issues, such as the purpose of elections and whether third parties should be represented, and questions of fact, such as the experience of countries with proportional systems. Opponents alleged that proportional representation resulted in corruption, gerrymandering, graft, weakness, and general decline in the whole standard of parliamentary government, whereas the British system produced efficient and strong governments. The best arguments for a change were put by a Labour member, Sir Robert Young, a product of Ruskin College,

[25] *The Times*, 1943, 14 Jan. 8d; 19 Jan. 6d; 7 Apr. 5e; 13 Apr. 5g; 16 Apr. 5e; 17 July, 5e; 20 July, 5d; 14 Sept. 5d.
[26] *The Times*, 2 Feb. 1944, 5b–c. See also *History of The Times* (1984), v. 52.
[27] *Electoral System*, 91.

Oxford, and by D. N. Pritt, KC, a formidable left-wing Labour MP who had been expelled from the party in 1940. Pritt stressed that one could decide who is to govern by choosing people who do almost exactly represent the real feeling of the country, and that one did not need to perpetuate a system which misrepresented the opinion of the electorate. This was the answer to the doctrine constantly reiterated since it was in effect accepted by the Royal Commission of 1910, that the purpose of a general election was not to produce a representative House of Commons but to choose a government. Less valid points were made by some of the speakers supporting a change, for instance that the war would have been avoided if the British had had proportional representation fifteen years ago; that the Conservatives might soon find themselves the third party, or that there could be a coalition of Conservatives and Labour after the war. Moreover it is unlikely that their opponents were impressed by the frequent references to the success of the single transferable vote in Tasmania, whose total population, it was said in a subsequent debate, was about the same as that of Croydon, with a parliament about half the size of the Croydon Borough Council.[28]

The Speaker's conference had thirty-two members besides the Speaker, Douglas Clifton Brown.[29] The parties were represented roughly in proportion to their strength in the Commons, not as in 1930 in proportion to their strength amongst the electorate, presumably because eight years had elapsed since the electorate had expressed its views; but the selection was intended to secure, as far as possible, the representation of various shades of opinion, different types of constituency, and all parts of the country. The result was 17 Conservatives, 9 Labour, 2 Liberal, one National Liberal, one ILP, one Independent Labour, and one Independent Progressive.[30]

---

[28] *HC Deb*. 396 (1 and 2 Feb. 1944), 1154–1237, and 1258–1367. Robert Young, 1872–1957. MP, Labour, 1918–31 and 1935–50. As an engineer he may have experienced the use of the single transferable vote in trade union affairs. D. N. Pritt, 1887–1972. MP, Labour and Independent Labour, 1935–50. His defence of the Soviet attack on Finland in 1939 was the occasion of his expulsion from the party.

[29] D. Clifton Brown, 1879–1958. MP, Conservative, 1918–23, and 1924–51. He had only been Speaker since Mar. 1943.

[30] See Appendix G for names of members.

The conference met on 16 February 1944 and reported its decisions on methods of election in May 1944.[31] The PRS had submitted a comprehensive resolution containing several statements of fact which the society thought the conference would have to accept. These were as follows:

> That the present method of election fails to produce results fully and truly representative of the views of the voters.
>
> That the principal reason for this failure is the distribution of the country into single-member constituencies (or double-member constituencies in which each elector has two votes), under which it may be observed,
>
> (*a*) there can be and has in fact been in the years 1922–3, 1924–9, and 1935 to date a majority in the House of Commons of one party based on a minority of votes for that party in the country;
>
> (*b*) coalition government has prevailed during the years 1918–22 and 1931 to date, and government by a single party, having no majority in the House of Commons, during the years 1923–4 and 1929–31;
>
> (*c*) there has not been at any time since the Speaker's Conference of 1917 a government formed by any one party supported by a majority of the voters.

As no record of the conference's proceedings is available, it is not known whether members disagreed with this account of the working of the existing electoral system, though it is difficult to see how they could have. What is clear is that most of them saw no reason to change the system by the adoption of proportional representation with the single transferable vote, or of the alternative vote. These were turned down by 25 to 4 and 20 to 5 votes respectively. The conference did not apparently consider any other electoral systems. Those in favour of proportional representation were presumably Harvey, M. Lloyd George, Pritt, and Rea.

The people who had been for some years pressing for a Speaker's conference on electoral reform had naïvely assumed that it would follow the model of the conference of 1916–17

---

[31] PP 1943–4, iii. 213. Conference on Electoral Reform and Redistribution of Seats, Letter from Mr Speaker to the Prime Minister, 24 May 1944.

which it was believed had held genuine discussions about the effects and merits of different systems. Nothing like this happened in 1944. According to one of the persons present, only one day was devoted to proportional representation, when Pritt was allowed to put the case for it; but this was a mere formality, for no one paid any attention to his arguments and the issue was not seriously discussed. The Conservative and Labour party organizations had probably decided against proportional representation before the conference started. So, even if Clifton Brown had been, like Lowther in 1916, sympathetic to a proportional system, the outcome could hardly have been different.

Having agreed that no change should be made in the method of election, the conference turned its attention to the other matters which had been referred to it and in due course bills were brought in embodying its recommendations. The PRS was naturally very disappointed by the conference's rejection of proportional representation, but decided to fight on in spite of the poor prospects of success. So in a further effort to put their case, they moved the rejection of the bill providing for the redistribution of seats which was passing through parliament in the autumn of 1944, because it did not include proportional representation. Supporters of this motion—Liberal, Labour, Independent, and Commonwealth—made a few points which had not been made for some time. Thus a new MP, Hugh Lawson (Commonwealth), an engineer who was capable of some simple mathematical thinking, pointed out that the existing system was so illogical it could result in one party getting all the seats if the other party's votes were spread evenly in straight fights. Megan Lloyd George (Liberal) admitted that proportional representation had some defects, but considered it infinitely preferable to the existing system. In a spirited speech she criticized the 'autocratic ring' in Arthur Greenwood's view that only two parties should exist. He, the deputy leader of the parliamentary Labour party, had said in the debate of 2 February 1944 that 'The people outside the two predominant parties should make up their minds under which umbrella they will come'. Pritt pointed out that proportional representation had not created new parties in the countries where it operated. Less persuasive was Commander King-Hall's plea that one should get back to eighteenth-century conditions when the division in parliament was not between political parties but between the government and the House.[32]

In opposing the motion the government spokesman, Osbert Peake (Conservative), made some scathing remarks about proportional representation. He referred to it as a mere 'algebraic formula' and said that if the aim of its supporters was to produce a parliament that was a cross-section of the community, this could be done by asking the Registrar-General to select 615 names out of a hat. He praised the speech made by the Labour ex-minister Pethick-Lawrence as 'the most powerful demolition of the case for proportional representation he had ever heard'. Pethick-Lawrence had argued *inter alia* that the object of democracy was not to reproduce in miniature the views of the electorate, and that in any case proportional representation would not result in a more representative House of Commons than the existing system.The motion to reject the bill was decisively defeated, by 202 votes to 18.[33] At the committee stage of the bill, an attempt was made by Harvey to get debated an amendment which would have provided for the single transferable vote as a limited experiment on the ground this had not been discussed at the second reading, but it was ruled out of order by the Speaker.[34]

The subject was not raised in the Lords when they were considering the bill, mainly, it seems, because they regarded it as a matter for the Commons.[35]

There was one further parliamentary discussion about proportional representation before the war ended. This was in 1945 on an amendment to the Representation of the People Bill moved by the Liberal Geoffrey Mander seeking to confer on local authorities optional powers to adopt a proportional system. Harvey pointed out that local government had not been discussed at the Speaker's conference, and Sir Percy Harris that

[32] Megan Lloyd George, 1902–66. MP, Liberal, 1929–51; Labour, 1957–66. King-Hall was the founder of the Hansard Society. MP, 1939–45, first National Labour, then Independent National.

[33] *HC Deb.* 403 (10 Oct. 1944), 1632–1708. Second reading of House of Commons (Redistribution of Seats) Bill.

[34] *HC Deb.* 403 (12 Oct. 1944), 1935.

[35] See Minutes of the Executive Committee of the PRS, 6 Dec. 1944. Simon had withdrawn as a vice-president of the society, and Samuel refused to move an amendment.

one-quarter of the twenty-eight London borough councils were drawn from one party. Several speakers supported the proposal on various grounds. However the chief feature of the debate was a violent denunciation of proportional representation by the Labour MP Ellen Wilkinson, who was then Parliamentary Secretary at the Ministry of Home Security. 'The problem of democracy', she said, 'and the object of voting was not to secure a kind of mathematical justice and a mathematical picture of a kaleidoscopic electorate. It is the job of getting government done in the simplest possible way.' She referred to 'that bedrock two-party system which most people regard as one of the fundamental factors in the success of our constitutional methods'. She did not stay in the chamber to listen to the angry responses she had stimulated or to the amazement of MPs at her account of democracy which, it was pointed out, Hitler would have been pleased to endorse. The other government spokesman, Maxwell Fyfe, argued the case against the amendment in more moderate terms, stressing that he did not think there was, as suggested by its supporters, a large non-politically-minded class of good candidates who would be attracted to local government if the change were made. The debate was also significant as the occasion on which a previously staunch supporter of proportional representation, Eleanor Rathbone, announced that she had doubts about it for parliamentary elections. She now felt it was a really difficult question on which there was much to be said on both sides. The amendment was defeated by 208 votes to 17.[36]

During the years 1931–45 there was little and increasingly little support for proportional representation amongst members of the two main parties, many if not most of whom wished overtly or privately that the Liberal party would fade away. Nor did they want to do anything to help candidates standing as independents, several of whom had been successful during the latter part of this period. There was one exception to this statement: Winston Churchill made several pronouncements in favour of electoral reform during the 1930s, advocating propor-

[36] *HC Deb.* 407 (23 Jan. 1945), 686–722. Ellen Wilkinson, 1891–1947. MP, Labour, 1924–31 and 1935–47. Her remarks are at 700–5.

tional representation for the great cities;[37] but being politically isolated, he had little influence. The case for a proportional system put so trenchantly by the Independent Labour MP D. N. Pritt carried no weight in either party; he was thought to be a Communist fellow-traveller and on his own admission was neither tactful nor patient. However the very different advocacy of T. E. Harvey, who was a deeply religious, idealistic Quaker, was no more persuasive, persistent though he was.

In spite of the decline in parliamentary support for proportional representation, membership of the PRS kept up quite well, averaging nearly 600 in the years 1932–45, and rising by 1945 to 726 as a result of growing interest in the subject towards the end of this period. But electoral reform was understandably not an issue at the general election of 1945. Even the Liberal party manifesto hardly referred to it and appeared to favour the alternative vote. Those who voted Liberal or for some of the smaller parties, i.e. Communist, Commonwealth, and Irish Nationalist, who all together numbered over two-and-a-half million, were probably at least sympathetic to proportional representation, but they constituted only about 10 per cent of the voters. Even allowing for the fact that in half the constituencies there was no chance of voting for these parties because they did not put up candidates in them, it seems impossible to accept the view of the secretary of the PRS expressed in 1944 that if a referendum on the issue was held the outcome would be favourable. The enthusiasts were as unrealistic as ever.

[37] See in particular Churchill's article in the *Daily Mail*, 29 May, 1935.

# XII

# Conclusion

INTEREST in voting theory was not shown in Britain until the early nineteenth century and even then it was confined to a small nucleus of people. By the 1830s some isolated experiments for parliamentary and local elections were suggested but not adopted. In the early 1850s a few thinkers with access to the main periodical journals began analysing the existing electoral system and proposing changes, one of which (the limited vote) received some encouragement from the government.

The scene altered dramatically in the late 1850s when Thomas Hare published his radical ideas. Bolstered by the enthusiastic support of John Stuart Mill, these aroused considerable interest. Though only a few people advocated Hare's complete electoral scheme, several were attracted by its key devices—the quota, and preferential voting with the transfer of surplus and useless votes. They launched campaigns pressing for changes in the electoral system to secure that the opinions of voters were represented in parliament in rough proportion to their support amongst the electorate. They showed what were, or could be, the effects of the existing simple majority system, emphasizing its erratic and distorting nature, especially if used in single-member constituencies. They proposed in its stead the single transferable vote in multi-membered constituencies.

From the 1860s onwards, the reformers introduced bills into parliament providing for proportional representation in parliamentary and local authority elections, and they seized every opportunity to try to amend any bill which was concerned with electoral matters, for example extension of the franchise, local government, Home Rule for Ireland, and school boards. They formed a society to advocate the cause. It aimed to educate the general public, and more particularly the political world and opinion formers. The case for proportional representation was explained and argued in books, pamphlets, periodicals, and at learned societies. In spite of all this assiduous activity and propaganda during the course of nearly ninety years, the reformers failed to get proportional representation adopted for British parliamentary or local elections, and have still not succeeded.

Many factors account for their failure. These fall into two groups: the mistakes and deficiencies of the reformers, and the problems posed by the attitudes and arguments of the opposition.

On the reformers' side, it was unfortunate that the first full scheme to be put forward (Hare's) was extremely complex. Most of the reformers backed a simpler scheme, but some of them remained loyal to Hare. It would have been better if they had frankly declared his plan impracticable.

Hare's case for a change in the electoral system was based largely on his view of British political life as deeply degenerate. His scheme was designed to improve *inter alia* the calibre of candidates and MPs. This argument for proportional representation was also much used by Leonard Courtney, who was one of the most important, if not the most important, advocate of the reform from 1884 until his death in 1918. However much substance there was in this picture of the political world, it was hardly designed to win friends amongst politicians. This was an example, among several which could be cited, of Courtney's shortcomings as a politician. Nor was it obvious to many people that proportional representation would, as was claimed, improve the quality of MPs.

Further, neither politicans nor indeed many others thought it realistic or desirable to try to eliminate parties from the political process, or even substantially to curtail their activities and influence. This was one of the motives behind Hare's voting theory; it was shared by Mill and much emphasized by Courtney and many other supporters of proportional representation since his time. They argued for a proportional system as a way of getting independent candidates elected. They also wanted to enable electors to choose between candidates from the same party who represented different views, without splitting the vote. This objective found little support among politicians, who are usually keen to foster unity in their party.

However acceptable their aims—to purify political life and improve the quality of MPs—the early reformers appeared and indeed were Utopian and naïve in thinking that, as Courtney put it in 1904, 'a comparatively simple change held the promise of a complete transformation'. They claimed too much for the electoral system they proposed, recommending it as a panacea for all political ills, including the elimination of bribery and corruption; and they alienated many politicians with their revivalist language, talking of 'the new birth', 'a new gospel', and 'the resurrection and liberation of the people'. Supported by an American Senate report, they claimed that the Civil War in the USA might have been averted if a better electoral system had been in operation. Even more amazingly the same claim was made about the two World Wars in relation to the British electoral system. On the other hand there appeared to be some justification for a similar suggestion regarding political and sectarian strife in Northern Ireland.

The fact that some advocates of a proportional system were motivated by their fears of democracy alienated supporters on the left of the political spectrum. This was evident not only at the start of the movement in the 1860s and 1870s, but also in the important 1917–18 debates and even in the 1930s.

The Left was also alienated by pleas for proportional representation as a safeguard against socialism, for some reformers feared that the existing system might give the Labour party an unwarranted majority in parliament. The Proportional Representation Society never used this argument, but the society had nevertheless a middle-class image, in spite of the secretary's constant efforts to recruit support in Labour circles. For many years its Executive Committee met in the Courtneys' drawing-room and appeared to be something of a family coterie. Keir Hardie was naturally offended when, calling at the house one day, he was shown down to the back door in the basement.

In recommending the single transferable vote, its advocates would have done better to put more emphasis on its success in Ireland rather than in the distant and smaller Tasmania. They might then have avoided sarcastic comments such as that made by an MP who asked, 'Is there no lesson to be learnt from Lithuania? How do they elect their borough councils in Yugo-slavia and aldermen in Lapland?'[1]

---

[1] *HC Deb.* 160 (23 Feb. 1923), 1475. The MP was the Conservative R. W. Barnett.

It is, and was, common to hold the Liberals responsible for the failure to get proportional representation adopted in this country. They should, it is said, have had in 1917–18 a greater sense of what their party's future interests required, and backed the reform then firmly and in greater numbers. Having failed to do this, they were thereafter impotent. To take this line is to accept the view that the issue should be decided in the light of self-interest and the fortunes of one's party, and not on considerations of fairness, justice, and the proper nature of representative government. If one believes, as did many supporters of proportional representation, that these are the crucial considerations, it is just as reasonable to hold responsible for its rejection the Conservatives who argued and voted against it. Even if one does accept the view that party self-interest should guide politicians, it can be said in defence of the Liberals in 1917–18 that they could not be expected to have foreseen the fate of their party after 1918.

It is true that in the 1920s the Liberals were not solidly in favour of proportional representation: several of them thought the alternative vote would be an adequate reform, and the most vigorous thinkers among them, active in the Liberal Summer School, were not interested in the subject. However even if they had been united on the issue and deeply committed to it, it is unlikely that they could have played their cards more successfully in 1924 when Labour was in office, given the government's hostility to making any agreement with them. By 1929 the Liberals were more united and convinced of the case for proportional representation, but they were unwilling to make it a condition of support for the Labour government, as they wanted to preserve their freedom of action on other issues. It is reasonable to speculate whether they might not have succeeded if they had not attached so much importance to independence.

Did the PRS adopt the wrong strategy in appealing for support from all the political parties, rather than concentrating on one of them? When writing about the tactics of the women's suffrage movement, Brian Harrison has pointed out that contempt for party loyalty was widespread among late Victorian reforming movements, following the examples of the earlier successful campaigns against slavery and the corn laws. He considers this was a mistaken strategy after the 1860s, when political parties had become the vehicles of popular participation and had relegated non-party pressure groups to a subordinate role, dependent for success on the precarious device of private members' bills.[2] This theory may be plausible when applied to the women's suffrage movement, but it would not seem to be applicable to the PRS either when it was founded in the 1880s or later. It would have been difficult in the early days to decide which party to concentrate on, and later the society's near identification with Liberals was a hindrance rather than a help to the cause. However it is undeniable that the desire to obtain cross-party support posed problems: these were evident right from the start when Hare and others were trying to interest working men in his scheme, and they have re-emerged at intervals ever since. For the arguments used by some advocates of proportional representation have alienated some potential supporters with different party-political sympathies.

Opposition to proportional representation took many different forms. In the early days of the campaign for a change in the electoral system, one of the main problems faced by the reformers was the unwillingness of many people, including prominent politicians, even to think about the subject. It was strange and, they were certain, difficult. The result was that they took no interest in the analysis of the working of the existing system, and were even more reluctant to address their minds to the remedies proposed for its alleged shortcomings. If they did listen to those suggesting a change, many of them professed not to understand either the basic case for, or principle of, minority or proportional representation, or the various schemes designed to implement proportionality. It was an attitude which continued well into the twentieth century, although it was more and more difficult to sustain plausibly when proportional systems were being used in many countries and even by illiterate Irish peasants.

A lack of interest in electoral matters has also been evident in much historical writing in the past, though less so in recent years due to the development of psephology. Thus political

---

[2] Brian Harrison, 'Women's Suffrage at Westminster 1866–1928,' in M. Bentley and J. Stevenson, *High and Low Politics* (1983).

historians when explaining the results of general elections have not always looked behind the figures of seats gained or lost, neglecting the evidence provided by votes. For instance they write of 'the country' decisively rejecting Home Rule for Ireland at the general election of 1886, and claim that the country was 'much more anti-home rule . . . than the house [of Commons]'.[3] In fact only just over half the voters (51 per cent) supported candidates opposed to Home Rule, and the percentage of MPs voting against the Home Rule Bill the previous month was slightly larger (52 per cent). Similarly when votes are looked at, the Liberal victory of 1906 turns out not to have been such a 'landslide' as it appears, for the Liberal share of the total vote had increased by only 4.4 per cent since 1900. Nor was the Liberal lead over the Conservative vote very substantial. There is therefore much less to explain than is usually thought.

Another problem for the reformers was the misrepresentation of their aims. It was often alleged that they wanted the minority or minorities to rule, and to deprive the majority of proper representation. It was also said that they wanted parliament to be an exact replica of the opinions of all voters. This was true of Hare and Mill, aiming as they did at 'personal representation', but their successors' goal was only rough approximation between votes and seats. They constantly pointed out that a minority would have to be fairly substantial to obtain representation with the scheme they recommended, namely constituencies returning between three and at the most a dozen members each.

Opponents stressed the antiquity of the existing system as an argument in its favour, and after 1885 they could also claim that it had been recently reviewed and maintained by agreement between the two main political parties. The reformers denied that there had been an adequate examination of the whole subject before the settlement of 1884–5 which in their view, by the wide adoption of single-member constituencies, made the situation even worse.

The opposition voiced various fears about the effects of proportional representation. The most important of these was

[3] R. C. K. Ensor, *England 1870–1914* (1936), 99; and N. Mansergh, *The Irish Question 1840–1921* (1965), 125.

weak government. As early as 1859 Bagehot foretold inaction if minorities were represented, and ever since then this objection has been repeated to great effect. By contrast the British electoral system was credited with producing strong government by usually over-representing in parliament the party with the most votes.

Another frequently voiced fear was that proportional representation would increase the power of party caucuses. This was fuelled by the activities of Birmingham Liberals when the limited vote was in operation (from 1868 to 1885), and it has been alleged as late as the 1920s that the same thing could happen with the single transferable vote. The opposite danger was also foreseen, namely that with proportional representation many cranks and faddists would get returned to parliament. This fear was still evident in the 1930s.

Other objections included the disadvantages of large constituencies: it was said that MPs would not be able to maintain personal contact with their constituents, and that the cost of electioneering would rise considerably.

Most of these objections were answered by the advocates of proportional representation, though usually with no effect; but greater problems were posed by opposition at a more fundamental level. It was difficult to find any common ground as a basis for argument against those who considered that democratic theory did not require majority support and who thought that democracy did not consist, as Ramsay MacDonald said, in 'counting noses'; that even gross misrepresentation of the electorate's opinions in parliament was not something to be regretted; that it was better to have a strong, firm, consistent government even if it had bad policies than a weak, well-intentioned one that wobbled. Here too Bagehot was the first person to express this view, but he was by no means the last. The same line was taken by Herbert Morrison in the 1920s and by the editor of *The Times* in the 1940s.

There was an equally unbridgeable gulf between those who thought that it was legitimate for the two largest parties to try to eliminate or at least to emasculate a third party, and those who considered such a policy unacceptable and indeed immoral in a country which claimed to value political freedom.

Nor was it easy to argue with opponents who openly distrusted logic, who used as terms of abuse such words as 'scientific', 'arithmetical', and 'mathematical', and who treated the subject flippantly.

It was easier to counter the assertion made often in the later years of the debate that coalitions were contrary to democracy, but the advocates of proportional representation have not always done this effectively.

Nor did the reformers manage to convince their opponents that they posed the issue wrongly when they maintained, as they so often did, that the purpose of an election was not to produce a representative assembly but to choose a government. This argument against proportional representation seems to have carried considerable weight, partly because the reformers did not stress firmly enough that the two objectives were compatible, namely that in electing a representative parliament the country was also choosing a government.

The advocates of proportional representation have included in their ranks many clever, even brilliant, people, but the politicians who have supported it have, with a few exceptions, such as Balfour and Snowden, not been central figures in their parties. This is true of Lubbock, Courtney, Amery, F. E. Smith (Birkenhead), C. A. Cripps (Parmoor), Alfred Mond, and for many years Churchill; it is even more true of less well-known characters such as Walter Morrison, R. A. Sanders (Bayford), Levy-Lawson (Burnham), W. C. Anderson, Aneurin Williams, William Anson, William Layland, Cecil Wilson, Robert Young, and D. N. Pritt.

The opposition, by contrast, has included many leading politicians: Gladstone, Bright, Disraeli, Joseph and Austen Chamberlain, Harcourt, Morley, Northcote, Ramsay Mac-Donald, Lloyd George for a time, Craig, Herbert Morrison, Attlee, and formidable characters such as Shaw-Lefevre (Eversley), Carson, and Walter Long. Even among the intellectuals and journalists who took part in the controversy, opponents of reform were more impressive than the advocates, although these included Hare, J. S. Mill, Professor J. E. Cairnes, Professor Westlake, C. L. Dodgson, C. P. Scott, H. G. Wells, J. A. Hobson, and L. T. Hobhouse. Against them were pitted Walter Bagehot, Herbert Spencer, Leslie Stephen, Frederic Harrison,

A. V. Dicey, Graham Wallas, Bernard Shaw, the Webbs, and many other Fabians.

It is quite often argued that the determining factor for politicians is not the abstract merits or demerits of various electoral systems, but the concrete benefits and disadvantages which a particular system will provide for the party or cause they support.[4] This is certainly true of some politicians at some times, but it was not true for many years during which the subject was debated. It was often not clear what effect the change proposed would have on party fortunes, and many politicians on both sides of the argument were genuinely interested in voting theory.

[4] See, e.g., Vernon Bogdanor, 'Electoral Reform and British Politics', *Electoral Studies*, 6:2 (Aug. 1987), 115–21.

# XIII

# Postscript, 1945–1990

THERE was little pressure for electoral reform after 1945 until interest in the subject revived in the 1970s. Membership of the PRS declined; even keen advocates of proportional representation felt that the question did not touch the country's main post-war problems. However the working of the electoral system was discussed by a few people after each general election.

The general election of 1945 resulted in considerable over-representation of Labour who, with 48 per cent of the vote, secured 61 per cent of the seats. The Conservatives were under-represented, winning 40 per cent of the vote but only 33 per cent of the seats. As most Conservatives had for many years not wished to change the electoral system, it would have been difficult for them to criticize it for treating them unfairly. The Liberals, as usual, were greatly under-represented. Some people suggested that the overthrow of Winston Churchill's government, which caused general surprise, was due largely to the intervention of over 300 Liberal candidates who received two-and-a-quarter million votes; but *The Times* in explaining and deploring the crushing defeat of the Conservative party did not take this line. It considered that the Liberal party was virtually extinguished and commented that 'The tendency of parliamentary government towards a two-party system continually reasserts itself, is probably inevitable, and is ultimately healthy'.[1]

The Liberals raised the issue of proportional representation in parliament in 1948 when the Representation of the People Bill was being debated, but the subject was hardly discussed. The government spokesman, Herbert Morrison, admitted that all mathematical criticisms of the existing electoral system were correct, but he considered that 'broadly speaking the system

---

[1] *The Times*, leader, 27 July 1945, 5b.

works'; it produced governments with strength and power behind them; even if he did not agree with these governments, he preferred the system to one which involved 'the making and unmaking and remaking of coalitions and bargains of all sorts'.[2]

At the general election of 1950, Labour secured 46 per cent of the vote and just over half (50.4 per cent) of the seats. It thus had a parliamentary majority of only five over all the other parties. This was due to the fact that, in contrast to the 1945 results, the Conservatives too were over-represented, winning 48 per cent of the seats with 44 per cent of the vote. The Liberals fared even worse than in 1945.

After the 1950 election, the advocates of proportional representation were quick to argue that the result made nonsense of the belief that the existing system, whatever its faults, could at least be relied upon to provide strong, stable government by one party with a substantial parliamentary majority; but the opponents of proportionality did not accept that one of their favourite arguments against it had collapsed. Once again some of them considered that the blame should be directed not against the electoral system but against the Liberals for putting up so many (475) candidates. A *Times* leader criticized 'the irresponsible spattering of the electoral map with hundreds of candidatures' for which there was no chance of support; Liberals should be forced to choose between the two other parties.[3] Other opponents of proportional representation, reluctant thus to deny freedom of electoral choice to any citizen, saw the 1950 election as an aberration, and were confident that the system would continue to produce exaggerated parliamentary majorities by translating even a narrow majority in votes into a majority in seats large enough to make strong and effective government possible.[4]

This prediction was only partly borne out by the results of the general election of 1951, for although one party, the Conservatives, obtained a parliamentary majority of 17 over all the

[2] *HC Deb.* 447 (17 Feb. 1948), 1111.

[3] *The Times*, 27 Feb. 1950, 5b.

[4] See, e.g., letter to *The Times*, 6 Mar. 1950, 5e, from Anthony Neville of Queen's College, Cambridge. This view was also expressed by D. E. Butler in his Appendix to H. G. Nicholas, *The British General Election of 1950* (1951), 328 and 333.

other parties (as contrasted with the previous Labour government's majority of 5), they had received a smaller number of votes than Labour. The fact that Labour had 26 fewer seats than the Conservatives in spite of winning over a quarter of a million more votes does not appear to have attracted much comment. This was obviously not to be expected from Conservatives. *The Times* described the new government as 'The Electors' Choice' and one Conservative MP considered that 'Our strange and illogical system, for all its absurdity, still gives the best and fairest result'.[5] But the paucity of Labour comment is remarkable. Moreover such concern as there was in Labour circles did not lead on to criticism of the electoral system or to an interest in proportional representation. The 1951 result was seen as a kink, a view supported by the leading psephologist's verdict that the electoral system's 'Capacity for producing decisive and even overwhelming parliamentary majorities from relatively narrow majorities in votes is in no way diminished'.[6] The Liberals alone criticized a system which in their view entrusted the fate of a great country to the greatest of all gambles.

At the general election of 1955, the Conservatives, who won, were somewhat over-represented, and Labour was a little under-represented. The defenders of the electoral system felt it was working better than it had recently, as the government secured an overall parliamentary majority of 60. They were even more pleased with the results of the general election of 1959, because it exaggerated the parliamentary majority of the winning party more than in 1955 and gave the government an overall majority of 100. The Conservative share of the vote had in fact gone down slightly compared with 1955, but their share of seats went up. They achieved this chiefly at the expense of the Liberals, though Labour was still under-represented with 44 per cent of the vote and only 41 per cent of the seats. Labour was naturally downcast by the massive Conservative majority in parliament, but were not moved to look more sympathetically on proportional systems. They waited for the system to work in their favour, and were rewarded in 1964, as, with almost the

---

[5] *The Times*, leader, 27 Oct. 1951, 7a, and letter from Henry Usborne, 22 Nov. 1951, 5f.

[6] D. E. Butler, *The General Election of 1951* (1952), 277.

same percentage of votes as in 1959 (44.1 as against 43.9), they secured over half the seats. But the system had not produced, as its defenders maintained it did, a strong, stable government, for, because the Conservatives were over-represented, Labour had a parliamentary majority of only 4 over all the other parties, in spite of the great under-representation of the Liberals.

However in 1966 the system worked markedly in favour of Labour, for with 48 per cent of the vote they obtained 58 per cent of the seats, and thus had an overall majority of nearly 100. By contrast the Conservatives were under-represented (though not badly) for the first time since 1945. The Liberals remained the chief sufferers. The two main parties therefore continued to support the existing electoral system at the Speaker's conference of 1965–7 which discussed methods of election amongst the many other matters referred to it. The voting at the conference against a change from the relative majority system in single-member constituencies to the single transferable vote was 19 to 1, the one dissentient being Eric Lubbock, the grandson of the founder of the PRS.[7] The PRS, now renamed the Electoral Reform Society, had been able to put its case to the conference, but it was no doubt right in feeling that many members had closed minds on the subject. It was also hampered subsequently by the fact that, as on previous occasions, the rules of the conference did not allow disclosure of the reasons for their decisions.[8]

When the recommendations of the Speaker's conference were embodied in a White Paper and then in a bill in the autumn of 1968, Lubbock raised the issue of proportional representation on three occasions in the Commons. He concentrated on the central arguments for electoral reform and pointed out that the British government recommended proportional systems for the constitutions of developing countries. Even before he had spoken, the Home Secretary, James Callaghan, had defended the *status quo* by saying that the purpose of an election was to elect a government and that a member of the public chooses his government best by choosing between those candidates whose

---

[7] Eric Lubbock, 1928–. MP, Liberal, 1962–70. Became Baron Avebury in 1971.
[8] PP 1965–6 XIII. 121; and PP 1966–7 XXVII. 417.

parties will form a government; he regretted this on behalf of the Liberal party, but it was 'one of the inexorable facts of life that third parties come up against when a general election arises'. This was in effect to rule out coalition government. Another minister, Merlyn Rees, when arguing against a change, referred to Professor Laski's (mocking) assertion that there were 949 different methods of proportional representation.[9] Rees was confident that 'our democracy works', one reason for which was 'the clear majority which is given to the government of the day'.[10]

The general election of 1970 resulted in over-representation of the Conservatives who won 52 per cent of the seats for 46 per cent of the vote, but Labour too was over-represented, though not by as much. Thus both the main parties benefited from the continued under-representation of the Liberals. The psephologists unusually admitted to the existence of 'chance' and 'accidental' factors.[11]

In the mid-1970s there was a sharp increase in interest in electoral systems and growing doubt about the legitimacy of first-past-the-post, leading to support for some form of proportional representation. The change was dramatic. Advocates of electoral reform were no longer treated, as Lord Avebury put it, as 'harmless and rather amusing cranks, like nudists or the eaters of nut-cutlets',[12] for they included several influential Conservatives, business men, industrialists, and many members of the general public.

The main stimulus to this development was given by the general elections of February and October 1974. Several aspects of the results in February aroused concern. One was that Labour received fewer votes but more seats than the Conservatives. Another was that though Labour with 301 seats was the largest party in parliament, it did not have a majority over all the other

[9] This is another instance of the fact that the London School of Economics and Political Science was a centre of hostility to a proportional system, due no doubt to the influence of the Webbs, Graham Wallas, and H. Finer.

[10] *HC Deb.* 770 (14 Oct. 1968), 39, and 775 (11 Dec. 1968), 462. Lubbock also spoke on 18 Nov. 1968.

[11] D. E. Butler and M. Pinto-Duschinsky, *The British General Election of 1970* (1971), 412–14.

[12] *HL Deb.* 359 (23 Apr. 1975), 903.

parties. Moreover it had received only 37 per cent of the total vote. Thirdly, the gross under-representation of the Liberals, who secured nearly 20 per cent of the vote but only 14 seats instead of the 122 they reckoned was their due, seemed more difficult than ever to defend, and excited sympathy in some who had never before evinced any interest in proportional representation. Regionally based parties also did better than usual, with the result that there were as many as 37 MPs unconnected with the Conservative or Labour parties. By June 1974 the Chief Whip declared that parliament was unmanageable.

The general election of October 1974 did not restore confidence in the British electoral system, for it resulted in a Labour government supported by only 39 per cent of the voters, with a majority of only 3 over all the other parties in parliament. The Liberals with 18 per cent of the vote suffered again disastrously, winning only 13 seats instead of the 118 which they reckoned a proportional system would have given them. The Scottish and Welsh parties increased their representation.

The election of February 1974 had stimulated the formation of the Conservative Action for Electoral Reform, on the initiative of Anthony Wigram, a property developer who was the chairman of the group until 1986. In the 1970s it had the committed support of about fifty Conservative MPs, some of whom became members of Conservative governments in the 1980s. A similar number of Conservative MPs said they did not entirely rule out electoral reform. The group also received support from members of the House of Lords. The subject was discussed at several Conservative party conferences.

Interest in electoral systems was also fostered in the 1970s by the need to decide what electoral method to adopt for direct elections to the European assembly/parliament, and to regional assemblies in Britain if they were set up as a result of pressure for devolution of power.

Advocates of proportional representation naturally recommended its adoption for British members of the European parliament, and many people, whilst not in favour of a proportional system for Westminster, thought it would have to be adopted for European elections, partly because all the other member states would be using proportional systems or the second ballot. But the select committee which considered the many issues involved in direct elections reported in August 1976, with only one dissentient (Jeremy Thorpe), in favour of using the first-past-the-post system.[13] A White Paper of April 1977 discussed three options: a single majority system, i.e. first-past-the-post; proportional representation with a list system, perhaps regional; and proportional representation with the single transferable vote.[14] The government's bill provided for a regional list system, but the Commons decided by a large majority in December 1977 to stick to the existing simple majority system, except for members from Northern Ireland. An effort was made in the Lords to reverse the Commons decision. Lord Banks (Liberal) pointed out that substantial minorities whose support was widely distributed over the country would not get represented in the European parliament and that the Scottish National party could be over-represented, but his amendment proposing a regional list system was lost. Among the arguments used against it was that it was difficult to understand and that it was totally alien to anything which had happened in this country before.[15]

As predicted by the advocates of proportional representation, electing MEPs by the first-past-the-post system in large constituencies has resulted in disproportionate results. The Conservatives have been twice, and Labour once, greatly over-represented, and, except for the Scottish Nationalists, parties other than Conservative and Labour have failed to get a single member returned in the three elections which have been held, in spite of getting substantial support; the Liberals obtained 13 per cent of the vote in 1979, the Alliance of Liberals and Social Democrats 20 per cent in 1984, and the Greens 15 per cent in 1989. Some British MEPs have found it difficult to defend these results when commented on critically by their colleagues in the European parliament, and this has made them question the electoral system used not only for British MEPs but also for the Westminster parliament.

[13] PP 1975–6 XII. Second Report of Select Committee on Direct Elections to the European Assembly.
[14] PP 1976–7 LX.
[15] *HL Deb.* 390 (13 Apr. 1978), 791–822. Desmond Banks, b. 1918, an insurance expert who was made a peer in 1974.

The three MEPs from Northern Ireland are elected by the single transferable vote method which had since 1973 been in use in that part of the United Kingdom for local government elections and the (short-lived) Assembly. This electoral method had been introduced in order to facilitate power-sharing between Catholics and Protestants.

In the late 1960s there was a demand for power to be devolved from Westminster and Whitehall to the various nations and regions of the country. The government appointed a Royal Commission on the Constitution (the Kilbrandon Commission) which reported in October 1973. The commission was not concerned with the electoral system used for the United Kingdom parliament, but it recommended that the regional assemblies which it proposed for Scotland and Wales should be directly elected by the single transferable vote system of proportional representation, with perhaps the alternative vote in single-member constituencies in sparsely populated areas in Scotland. But the bill introduced by the Labour government in January 1977 to create regional assemblies did not provide for their election by a proportional system. An attempt was made to amend the bill by substituting the additional members system for first-past-the-post, but this was defeated after a long debate.[16] The assemblies have not been set up, but pressure for them continues, and this inevitably involves discussion of how they should be elected.

A new argument for proportional representation emerged in the mid-1970s. This was that the economic health of the country was suffering from violent changes of policy, which were due to swings in the electoral pendulum, resulting in alternating governments which reversed each other's economic and industrial measures. Politics, it was said, had become 'adversarial', and this was inimical to the good conduct of the nation's affairs. The remedy proposed was a change in the electoral system, in order to give better representation to the electorate's views which were, it was maintained, more stable and centrist than those which usually dominated in government.

[16] *HC Deb.* 924 (25 Jan. 1977), 1227–1452. The movers of the amendment were John P. Mackintosh (Labour) and Anthony Kershaw (Conservative). For additional members systems, see Glossary.

This thesis was expounded in 1975 in a book entitled *Adversary Politics and Electoral Reform*. The term 'Adversary Politics' was probably suggested by an article in the *Economist* in May 1974 discussing whether the government was likely to hold an election in June. It considered that 'it will take more than another general election to convince British politicians that the adversary game on which they have all been brought up has been played out'.[17] The editor of the book was Professor S. E. Finer, who had not previously been in favour of proportional representation. All the contributors were academics, but their ideas aroused considerable interest amongst business men and industrialists, and generally in Conservative circles where alarm was felt at the alleged influence of left-wing extremists on the government. The book and its main theme were referred to in parliamentary debates, and inspired pamphlets from right-wing pressure groups arguing that industry needed electoral reform.

As a result of all this increasing interest in the subject, the Hansard Society for Parliamentary Government sponsored a commission under the chairmanship of the historian Lord Blake to make an objective and comprehensive study of the subject. The membership of the commission was unusual, as it consisted mostly of people not involved in the academic study of politics. The commission's report, which came out in June 1976, examined the subject from a broad perspective, showing how an electoral method could affect the working of the whole political system. It set out clearly and incisively the requirements which it thought an electoral system should achieve, the case for and against the present system, and the criteria for a new one. It concluded emphatically that electoral reform was necessary, but it was restrained in its recommendation, which was on balance not the single transferable vote but a variant of the German additional members system. Three-quarters of the House of Commons were to be elected in single-member constituencies by first-past-the-post, and one quarter regionally according to a formula which would produce party proportionality.

One spin-off of the report was the creation in 1976 of a National Committee for Electoral Reform, chaired by Lord

---

[17] *Economist*, 11 May 1974, 14.

Harlech, a Conservative, and directed by a Liberal, Richard Holme. It aimed to co-ordinate all the various bodies and people advocating electoral reform, including the groups formed by the political parties, but its existence and activities were not altogether welcomed by the Conservative Action group, partly because of its impact on fund raising. In 1983 it launched the Campaign for Fair Votes and obtained one million signatures asking for a referendum on proportional representation. For several years it was, perhaps wisely, neutral as between proportional systems, but in the end it settled on the single transferable vote, as had the Conservative Action group after lengthy battles. The National Committee appears at present to be moribund.

Because the Hansard Commission and the National Committee were financed by industry, they have been regarded with some suspicion in Labour circles, a suspicion inevitably encouraged by the emphasis put by many advocates of electoral reform on its role in curbing the influence of left-wing politicians. Even the Liberal leader Jeremy Thorpe saw proportional representation in November 1974 as a means of guaranteeing that there would never again be a socialist government, and a *Times* leader of 9 October 1975 pleaded for electoral reform to keep the 'wild men of the left' from influence and power.

Conservative support for electoral reform was, it seems, at its height between 1975 and 1979, and though it continued thereafter for a time, especially in the City of London and among leading industrialists, it was not so vigorous as previously, no doubt because in the three general elections since then the existing system worked very much in favour of the Conservatives. Thus in 1979 they secured 53 per cent of the seats with 44 per cent of the vote, in 1983 61 per cent of the seats with 42 per cent of the vote, and in 1987 58 per cent of the seats with 42 per cent of the vote. This over-representation was achieved not by the under-representation of Labour, who were over-represented by small amounts at all these elections, but by the great under-representation of the Liberals and Social Democrats.

In spite of these successes at general elections, unease about the working of the electoral system was manifested in some Conservative quarters. Rees-Mogg, when retiring as editor of *The Times* in 1981, feared that it could lead to a government of the hard Left; he wanted a system which was less of a gamble.[18] After the 1983 election, a *Times* leader entitled 'Disproportionate Representation' had to admit that the system was more than ever 'out of kilter', and whilst praising it for producing decisive results and coherent government, warned that the political system might no longer be regarded as legitimate if there was not a recognizable correspondence between voting preferences and the parliamentary results.[19] Proposals to allow local authorities to adopt the single transferable vote were supported by many Conservative peers in the mid-1980s.[20]

Despite distrust of the motivation of many electoral reformers, a Labour Campaign for Electoral Reform was founded in March 1976. At first it had few members and many of these defected to the Social Democratic party in the early 1980s. However Labour's defeat in 1983 created some interest in electoral reform, mainly it seems because the Conservatives obtained 400 seats in a parliament of 650. It was said that the existing electoral system no longer 'worked for Labour', though in fact the main victims in 1983 were the Liberals and Social Democrats who with 26.3 per cent of the vote secured only 3 per cent of the seats. Labour with 27.6 per cent of the vote at least won 32 per cent of the seats. The discussion about what should be done became confused: some Labour supporters favoured an electoral pact between the opponents of Toryism; others argued for a different electoral system, embodying proportional representation. It was difficult at that moment to base the case for electoral reform on the interests of the Labour party; as this became clearer the Labour Campaign widened the issue and argued against the existing system on the ground that it was not democratic or fair. It faced up to the contentious issue of coalition government, arguing that any party which lived in the real world had to accept the possibility of compromise and coalition.

The results of the 1987 general election, which repeated fairly closely those of 1983, gave a further impetus to the Labour

[18] *The Times*, 7 Mar. 1981, 14c.
[19] *The Times*, 11 June 1983, 9a.
[20] *HL Deb.* 439 (18 Feb. 1983), 452–495; and *HL Deb.* 460 (4 Mar. 1985), 1160–94. The bills were introduced by Lord Blake, the president of the Conservative Action Group.

Campaign. Resolutions calling for a change in the electoral system have been submitted to Labour party conferences, and by 1990 one was passed calling on the National Executive Committee to set up a working party on electoral reform to consider elections to the House of Commons as well as to other bodies such as the European parliament, devolved assemblies, and a new second chamber.[21] The Campaign's membership has increased considerably. It includes some MEPs, trade union officers, Labour councillors, and most importantly a substantial number of Westminster MPs. The Campaign is using a mixture of arguments. Some of its leaders boldly detach the cause of electoral reform from Labour's electoral prospects and see it as a question of principle. They argue that a party which believes in democracy, equality, and fairness cannot support the existing system even if it works in Labour's favour and gives them a good parliamentary majority with much less than half the country's votes. Others are more concerned to show that a commitment to electoral reform would help Labour to win the next election. The Campaign has decided not to support any particular proportional system.

By 1990 the outlook for success appeared to the reformers more hopeful than at any time previously. Interest in and support for proportional representation was not confined to a small group of zealots. Most advocates had narrowed down their arguments to the essentials of the case, and opponents had been forced to take the subject seriously. It might not be absurd for the reformers to celebrate, though with modest optimism, the centenary of Thomas Hare's death in 1891.

[21] A working party has been set up under the chairmanship of Professor Raymond Plant.

# Appendix A

## THE HARE SCHEME AND WORKING-CLASS REPRESENTATION

Would Hare's scheme have helped working men to obtain greater representation in parliament than they actually did during the years 1868 to 1900?

The Reform Act of 1867 made the working classes for the first time a considerable voting power in many borough constituencies, and after further legislation in 1884 in county constituencies as well; but their representation in parliament either by working-class MPs, or by MPs backed by working men's organizations, was well below their voting strength.

Thus at the general election of 1868 none of the seven candidates supported by the Reform League was successful, though they received all together a quite substantial number of votes (15,000). If the Hare scheme had been in operation, and if the voters supporting these candidates had used the chance given them of indicating their preferences on their ballot papers, they would have been able to secure some representation in parliament, probably at least three MPs.

In 1874 considerable attention was focused, as it has been since, on the fact that two working-class men were returned to parliament at the general election of that year. But if the Hare scheme had operated then, the 27,000 votes given to the thirteen candidates standing in what can be called 'the labour interest' would probably have secured not just two but perhaps five representatives in parliament.

The position improved in 1885 in the sense that the number of MPs representing the labour interest had increased, but both then and later it was greatly under-represented in relation to the number of votes its candidates received. This was particularly true of the general elections of 1895 and 1900 at which unsuccessful labour candidates received a large number of votes which were, on Hare principles, wasted— 102,000 in 1895 and 114,000 in 1900. In 1895 the wasted votes included 44,325 for the twenty-eight Independent Labour Party candidates. If the Hare scheme had operated, and if ILP supporters had used their preferences to vote solidly for these candidates, they should have been able to return some MPs—perhaps as many as four or five—instead of none.

The term 'labour interest' is used here to include Lib.-Labs., Liberals put up by trade unions and other working men's organizations, candidates sponsored by the ILP, the SDF, and other fringe parties of the Left.

There are admittedly difficulties involved in making these calculations. The number of votes received by unsuccessful candidates is known, but any estimate of the extra successes if the Hare scheme had operated is bound to be tentative, because it rests on certain assumptions about the behaviour of the electorate. However there can be little doubt that during the years 1868 to 1900 working men's interests would have been better represented in parliament if the Hare scheme had been in operation.

This was the view of several contemporaries. Thus in 1868 Mill thought that the only complete remedy to the absence of working men in parliament was 'the adoption of Personal Representation, by which the electors would be enabled to group themselves as they pleased, and any electors who chose to combine could be represented, in exact proportion to their numbers, by men of their own personal choice' (L 1352, 7 Dec. 1868). A pamphlet of 1869 thought that even a simplified version of the Hare scheme (constituencies of seven members with the single transferable vote) would enable working men to return about forty representatives of their own class; George Odger would have needed only 3,000 votes in 1868 and could have entered parliament (*Representation of Minorities, with a Scheme of Redistribution showing the probable results of equal justice to all*, by a Merchant, 1869). Mrs Fawcett too pointed out that Odger always lost, and that he would get into parliament if he was an all-England candidate (*Macmillan's Magazine*, Sept. 1870). Odger, who was the most prominent of working-class Radicals, made several unsuccessful attempts to enter parliament between 1868 and 1874. He only actually fought one general election (1874) and one by-election (1870), but he failed to be selected by the local Liberal constituency party or withdrew at that stage three times. Mill thought very well of him and wanted to see him in parliament.

At the time of the franchise extension of 1884, it was said by one advocate of the single transferable vote that such a change in the electoral system would make it much easier for working men to return labour representatives to parliament (*Proportional Representation. An Address to Working Men*, by S. Neil, n.d. but c.1885).

# Appendix B

## SPEAKER'S CONFERENCE, 1916–1917

*Members*

| | |
|---|---|
| Chairman | The Speaker, J. W. Lowther. |
| Unionist | Sir F. Banbury, Sir W. Bull, Lord Burnham, Sir J. Craig, Sir R. Finlay, Sir J. Larmor, D. MacMaster, Sir H. Page-Croft, B. Peto, Lord Salisbury, Sir Harry Samuel, E. R. Turton, Sir R. Williams. |

In December 1916, Banbury, Craig, and Salisbury were replaced by G. A. Touche, E. M. Archdale, and Lord Stuart of Wortley.

| | |
|---|---|
| Liberal | Sir R. Adkins, Sir J. Bethell, W. Davies, W. H. Dickinson, Lord Gladstone, Lord Grey, G. Lambert, J. Mac-Cullum Scott, W. M. R. Pringle, Sir J. Simon, Lord Southark, A. Williams. |
| Nationalist | P. J. Brady, Maurice Healy, T. P. O'Connor, T. Scanlan. |
| Labour | F. Goldstone, S. Walsh, G. J. Wardle. |

# Appendix C

## PARLIAMENTARY DECISIONS ON PROPORTIONAL REPRESENTATION, 1917–1918

### Commons

| | Votes | Majority against |
|---|---|---|
| 12 June 1917 | 149 v. 141 | 8 |
| 4 July 1917 | 201 v. 169 | 32 |
| 22 Nov. 1917 | 202 v. 126 | 76 |
| 5 Dec. 1917 | 181 v. 117 | 64 For Ireland |
| 30 Jan. 1918 | 223 v. 113 | 110 |
| 5 Feb. 1918 | 238 v. 141 | 97 |
| 13 May 1918 | 166 v. 110 | 56 |

### Lords

| | Votes | Majority in favour |
|---|---|---|
| 22 Jan. 1918 | 131 v. 42 | 89 |
| 29 Jan. 1918 | No division | — |
| 4 Feb. 1918 | 86 v. 35 | 51 |

# Appendix D

## PARLIAMENTARY DECISIONS ON ALTERNATIVE VOTE, 1917–1918

### Commons

|  | Votes | Majority in favour |
|---|---|---|
| 9 Aug. 1917 | 125 v. 124 | 1 |
| 22 Nov. 1917 | 150 v. 121 | 29 |
| 31 Jan. 1918 | 180 v. 172 | 8 |
| 5 Feb. 1918 | 195 v. 194 | 1 |
| 6 Feb. 1918 | 184 v. 166 | 18 |

### Lords

|  | Votes | Majority against |
|---|---|---|
| 22 Jan. 1918 | 66 v. 9 | 57 |
| 4 Feb. 1918 | 66 v. 29 | 37 |
| 6 Feb. 1918 | 74 v. 33 | 41 |

# Appendix E

## THE PROPORTIONAL
## REPRESENTATION SOCIETY

| Year | No. of Subscribers | Subscriptions in £ | Year | No. of Subscribers | Subscriptions in £ |
|---|---|---|---|---|---|
| Jan. 1884– | | | | | |
| Mar. 1885 | 105 | 1,300 | 1930 | 595 | 2,026 |
| 1885–8 | ? | 51 | 1931 | 605 | 1,974 |
| 1906 | 97 | 229 | 1932 | 593 | 1,551 |
| 1907 | 135 | 155 | 1933 | 561 | 1,697 |
| 1908 | 318 | 602 | 1934 | 563 | 2,229 |
| 1909 | 339 | 460 | 1935 | 567 | 2,168 |
| 1910 | 357 | 638 | 1936 | 629 | 2,020 |
| 1911 | ? | 842 | 1937 | 600 | 1,856 |
| 1912 | 561 | 2,027 | 1938 | 572 | 2,005 |
| 1913 | 648 | 1,746 | 1939 | 623 | 1,814 |
| 1914 | ? | 1,665 | 1940 | 547 | 1,144 |
| 1915 | 389 | 826 | 1941 | 531 | 1,221 |
| 1916 | 385 | 791 | 1942 | 576 | 1,178 |
| 1917 | 481 | 1,585 | 1943 | 607 | 1,201 |
| 1918 | 534 | 2,342 | 1944 | 650 | 1,351 |
| 1919 | 547 | 3,431 | 1945 | 726 | 1,248 |
| 1920 | 648 | 4,000 | | | |
| 1921 | 650 | 4,000 | | | |
| 1922 | 802 | 3,996 | | | |
| 1923 | 770 | 3,839 | | | |
| 1924 | ? | 2,692 | | | |
| 1925 | 767 | 2,537 | | | |
| 1926 | 581 | 2,294 | | | |
| 1927 | 692 | 2,573 | | | |
| 1928 | 593 | 2,271 | | | |
| 1929 | 674 | 2,281 | | | |

# Appendix F

## CONFERENCE ON ELECTORAL REFORM, 1930

*Members*

Chairman        Lord Ullswater.

Labour          W. M. Adamson, Lord Arnold, Sir E. N. Bennett, J. S. Clarke, G. Dallas, Ben Gardner, Marion Philips, J. Westwood.

Conservative    Lord Bayford, Capt. R. C. Bourne, Lord Hugh Cecil, Sir S. Hoare, Sir H. O'Neill, Sir B. Peto, A. N. Skelton, Oliver Stanley.

Liberal          Lord Craigmyle, Megan Lloyd George, Sir D. Mac-Lean, Sir H. Samuel, Sir A. Sinclair.

# Appendix G

## SPEAKER'S CONFERENCE ON ELECTORAL REFORM AND REDISTRIBUTION OF SEATS, 1944

*Members*

| | |
|---|---|
| Chairman | The Speaker, Douglas Clifton Brown. |
| Conservative | P. Buchanan-Hepburn, A. Erskine-Hill, Arthur Evans, Sir Douglas Hacking, Sir Austin Hudson, G. C. Hutchinson, H. W. Kerr, Sir Joseph Lamb, Duncan MacCallum, Viscount Margesson, Sir Joseph Nall, Sir Hugh O'Neill, M. Petherick, K. Pickthorn, R. D. Scott, R. H. Turton, Sir Herbert Williams. |
| Labour | Mrs J. L. Adamson, Lord Ammon, W. Foster, W. Glenvill-Hall, Wallis Green, James Griffiths, J. H. Parker, F. W. Pethick-Lawrence, A. Woodburn. |
| Liberal | Megan Lloyd George, Lord Rea. |
| Liberal National | T. Magnay. |
| Independent Labour | D. N. Pritt. |
| ILP | James Maxton. |
| Independent Progressive | T. E. Harvey. |

# Glossary

**absolute majority**   More than half of all the votes.

**additional members systems**   In these a certain proportion (for example, one-half or three-quarters) of seats are directly elected in single-member constituencies, using the first-past-the-post system. The remaining seats are allocated to the parties by regions in such a way as to bring about some degree of proportionality.

**alternative vote**   In a single-member constituency, voters may number the candidates in order of preference. If a candidate gets an absolute majority, he is declared elected. If none does, the candidate with least votes is eliminated, and the votes of his supporters are transferred to whichever of the remaining candidates they had marked as their next preference. This procedure is repeated if necessary until a candidate has an absolute majority.

**block vote**   Each voter in a multi-member constituency has as many votes as there are seats to be filled. It is widely used in local government elections in Britain. The term has a different sense when it is used to describe the casting by a trade union delegate at conferences of as many votes as there are members of his union.

**cumulative vote**   In a multi-member constituency, where voters have as many votes as there are seats to be filled, a voter can if he likes accumulate his votes on one or more candidates.

**first-past-the-post**   The candidate with the most votes is elected even if he has not got an absolute majority. Also known as the relative, or simple, majority system.

**Hare system**   Hare put forward different schemes from time to time, but the essence of his system is as follows. The whole country is one constituency. The voter indicates on his ballot paper, on which all the candidates are listed, an order of preference comprising as many candidates as he wishes to support. A candidate is elected if he obtains the quota (q.v.). If a candidate secures more than the quota, his surplus votes are transferred to the next candidate preferred by his supporters. If necessary, candidates at the bottom of the poll are eliminated and their votes transferred to other candidates. These processes continue until the full number of MPs has been elected.

**limited vote**   In a multi-member constituency, each elector has fewer votes than the number of seats to be filled, for example two votes in a three-member constituency. It was sometimes known as the restricted vote.

**list systems** A form of proportional representation in which electors vote for a list of candidates drawn up by a party. There are many types of list systems. The list can be a national one, a regional one, or a constituency one. In some list systems the elector can alter the order of the candidates on the list, and in some he can distribute his votes amongst candidates on other lists, or accumulate votes on one particular candidate.

**multi-member constituency** A constituency returning two or more members.

**personal representation** A term used mainly by Hare and Mill to denote the representation of the opinions of all, or almost all, the persons who constitute the electorate, in order to prevent their votes being useless. They also recommended that every section of the electorate should be represented in proportion to its numbers.

**plural vote** Some electors but not others have more than one vote, for example because they are University graduates or have a business or property in the constituency.

**proportional representation** An electoral system which is intended to bring about the representation of voters in proportion to their numbers.

**quota** The number of votes which in the Hare and single transferable vote systems (qq.v.) necessarily secures the election of a candidate. The correct way of calculating it is to divide the total number of votes polled by one more than the number of seats allotted to the constituency and then to add one to the result so obtained.

**relative majority** More votes than any other candidate. Same as first-past-the-post and simple majority.

**scrutin de liste** Same as block vote.

**second ballot** If no candidate has received an absolute majority, i.e. more votes than all his opponents combined, a second election is held. Sometimes all the candidates are allowed to stand again; sometimes candidature is limited, for example to the top two, or to those with a certain percentage of the votes.

**simple majority** Same as relative majority and first-past-the-post.

**single-member constituency** A constituency returning only one member.

**single transferable vote** A form of proportional representation in which electors in a multi-member constituency, returning at least three members, can place candidates in order of preference by putting 1, 2, 3, etc. against their names. Any candidate who receives the quota of votes is elected. His surplus votes, i.e. those in excess of the quota, are transferred in the correct proportion to the second preferences of the voters who voted for him. This process is repeated until enough candidates have obtained the quota. If not enough have, the lowest candidate is excluded and the second preferences of his supporters are transferred appropriately. This process may also have to be repeated.

# Bibliography

Beneath are listed only a small selection of the large number of sources used in the writing of this book. The place of publication is the United Kingdom unless otherwise stated.

## I. MANUSCRIPT SOURCES

Avebury papers. British Library. Additional MSS.
Courtney papers. London School of Economics and Political Science.
Fischer Williams. Letters to Lady Courtney. In the author's possession.
Hare papers. St John's College, Oxford.
Hare family documents. In possession of David Roberts.
Howell Collection. Bishopsgate Institute, London.
Proportional Representation Society. Correspondence, and Minutes of Meetings. Electoral Reform Society, London.
Templewood papers. Cambridge University Library.

## II. PARLIAMENTARY DEBATES

*Parliamentary debates at Westminster and in Northern Ireland.*

## III. PARLIAMENTARY PAPERS

1839 XVII. Third Annual Report of the Colonial Commissioners for South Australia.
1854 XXVI. Commission of Enquiry into the Corporation of London.
1860 XII. House of Lords Select Committee on the Elective Franchise in Counties and Boroughs.
1864 LXI. Report on the Election of Representatives for the Rigsraad.
1866 XIII. Select Committee on Metropolitan Local Government.
1884–5 XI. Select Committee on School Board Elections (Voting).
1888 XXXV. Royal Commission on Elementary Education Acts.
1907 LXXXVII. Reports from His Majesty's Representatives in foreign countries and in British Colonies respecting the application of the principle of proportional representation to public elections.

1907 HL VII. House of Lords Select Committee on the Municipal Representation Bill.

1910 XXVI. Royal Commission on Systems of Election.

1917–18 XXV. Conference on Electoral Reform. Letter from Mr Speaker to the Prime Minister.

1918 VIII. Royal Commission on Proportional Representation, appointed in pursuance of the Representation of the People Act, 1918, section 20(2), with the scheme prepared by the Commissioners.

1923 XII. Royal Commission on London Government.

1929–30 XIII. Conference on Electoral Reform. Letter from Viscount Ullswater to the Prime Minister.

1943–4 III. Conference on Electoral Reform and Redistribution of Seats. Letter from Mr Speaker to the Prime Minister.

1966–7 XXVII. Conference on Electoral Law. Letter from Mr Speaker to the Prime Minster.

1973–4 XI. Royal Commission on the Constitution.

1975–6 XII. Second Report of Select Committee on Direct Elections to the European Assembly.

1976–7 IX. Direct Elections to the European Assembly. White Paper.

## IV. PROPORTIONAL REPRESENTATION SOCIETY

*Annual Reports, pamphlets, and journal,* Representation, *1908–27.*

## V. *THE TIMES* NEWSPAPER

## VI. CONTEMPORARY WORKS

Amedroz, H. F., *The Franchise* (1858; 2nd edn., 1865).

—— *The Reform Measure of 1885, and subsequent General Election, with its bearing on Proportional Representation* (1886).

Anon. 'Representation of Minorities', *Spectator* (18 Oct. 1851).

—— 'Mr Hare on Representation', *Saturday Review* (26 Feb. 1859).

—— Review of Hare's *Treatise*, *Westminster Review*, 18 NS (July 1860).

Bagehot, W., 'Parliamentary Reform', *National Review*, 8 (Jan. 1859).

—— Review of Mill's *Representative Government*, *Economist* (18 May 1861).

—— *The English Constitution* (1867).

Baily, W., *A Scheme for Proportional Representation* (1869).

—— *Proportional Representation in Large Constituencies* (1872).

Baines, J. A., 'Parliamentary Representation in England illustrated by the Elections of 1892 and 1895', *Journal of the Royal Statistical Society*, 59 (Mar. 1896).

Bompas, H. M., *A Modification of Mr Hare's Scheme* (1870).

Boyd-Kinnear, J., 'Practical Considerations on the Representation of Minorities', *Fortnightly Review*, 4 os (Feb. 1866).

Cecil, Lord H., 'Proportional Representation', *Contemporary Review*, 116 (Dec. 1919).

Colchester, Lord, 'The Evil of Ignoring Minorities', *Nineteenth Century*, 61 (Apr. 1907).

Corbett, J. R., 'Recent Electoral Statistics', *Transactions of the Manchester Statistical Society* (1906–7).

Courtney, L. H., 'Political Machinery and Political Life', *Fortnightly Review*, 20 NS (July 1876).

—— 'The Representation of Minorities', *Nineteenth Century*, 6 (July 1879).

—— 'Proportional Representation: Objections and Answers', *Nineteenth Century*, 17 (Feb. 1885).

—— *The Working Constitution and its Outgrowths* (1901).

—— 'The Decline of Parliament', *Monthly Review*, 17 (Dec. 1904).

—— 'The Regeneration of Parliaments', *Contemporary Review*, 87 (June 1905).

—— 'Proportional Representation: A Reply', *Albany Review*, 2 (Dec. 1907).

—— 'Home Rule', *Contemporary Review*, 102 (July 1912).

Dicey, A. V., 'The Referendum and its Critics', *Quarterly Review*, 212 (Apr. 1910).

—— *Introduction to the Study of the Law of the Constitution* (8th edn., 1915).

Dobbs, A. E., *General Representation: On a Complete Readjustment and Modification of Mr Hare's Plan* (1871).

Dodgson, C. L., *The Principles of Parliamentary Representation* (1884).

Droop, H. R., *On Methods of Electing Representatives* (1868).

—— 'On Methods of Electing Representatives', *Journal of the Statistical Society*, 44 (June 1881).

Fabian Tracts. No. 53, *The Parish Councils Act* (1894).

—— No. 153, *The Twentieth Century Reform Bill* (1911).

—— No. 211, *The Case Against Proportional Representation* (1924).

Fawcett, H., *Mr Hare's Reform Bill Simplified and Explained* (1860).

Fawcett, M. G., 'Proportional Representation', *Macmillan's Magazine*, 22 (Sept. 1870).

—— 'A Short Explanation of Mr Hare's Scheme of Representation', *Macmillan's Magazine*, 23 (Apr. 1871).

Fischer Williams, J., *Proportional Representation and British Politics* (1914).
—— *The Reform of Political Representation* (1918).
Gilpin, T., *On the Representation of Minorities of Electors to act with the Majority in Elected Assemblies* (Philadelphia, 1844).
Grant Robertson, C., 'The Future of Parliamentary Democracy', *Contemporary Review*, 153 (Jan. 1938).
Greg. W. R., 'The Expected Reform Bill', *Edinburgh Review*, 95 (Jan 1852).
—— 'Representative Reform', *Edinburgh Review*, 96 (Oct. 1852).
—— 'Parliamentary Purification', *Edinburgh Review*, 98 (Oct. 1853).
Grey, A., 'Proportional Representation and Freedom from the Caucus', *Nineteenth Century*, 73 (June 1913).
Grey, Earl, *Parliamentary Government considered with Reference to the Reform of Parliament* (2nd edn., 1864).
Hare, T., *The Machinery of Representation* (1857).
—— *A Treatise on the Election of Representatives, Parliamentary and Municipal* (1859; further edns. in 1861, 1865, and 1873).
—— Representation in Practice and Theory', *Fraser's Magazine*, 61 os (Feb. 1860).
—— 'Representation of Every Locality and Intelligence', *Fraser's Magazine*, 61 os (Apr. 1860).
—— 'Suggestions for the Improvement of Our Representative System: The University Elections Act of Last Session', *Macmillan's Magazine*, 5 (Feb. 1862).
—— 'Ideal of a Local Government for the Metropolis', *Macmillan's Magazine*, 7 (Apr. 1863).
—— 'An Electoral Reform', *Fortnightly Review*, 2 os (Oct. 1865).
—— 'The Keystone of Parliamentary Reform', *Fortnightly Review*, 3 os (Jan. 1866).
—— 'Individual Responsibility in Representative Government', *Fortnightly Review*, 4 os (Mar. 1866).
—— 'A Note on Representative Government', *Fortnightly Review*, 18 ns (July 1875).
—— 'The Reform Bill of the Future', *Fortnightly Review*, 23 ns (Jan. 1878).
Harrison, F., *Parliament before Reform* (1867).
—— *The Revival of Authority* (1873).
—— *Thoughts on the Theory of Government* (1875).
Hobart, V. H., 'Parliamentary Reform', *Macmillan's Magazine*, 13 (Jan. 1866).
Hobhouse, L. T., *Liberalism* (1911).
Hobson, J. A., *The Crisis of Liberalism: New Issues of Democracy* (1909).
Humphreys, J. H., *Practical Aspects of Electoral Reform: A Study of the General Election of 1922* (1923).

Jenks, E., 'Doubts of Proportional Representation', *Albany Review*, 2 (Nov. 1907).

Knatchbull-Hugessen, E. H., 'Redistribution of Political Power', *Macmillan's Magazine*, 27 (Nov. 1872).

Lecky, W. E., *Democracy and Liberty* (1896).

Lewis, G. C., 'Marshall and the Representation of Minorities', *Edinburgh Review*, 100 (July 1854).

Lubbock, J., *Representation* (1885).

MacDonald, J. R., 'The Second Ballot and Party Government', *Independent Review*, 5 (Feb. 1905).

—— *Socialism and Government* (1909).

—— *The Socialist Movement* (1911).

—— *Socialism: Critical and Constructive* (1924 edn.).

Marshall, J. G., *Minorities and Majorities: Their Relative Rights. A Letter to Lord John Russell on Parliamentary Reform* (1853).

—— *The New Franchise: How to Use it*. An Address to the Working Men of Leeds (1867).

Maurice, F. D., 'The Suffrage Considered in Relation to the Working Class and to the Professional Class', *Macmillan's Magazine*, 2 (June 1860).

Mill, J. S., *Thoughts on Parliamentary Reform* (1859).

—— 'Recent Writers on Reform', *Fraser's Magazine*, 59 os (Apr. 1859).

—— *Considerations on Representative Government* (1861).

—— *Autobiography* (1873).

—— *Later Letters*. In *Collected Works of John Stuart Mill*, ed. F. E. Minneka and D. N. Lindley (Toronto and Buffalo, 1972–81).

Moore, T., *The Representation of the People: A Plea for Free Voting and Elective Equality by the Method of Mr Hare* (1879).

Ostrogorski, M. Y., *Democracy and the Organisation of Political Parties* (1902).

Rigby Smith, J., *Personal Representation: A Simplification, Adaptation to the Ballot, and Defence of Mr Hare's Scheme of Electoral Reform* (1868).

Robertson, J. M., 'Proportional Representation', *Edinburgh Review*, 226 (July 1917).

Russell, Lord J., *An Essay on the History of the English Government and Constitution* (1865 edn.).

Salisbury, Lord, 'The Value of Redistribution: A Note on Electoral Statistics', *National Review*, 4 (Oct. 1884).

Seebohm, F., 'Proportionate Representation', *Contemporary Review*, 44 (Dec. 1883).

Shaw-Lefevre, G. T., 'The Representation of Minorities', *Contemporary Review*, 45 (May 1884).

Shaw-Lefevre, G. T., 'Representation and Misrepresentation: I. The Crusade for Proportional Representation', *Fortnightly Review*, 37 NS (Feb. 1885).

Spence, C. H., *A Plea for Pure Democracy: Mr Hare's Reform Bill Applied to South Australia* (Adelaide, 1861).

—— *An Autobiography* (Adelaide, 1910).

Spencer, H., 'Representative Government: What is it Good for?', *Westminster Review*, 12 NS (Oct. 1857).

Stephen, L., 'Reform', *Macmillan's Magazine*, 15 (Apr. 1867).

—— 'Order and Progress', *Fortnightly Review*, 17 NS (June 1875).

—— 'The Value of Political Machinery', *Fortnightly Review*, 18 NS (Dec. 1875).

Wallas, G., 'The American Analogy', *Independent Review*, 1 (Dec. 1903).

Walpole, S. H., 'Parliamentary Reform, or the three Bills and Mr Bright's Schedules', *Quarterly Review*, 106 (Oct. 1859).

—— 'Reform Schemes', *Quarterly Review*, 107 (Jan. 1860).

## VII. BIOGRAPHIES, AUTOBIOGRAPHIES, DIARIES

*The Life-Work of Lord Avebury, 1884–1913*, ed. A. Grant Duff (1924).

Begbie, H., *Albert, Fourth Earl Grey, a Last Word* (1917).

Goldman, L. (ed.), *The Blind Victorian, Henry Fawcett and British Liberalism* (1959).

Gooch, G. P., *Life of Leonard Courtney* (1920).

Hutchinson, G., *Life of Sir John Lubbock*, 2 vols. (1914).

Leventhal, F. M., *Respectable Radical: George Howell and Victorian Working Class Politics* (1971).

Lowther, J. W., *A Speaker's Commentaries* (1925).

Pumphrey, R. J., *The Forgotten Man—Sir John Lubbock, FRS*. Notes and Records of the Royal Society of London, 13, No. 1 (June 1958).

*Real Old Tory Politics: The Political Diaries of Sir Robert Sanders, Lord Bayford, 1910–35*, ed. John Ramsden (1984).

Scott, C. P., *Political Diaries 1911–28*, ed. T. Wilson (1970).

Snowden, P., *Autobiography* (1934).

Stephen, L., *Life of Henry Fawcett* (1885).

Westlake, J., *Memories of John Westlake* (1914).

## VIII. OTHER WORKS

Black, D., *The Theory of Committees and Elections* (1958).

Bogdanor, V., *The People and the Party System* (1981).

Bogdanor, V. (ed.), *Liberal Party Politics* (1983).
—— (ed.), *Representatives of the People* (1985).
Bonnefoy, G., *La Représentation proportionnelle* (Paris, 1902).
Butler, D. E., *The Electoral System in Britain since 1918* (1963).
—— *British General Elections since 1945* (1989).
—— 'Modifying Electoral Arrangements', in *Policy and Politics: Essays in Honour of Norman Chester*, ed. D. Butler and A. H. Halsey (1978).
Carstairs, A. M., *A Short History of Electoral Systems in Western Europe* (1980).
Craig, F. W. S., *British Electoral Facts 1832–1980* (1981).
Finer, S. E. (ed.), *Adversary Politics and Electoral Reform* (1975).
Flandin, P.-E., *La Question de la représentation proportionnelle en Angleterre et dans les colonies anglaises, le vote transférable* (Paris, 1914).
Hansard Society for Parliamentary Government, *Commission on Electoral Reform. Report* (1976).
Hart, M., 'The Decline of the Liberal Party in Parliament and in the Constituencies, 1914–1931', D. Phil. thesis (Oxford, 1982).
Hoag, C. G. and Hallett, G. H., *Proportional Representation* (New York, 1926).
Humphreys, J. H., *Proportional Representation* (1911).
Lakeman, E., *How Democracies Vote* (4th edn., 1974).
MacKenzie, W. J. M., *Free Elections* (1958).
Pugh, M., 'The Background to the Representation of the People Act, 1918', Ph.D. thesis (Bristol, 1974).
—— *Electoral Reform in War and Peace 1906–18* (1978).
Robertson, J. M., *Electoral Justice* (1931).
Ross, J. F. S., *Elections and Electors* (1955).
Rowe, E. A., 'The British General Election of 1929', B. Litt. thesis (Oxford, 1959).

# Index